THE RECONST OF ED
Quality, Equality ...

Edited by

Judith D. Chapman
William L. Boyd
Rolf Lander
David Reynolds

CASSELL

Cassell
Wellington House
125 Strand
London WC2R 0BB

212 Park Avenue South
New York
NY 10003

First published 1996

British Library Cataloguing-in-Publication Data
A catalogue record for this book is available from the British Library

ISBN 0–304–33176–7 (hardback)
      0–304–33179–1 (paperback)

Typeset by Action Typesetting Limited, Gloucester
Printed and bound in Great Britain by
Redwood Books Limited, Trowbridge, Wiltshire

Contents

Contents

Contributors

David Aspin is Professor of Education at Monash University, Melbourne, Australia.

William Boyd is Professor of Education at Pennsylvania State University.

Judith Chapman is Professor of Education at The University of Western Australia, Perth, Australia.

James G Cibulka is Chair, Department of Educational Policy, Planning and Administration at the University of Maryland in the United States.

Christine E Deer is Professor of Education at the University of Technology, Sydney, Australia.

Jeffrey Dunstan is an educational consultant in Melbourne, Australia.

Leslie C Eliason is Assistant Professor at the Graduate School of Public Affairs, University of Washington, Washington.

Kjell Granström is Associate Professor and lecturer at the Department of Education and Psychology at the University of Linköping, Sweden.

Gunnel Gustafsson is Professor at the Department of Political Science at the University of Umea, Sweden.

Rolf Lander is Associate Professor and Lecturer at the Department of Education and Educational Research at the University of Göteborg, Sweden.

Jon Lauglo is Professor of Sociology at the Department of Sociology and Political Science at the University of Trondheim in Norway

Anders Lidström is a Research Associate at the Department of Political Science at the University of Umea, Sweden.

Ulf P Lundgren is Professor and Director General of the National Agency for Education in Sweden.

Kerstin Mattsson is Head of Department at the National Agency for Education in Sweden.

David Reynolds is Professor of Education at the University of Newcastle.

Brian Spicer is Senior Lecturer in Education at Monash University, Melbourne, Australia.

Hywel Thomas is Professor of Economics of Education and Head of the School of Education at the University of Birmingham.

Series Editors' Foreword

Educational decentralization is a key strategy in the panoply of policy options open to national governments. During the past ten to fifteen years decentralization has characterized the educational reform agenda in most western countries. The key challenge, as a recent OECD report makes clear, is to find a balance between the increasing demands for centrally determined policy initiatives and quality control, and the encouragement of locally developed school improvement efforts.

Much of the research on the implications of decentralization policies has occurred at the school level. This research has helped us to understand the complexities of school change and school improvement. The literature on decentralization at the national and international levels, however, has largely been neglected. This is unsurprising given the breadth and complexity of the task. It is for this reason that Judith Chapman, Bill Boyd, Rolf Lander and David Reynolds, editors of *The Reconstruction of Education*, are to be congratulated on the boldness of their concept for this book.

Drawing on a wide range of experiences and perspectives the editors and contributors attempt to compare the experiences of decentralization in Australia, Sweden, the United Kingdom and the United States of America. The focus of the book is on two key issues in this process: the balance between centralization and decentralization in differing national contexts; and the impact of this balance on the quality of schooling. As a consequence the work sheds light on a key debate on the effectiveness of 'top-down' and 'bottom-up' strategies for educational reform.

Although the book does not claim to offer a definitive assessment of the impact of decentralization, it does highlight issues of effectiveness, equality, financial delegation, and professional development and management of change across a number of national and cultural contexts. As such the book presents a map of the territory of decentralization that is broad in scope as well as raising a series of issues in depth. *The Reconstruction of Education* is an invaluable record of an international educational system in transition.

David Hopkins
David Reynolds

Introduction and Overview

INTRODUCTION

In this book we report on a cross-national enquiry comparing education policy in four nations that vary significantly in their approaches to the governance of education: Australia, Sweden, the United Kingdom and the United States of America. The central objectives of the book are to analyse and compare (a) the particular balance that each of the four nations has struck between centralization and decentralization in governance arrangements, and (b) the consequences of this balance for quality, equality and control in the provision of schooling.

In most developed democracies one can see a tension in education policy between four competing values: quality, equality, liberty and efficiency. Policies rarely can be developed that do not involve some sort of 'trade-off' between these competing values. In trying to deal with these trade-offs, nations tend to produce their own distinctive approaches to education policy and governance. There is a good deal of evidence, however, that over time nations will endeavour to make adjustments to create a better balance between the advantages and disadvantages of their particular approach. These adjustments often involve alterations in the balance struck between centralization and decentralization in governing education.

During the early 1980s, the main emphasis in school improvement efforts in most developed nations was on a school-based approach. However, in the last half of the 1980s and the early 1990s the emphasis in policy and governance shifted more towards an approach based upon centrally determined quality control. The shortest explanation for this change may be found in worldwide developments, particularly in the economic sphere, that have spilled over national boundaries and created mounting pressures for improved schooling. As developed nations have increasingly become post-industrial societies and knowledge economies, their needs for more effective schooling have escalated. In this context, the old bottom-up, school-based approach has seemed too slow and uncertain of producing desired improvements. Consequently, governments have felt increasing pressures to design and implement centrally controlled standards and accountability schemes for their school systems.

However, although the context has changed, the fundamental issue remains the same: how can governments best promote quality, equality and effectiveness in schooling? If bottom-up, school-based approaches seem slow and unreliable, top-down, centrally mandated approaches have equal deficiencies. Typically, they are inclined to rigidify schools through heavy bureaucratic rules and procedures. Yet research has long shown that school improvement requires flexibility and extensive staff input and commitment at the school level, qualities that bureaucracy tends to put an end to.

1

It is not surprising, then, that in the mid-1990s much of the current research and policy debate focuses on ways to strike a balance or forge a synthesis between the opposing top-down and bottom-up approaches to school improvement. Indeed, in a number of countries the current thrust in education policy couples increased control from the centre with increased discretion at the school site level. Thus, there is a strong need for research that compares current national approaches for dealing with the tensions and trade-offs – in governance and policy outcomes – involved in efforts to resolve the contradictions between centralization and decentralization in education policy.

By means of the cross-national comparisons made possible through this edited collection, it is hoped that the reader will come to understand better the relative strengths and weaknesses of the means employed by different central, state and local agencies of government to try to ensure quality, equality and control in the provision of education in schools.

Each of the four countries under investigation has a unique history in the control and governance of education:

1 In Australia there is a federal system with six states and two territories, each with their own state or territory-wide education system. Traditionally, states have operated highly centralized state-wide systems, which only in the last two decades began to undertake serious efforts at decentralization and devolution.

2 The USA also has a federal system but, of the 50 states, only one (Hawaii) runs a state-wide school system. Throughout the rest of the United States there are over 15,000 school districts. Countering the fragmentation which has resulted from this decentralized approach, there has been, since 1954, a shift towards greater federal and state regulation of local districts in the interests of greater equality and effectiveness.

3 The goal of equality has also been fundamental in Sweden, in this instance, to the maintenance of a highly centralized national system of education. In the last decade, however, responding to broader political and economic influences which have been impacting on the entire public sector, the education system has been undergoing a process of decentralization to municipal authorities and schools.

4 In the United Kingdom the principle of decentralization was enshrined in the 1944 Education Act. This gave a high degree of autonomy in matters of staffing, curriculum choice and methods of assessment, not only to different Local Education Authorities (LEAs), but also to principals of individual schools. This principle, with suitable modifications, was sustained as a virtual article of faith in local organization and administration of publicly maintained educational institutions from primary through to tertiary. In recent years, however, a new Education Act has been put into place. This has set up central funding of LEAs through the rate support grant, established a national curriculum, introduced a system of national assessment and testing, dictated

teachers' conditions of service, and arrogated to the government minister no fewer than 178 new centralizing powers.

CONTENTS OF THE BOOK

The book begins with an analysis of different forms of decentralization and their implications for education. Jon Lauglo argues the case for disaggregating the notion of 'decentralization' and presents a range of types of administrative and governance arrangements which differ as to their rationale. Under the rubric of 'political' rationales, for instance, he identifies: federalism, populist localism, participatory democracy and liberalism. Under rationales that mainly concern quality and efficiency he points to: pedagogic professionalism, management by objectives, the market mechanism and deconcentration.

In the following three chapters some of these forms of 'decentralization' are subjected to more intensive analysis. In Chapter 2, David Aspin draws upon experiences in the United Kingdom and Australia to illustrate 'The Liberal Paradox'. William L. Boyd, in Chapter 3, discusses market-oriented decentralization trends, with particular reference to the United Kingdom and the United States of America; while in Chapter 4, Leslie Eliason analyses some of the tensions between market-oriented reform and the concern for participatory democracy in the United States of America and Sweden.

The next two chapters address the implementation of these policy approaches and the overall effects for schools. James Cibulka, in Chapter 5, provides an analysis of the policy implementation process in Great Britain and the United States of America, while in Chapter 6, David Reynolds offers a synthesis of the research on school effects from decentralization drawn from experiences around the world.

The effects of decentralization for functional areas of schooling relevant to ensuring quality, equality and control are the subject of the remaining half of the book. In Chapter 7, Ulf Lundgren and Kerstin Mattsson discuss 'Decentralization by or for School Improvement' in Sweden. The Swedish experience also provides the focus for Gunnel Gustafsson and Anders Lidström in Chapter 8, as they consider 'Redefining the Concept of Educational Equality through Decentralization'. In Chapter 9, Christine Deer reports on experiences of the impact of decentralization on curriculum in Australia, with the impact on teachers in Sweden, being discussed by Kjell Granström in Chapter 10 and the impact of decentralization on school leaders in the United Kingdom being discussed by Hywel Thomas in Chapter 11. The book closes with an examination of 'System Restructuring School-based Management and the Achievement of Effectiveness in Australian Education' by Judith Chapman, Jeffrey Dunstan and Brian Spicer.

AN OVERVIEW OF DECENTRALIZING TRENDS IN SELECTED COUNTRIES

In order to assist the reader to understand the context within which changes have taken place, a brief description of the decentralizing trends in Australia, Sweden, the United States of America and the United Kingdom follows.

Australia

The Commonwealth of Australia is composed of six states and two territories. The Commonwealth Government is considered to be relevant to national interests, however education is primarily the responsibility of the government of each individual state or territory.

In the early 1970s the Commonwealth Government undertook a large-scale inquiry into education. The Karmel Report, which resulted from that inquiry, recommended a movement away from the traditional, centralized system of school administration to greater decentralization in decision-making. To enable this, the newly created Schools Commission injected funds for educational reform on a massive scale in 1974, closely tying funding for innovation to evidence of community involvement and school-based decision-making.

The Commonwealth initiatives reinforced decentralizing trends in many of the states and territories. In the Australian Capital Territory school system which was newly created in 1974, for instance, organizational structures were based on respect for principles associated with community involvement and participative decision-making. For the first time in Australia's educational history a school system existed which was not organized along highly centralized bureaucratic notions of authority and control.

In the administration of some of the large state systems, forces were also in operation to influence the decentralization trend. In these states, the administrative structures which were established under the Education Acts of the late nineteenth century had created highly centralized state systems in which major functions were under the supervision of each state Education Department located in the particular state capital. The chief executive officer was the Director General, who was responsible to the Minister of Education and the State Parliament for the administration of the Education Act. Major decisions, both professional and managerial, were made by senior officers of the Education Department. The school principal acted as an agent of the Department, implementing policies and decisions made by officials in the central state office.

Gradually, in most states during the late 1960s and 1970s some elements of power were relinquished by the centralized state authorities. Recognizing that the traditional system could no longer provide effective administration for rapidly expanding and increasingly complex systems of schools, it became the policy of a number of state governments to decentralize administrative arrangements. During the 1970s the process had two distinct dimensions: one of these was associated with the creation of administrative regions and the other with the granting of increased responsibility to the principals of schools.

During the 1980s, in some states, this administrative reorganization was further expanded to achieve increased devolution of authority and responsibility to the community of the school. In states such as Victoria and Western Australia, the possibilities for school improvement and school development were seen to be enhanced through democratic, school-based decision-making which required a revised management role for principals. Particular emphasis was placed on collaborative decision-making by all partners in the school community and the creation of a responsive bureaucracy with the main function of serving and assisting schools.

4

Throughout the decade of the 1980s in Australia many politicians, educational interest groups, policy-makers and school-based personnel supported the notion that a school that was relatively autonomous, self-appraising and aware of its own strengths and weaknesses was most able to address problems of quality. In the 1990s, however, there have been more specific, direct and short-term approaches to the quality issue. This is in response to concern about the relationship between education, the state of the economy and national competitiveness. As a result policy-makers and central administrations are placing greater emphasis on setting quality targets and monitoring the achievements of schools. The immediate challenge facing Australian education is to resolve the dilemmas and unquestionable tensions which exist between an emphasis on school improvement through decentralized management and the emerging politically and economically motivated concern for centrally determined quality control.

Sweden

Centralization of the Swedish school system evolved over about 100 years from the 1860s to the 1970s. It achieved the integration of many different kinds of education into a relatively coherent structure: a comprehensive school with pupils between the ages of 7 and 15, and vocational and academic upper secondary programmes within the same organization.

Centralism backed up quality and equality efforts by funding and by direct regulation. Teachers and principals were formally employed and paid for by the state, and their terms regulated in detail. In-service training, previously arranged by teacher unions, was taken over by state agencies. In order to support the implementation of the comprehensive school 24 regional state administrations were built up, complementing the National Board of Education. Their duties were both support and inspection. As streaming was forbidden, except in English and mathematics, inspectors were on guard against informal ability grouping. During 1970–80 a rather ambitious policy of remedial teaching and integration of special education into ordinary classrooms was implemented, making the system even more comprehensive.

The curriculum for Grades 7–9 maintained an expensive subject specialization. It therefore offered an important motive for the successive rationalization of the Swedish municipalities, which decreased in numbers from about 2,500 to about 280, and thereby increased their population and tax-paying potential. (Today the median municipality has 16,000 inhabitants, the biggest 680,000.) An equal standard of schooling became easier to pay for. Municipalities could have bigger administrative staffs, which they needed in order to carry out their obligation to implement state legislation in all fields of welfare policy.

Equity was given as the primary political reason for the integration movement, but research gave evidence of relative ineffectiveness in terms of equal opportunities; the choice patterns of social strata were little affected. On the positive side, however, the reforms made a longer, uniform compulsory programme possible, and upgraded vocational education. In the long run most important may have been the pluralistic admission rules at each stage, which made further education a realistic possibility for most people (Härnqvist, 1989). State-supported municipal adult education also played a most decisive role in this flexibility (Ball and Larsson, 1989).

It seems that the system so far has produced homogenous quality throughout the country. International comparisons in mathematics and science from 1970 and 1983 show that Swedish comprehensive schools had a very small inter-school variation, together with other Scandinavian countries and Japan. The top achievers in the upper secondary schools also match the best pupils elsewhere. The conclusion has been drawn that an even distribution within classes of pupils with different achievement levels and social backgrounds is of vital importance in order to have good and uniform results (Pyddoke, 1994).

Despite the positive benefits of centralism, decentralization has been a topic of political debate in Sweden since the 1970s. The Social Democratic party (in government since 1936 except for the periods 1976–81 and 1991–94) was slow in adopting decentralizing measures, originally mostly advocated by the Liberal and Conservative parties. But in the late 1980s Social Democrats suddenly speeded up reform policy.

Three stages characterize reform efforts in decentralization:

1　From the late 1970s efforts were made to restructure the local school as a more efficient organization. This was done without political conflict.

2　Culminating in 1991, the municipalities were given back many, or most, control measures for their own school system from the state, and the state-governing system emphasized evaluation of goals.

3　Since 1991 state and municipal reforms have started trying out competition as a decentralization measure. Conflict about means and ends grew with the radicalization of reforms.

The so-called SIA-commission (1974) claimed that instruction needed to be planned and evaluated collectively in order to be more systematic. It advocated team teaching in what were known as working units, and working plans as the tools of development. This was taken into the curriculum reform of 1980. Systematic collaboration started to flourish at the primary level, but was still not the rule at secondary level (Ekholm et al., 1987). The commission also proposed compulsory state education for school leaders (see, for example, Pettigrew et al., 1982). The commission's ideas about citizen participation in instruction and local school boards were not successful because of teacher resistance.

The next important step was taken by the Social Democratic government with the reform of 1991. In order to balance municipal power and to uphold national aims of equal standards of schooling, the policy of management by objectives, or 'goal-steering', was introduced. In order to underline the dramatic shift of policy, the government abolished the National Board of Education in 1991, and established a new administrative body, the National Agency of Education (NAE), with evaluation and assessment as its main functions. NAE uses a rather sophisticated assessment system, partly aiming at productivity studies. It develops national tests of knowledge and attitudes which are ambitious regarding their performance assessment methods. Instead of an inspectorate it has a field organization staffed by 90 'evaluation generalists', who conduct yearly evaluations on issues such as governing, resources and choice.

After the reform of 1991, it soon became clear that municipalities were not reluctant to exert their new power over schools through their principals. Many boards dismissed their principals, rehired some and appointed new ones. The latter were often taken from the municipal pre-schools, as these were seen by many politicians as having better leadership, and through that better staff collaboration, than most schools. By this municipalities also signalled that a principal should regard him- or herself as a representative of the employer and not only as a guardian of the state curriculum and *primus inter pares* among teachers.

The election of 1991 gave power to a new government ideologically dominated by the Liberals and the Conservatives, both Ministers of Education and the Prime Minister being Conservatives. The election also shifted power at the municipal level, three-quarters of the municipalities obtained a 'burger' party majority. A 'choice revolution' was launched. Its most important tools are a voucher system and a support system for private schools.

Parents and pupils who decide to move to another school (private or municipal), and do not compete for admission with children in the neighbourhood, take their share of the total municipal school grants with them. The municipality may decide how dependent its schools shall be on the voucher. The municipality of Nacka, for instance, last year allocated 85 per cent of its school resources directly to schools by counting pupil heads, and 15 per cent by other principles. The municipality of Umea had a proportion of 73:27 per cent for per pupil grants and other grants. Private schools, however, are always guaranteed no more and no less than 85 per cent of municipal costs per pupil. These schools are allowed to charge fees within 'reasonable' limits. Private schools rapidly increased in numbers in the big cities, but so far they serve less than 2 per cent of pupils aged 7 to 15.

The 85 per cent rule became one of the most controversial parts of the new policy. Critics claim that it is at least 10 per cent higher than is reasonable. The 15 per cent difference is meant to compensate the public school for taking care of children with handicaps, learning problems, in need of instruction in their native language, etc., i.e. the kind of pupils who do not go to private schools as often, and the reason why these schools have a lower per capita funding. If this difference is too low, then 'ordinary' pupils in public schools have less to share than pupils in private schools (Arnman and Jönsson, 1993). The national association of independent schools has sponsored an investigation of 171 of the 250 schools, and claims that about one-third of them recruit handicapped children and offer instruction in native languages. This means that they take on a social responsibility, the association argues. Eighty per cent of the schools are said to survive a reduction of grants to 75 per cent of the average municipal costs (Lane, 1995).

Despite the preparedness of municipalities to exercise aspects of their power, it has taken time for municipalities to learn to use their new governing measures in the interests of quality and equality: they have problems upholding a clear relationship between the school plan and the municipal budget and the school plan and working plans (Skolverket, 1993); local evaluations and assessment systems are exercised from a very limited experience basis (Lander, 1994); it is difficult to assess the productivity of schools regardless of governing system; there are no precise performance standards, and the cost accounting carried out by municipalities is very unreliable (Edström-Fors and Gunnarsson, 1994).

Markets aim at giving citizens influence by exercising the so-called 'exit' solution, as compared to 'voice'. 'Voice' implies taking part in political discourse by different means. There are some indications that contracting has reduced the possibilities of 'voice'. For functions of political democracy that are dependent on the number of political representatives, it sharpens the old problems of contact between citizens and politicians. Compared to municipalities with a traditional organization, there are 19 per cent less individual politicians in market-oriented organizations than expected (Bäck, 1993). There have also been considerable complaints from unions, journalists, and others that municipalities with market-oriented organizations tend to shield themselves from public scrutiny. Competition and the recruitment of business leaders to municipal posts seem to have brought about a manner of protecting what is seen as business secrecy.

Both the voucher system and the 85 per cent rule should be changed, according to promises made by the Social Democrats in the 1994 elections. A committee has been appointed to suggest solutions for the next school year, but one of the new ministers has been heard giving some credit to a voucher system of some kind. The dominant Social Democratic view, nevertheless, is to uphold the status and power of political government, because they see schooling as an instrument for societal change. If the political arena is reduced, they argue, change is bound to be less influenced by people of low and average incomes. Far-reaching choice, it is feared, will reduce the equity which has for so long characterized education in Sweden.

The United States of America

In the United States, as in many western democracies, there has been a tight nexus in education policy between quality, equality and control. The civil rights movement of the 1960s, and associated efforts to end racial segregation in schools and other public facilities, produced a heavy emphasis on the goal of equity for all Americans. In the decentralized US political context, pursuit of this goal required strong intervention on the part of the Federal Government into the affairs of state and local governments. By law and tradition, the governance of public schooling in the USA is a highly decentralized undertaking. Legally, education is a state function, but all states except Hawaii have, by tradition, delegated the actual administration of schooling to local schools districts. With some 15,000 school districts across the 50 states, education is, in fact, the most local of all forms of government.

Strong federal intervention in this sector was necessary because history had shown that the cherished value of 'local control' of education too often produced what Katz (1971) called 'democratic localism', a tyranny of the local majority over the rights and interests of minorities, and especially over African-Americans. The 1954 Supreme Court decision ending the 'separate but equal' doctrine permitting racial segregation, and the subsequent federal passage and enforcement of the Civil Rights Act of 1964, put the central government on a collision course with local and state governments involved in the traditions of racism, racial discrimination and white rule.

After more than a decade of strong federal efforts to assure equity and social justice in schooling and other public services, a reaction began to grow against aggressive 'big government' and the redistributive social programmes of the 'Great Society', including 'affirmative action' (positive discrimination) practices. In education, by the late 1970s concerns were mounting about declining student test scores on standardized achievement tests. Neo-conservative critics asserted that quality and standards in schools had been sacrificed in favour of an excessive focus on equity during the 1960s and 1970s.

The reaction against the aggressive federal role culminated in the election of Ronald Reagan in 1980. In keeping with campaign pledges, the Reagan administration scaled down the Federal Government and encouraged the states to take over leadership in areas such as education. Reagan's election paralleled Margaret Thatcher's ascension to power in Britain in 1979; both represented the triumph of neo-conservative opinion over defenders of the welfare state, and in both cases equity was replaced as a priority in education policy by quality or 'excellence'.

What has come to be called the 'first wave' of the US reform effort began with the release of 'A Nation at Risk,' the Report of the National Commission on Excellence in Education (April 1983). The 'first wave' effort was promoted by a belief that the USA was losing its economic competitiveness in the increasingly competitive world marketplace. 'A Nation at Risk' launched the 'excellence' movement, which was characterized by the view that the USA must intensify what it was already doing: increase rigour, raise graduation standards for students and teachers and extend the school year.

By 1986 a 'second wave' of reform began, characterized by a belief that 'intensification' is not enough; rather, the USA must restructure schools, empower and professionalize teachers and give school choice to parents. The 'second wave' was exemplified by the Carnegie Task Force report, 'A Nation Prepared' (1986), and by the National Governors Association report, 'Time for Results' (1986). The second wave brought an exploration of ways to bring about more comprehensive reform, in the hope of moving beyond 'incremental' tinkering with the system. (This impulse became the seed for the 'third wave' discussed below.)

Emblematic of this sentiment was the first 'education summit', convened in 1989 by President Bush at Charlottesville, Virginia, and attended by the nation's governors (including then Governor Clinton). At this 'summit' meeting, agreement was reached in principle on six *national* education goals to be achieved by the year 2000. This was a stunning departure from the jealously guarded and legally supported US tradition of state and local control of education.

Subsequently, Bush proposed the 'America 2000' education strategy to pursue the national goals. Bush's plan also proposed (but did not achieve) government funding for parental and student choice between public and private schools.

Since 1990, a 'third wave' of reform has gathered momentum behind the view that intensification and piecemeal school restructuring are not enough: the USA needs fundamental 'systemic' reform. According to its advocates, systemic reform requires state and national curriculum frameworks and standards, and associated 'high stakes' testing geared to 'world class' standards. The demanding new standards are needed, advocates claim, to replace the 'de facto' low standards widely in effect, which perpetuate low expectations and minimal achievement. Moreover, beyond the school, deteriorating social and family conditions require (a) co-ordinated, 'school-linked' social and health services for at-risk children and families, and (b) rebuilding the community and societal environment to support healthy families and learning. Together, these academic and social objectives produce a sweeping reform agenda.

When the Clinton administration came to power, it renamed Bush's 'America 2000' plan, calling it 'Goals 2000'. Apart from deleting the controversial private school 'choice' proposal, the plan essentially was adopted almost intact, demonstrating the broad, bipartisan support for this education strategy. It should be emphasized, however, that school 'choice' is still very much on the agenda, but mainly in the form of 'charter school' plans being adopted by many states.

Charter schools laws permit the creation of new or reconstituted 'independent' public schools that are largely free of bureaucratic control, but are held accountable for results or student outcomes agreed upon in the 'charter' authorizing their creation. British observers will recognize that the charter schools idea parallels, in some ways, the opted-out, grant-maintained schools brought into being by the 1988 Education Reform Act.

President Clinton's 'Goals 2000: Educate America Act' was passed on 26 March 1994, bringing to a head the effort to formalize a 'systemic' reform plan. For the United States it is almost as significant as Britain's 1988 Education Reform Act. The act codifies the national education goals (adding two new goals) and establishes national, 'world-class' standards for what every child should know.

It formally authorizes an 18-member National Education Goals Panel responsible for overseeing and reporting on progress towards the eight national goals (the panel includes two presidential appointees, eight governors, four members of Congress and four state legislators); creates a 19-member National Education Standards and Improvement Council charged with developing voluntary national curriculum content and student performance standards, and also national 'opportunity to learn' standards; and creates a 28-member National Skill Standards Board that will fund the development of voluntary skill standards for specific occupations.[1]

The Act authorizes $400 million in grants for states that submit reform plans including content and performance standards; opportunity standards or strategies; assessment systems; strategies for aligning curricula and assessments with content and performance standards; and professional development strategies. States make sub-grants to school districts to implement local plans.

The Goals 2000 Act has already greatly intensified the 'politics of the curriculum', and the potential implications are staggering. A legal expert, Stephen Arons, has asserted that Goals 2000 poses a threat to freedom and believes that conflicts over 'official knowledge' loom in the future. Examples of this problem are already evident:

- Federal funding was terminated on 20 March 1994 for development of voluntary national standards for English and the language arts by the National Council of Teachers of English and the International Reading Association.

- Also in March, the National Science Foundation cut off funding for Rhode Island's state-wide effort to reform mathematics and science education.

- Nationwide, the Christian 'Religious Right' in the United States

has mobilized a huge and highly organized movement to stop what
they see, in the systemic reform movement, as a potential for
'thought control' and the imposition of alien and anti-Christian
values.

The 'Religious Right' is especially opposed to reforms that emphasize outcomes-
based education (OBE), critical thinking, values clarification, multicultural
education and tolerance for alternative lifestyles and cultures. By grass roots political action at the local level, they are seeking to gain control of local school boards
to ensure that things they oppose are kept out of the public schools. Their power
to determine policy and practice in US education will be tested as the next presidential elections approach.

The United Kingdom

Decentralization initiatives in England and Wales have been proceeding now for
over a decade (Scotland and Northern Ireland have separate arrangements that
have not undergone policy changes at the same pace nor in the same direction).
Four separate Acts of Parliament in 1986, 1988, 1989 and 1993 have fundamentally changed the balance of power between educational 'providers' and the
'consumers' of education (parents in this case, rather than children). The Acts
have also fundamentally changed the balance of power between the various
'provider' groups, with decentralization of power away from provider groups at
levels above the school (the local educational authorities) towards the school level
itself. At the same time as the decentralization of some powers and responsibilities has paradoxically taken place, there has been increasing centralization of
control over the curriculum content of schools, over the criteria by which schools
are evaluated and over, in the most recent Act, the attempts made at improvement
by poorly performing schools.

In 1980, the first of the Conservative Government's Education Acts required
schools both to publish their levels of academic achievement in public examinations and to make available to parents of pupils information about the internal
processes of the school, its disciplinary policy, its formal organization and its range
of curriculum contents. The Act also gave parents the right to express a preference for which school their child should attend, although the local education
authority could still restrict the operation of that choice by setting limits to the
numbers of pupils that each school could admit.

In 1986, the second Education Act gave parents legal representation on the
governing board of each school, with elections to be held to appoint the parent
representatives. The balance of forces on each governing body became approximately one-third parents, one-third appointed by the Local Education Authority
and approximately one-third representatives of the staff/headteacher.

In 1988, the Education Reform Act further radically restructured the educational system in the following ways:

1 Schools were given control over their own budgets, initially for
   secondary and the larger elementary schools but from 1992 for all
   schools. Schools' budgets were to be mostly based on the number
   of pupils in each school: 75 per cent of the total resources

11

allocated to schools were to reflect simple numbers, with only a quarter of the resources being used to 'positively discriminate' in any way.

2 Individual school governors and headteachers were given increased powers in such areas as the appointment of staff, the determination of headteacher and staff salaries, the general organization of the school and the like.

3 The new 'empowered' schools, given apparently substantial freedom to determine their own priorities, were to compete against each other in an 'educational market', in which parents were given greatly increased powers. This came through abolishing the Local Education Authorities' rights to restrict the exercise of parental choice, since schools were set free to expand or contract in numbers as the exercise of parental market choice determined.

4 While the rhetoric of the Act, and the debate that preceded it, was one of giving consumers power to choose their children's schools and of parental determination of the goals and means of the system, power in certain educational policy areas was heavily centralized to the national state:

   a the National Curriculum of core and foundation subjects was introduced, whereby both elementary and secondary schools were required by law to teach a certain range of subjects, a certain range of curricular content and to aim at a certain centrally determined set of curricular objectives;

   b a system of nationally administered and determined testing of pupils in the three 'core' subject areas of mathematics, English and science was introduced at ages 7, 11, 14 and 16, the phasing of tests at different ages to be gradual until 1995 when the entire apparatus was to be in place. The results of the tests were to be published and given to the parents of each individual child, with the results of all schools to be published also, together with certain contexting data on the schools' catchment areas.

5 To increase the variety of 'types' of schools which would be functioning in the educational market, schools were to be permitted to become autonomous, self-governing, 'grant-maintained' institutions which were to be centrally funded and independent of the Local Education Authorities.

The 1993 Education Act, introduced as a White Paper for discussion in the summer of 1992 and controversially becoming legislation in spring 1993, introduced even more inducements to schools to take the 'independence' offered in the 1988 Act, and also included further centralizing initiatives concerning 'ineffective' schools. Schools could now 'opt out' and become grant-maintained, independent institutions in clusters or groups, and the procedures for initiating moves to grant-maintained or opt-out status were made more simple. Crucially,

Local Education Authorities, having lost much of their control over the individual school organizations, were to lose their remaining major function of resource determination, allocation and transfer whenever the proportion of pupils of a given sector (elementary or secondary) which had opted out exceeded 10 per cent.

We have not space here in this brief description of country policies to outline changes in the further and higher education sectors of the universities and colleges that deal with the 16 to 19 age group and the 18 to 21 age group respectively. Such accounts are available elsewhere (e.g. Hargreaves and Reynolds, 1989; Ball, 1990). What it does seem important to do here, however, is to briefly examine the political, social and economic factors that have been responsible for one of the most dramatic and far-reaching changes towards reconstruction through decentralization (and the concomitant centralization outlined above) that has been undertaken anywhere.

First, it seems likely that the transfer of power to schools within centrally agreed frameworks in part reflects on the fiscal crisis of the UK that was a central economic feature of the 1980s and 1990s. Privatization of the educational system towards greater reliance upon parental contributions has occurred as services formerly provided by schools became available only on payment (e.g. school music, school societies, school trips), and as schools have needed to ask parents more and more to donate their own money simply to make it possible to run schools at all. Politically, it would have been difficult to raise revenue from parents without giving them an increased role in the determination of educational priorities and without decentralizing power to them.

In addition, the increasing irrelevance and lack of power of the 'meso' level of the education authority means that the cost of education to central and local government can be reduced by the dismantling of the sector, an event seen more and more in England and Wales as the effect of opting out schools reduces local educational resources and lowers the quality of the services they are able to provide to the schools that remain under their theoretical administrative authority.

Second, it seems likely that the increased competition from Pacific Rim economies and from the countries of the European Union has generated a need for increased system effectiveness for the England and Wales educational system, given that only 35 per cent (approximately) of pupils in English and Welsh schools achieve the basic five public examination passes which are held to be the equivalent of the comparable German and Japanese qualifications at age 16. The latter are obtained by up to 70 per cent of those two countries' young people. The use of parents as 'standards monitors' and 'watchdogs' is a cheap, apparently cost-effective and decentralized way of ensuring that system quality is improved, with the publication of schools' results and the transfer of powers to schools designed to ensure the 'levelling up' of standards by the stigmatizing of schools doing relatively poorly in the education 'market'.

Third, it is undoubtedly the case that the collapse of the beliefs and tenets of the liberal, social engineering-based dream of the 1960s and 1970s led to a desire, reactively, to do something very different with the levers of control that existed within the education system. The liberal or Fabian dream of the past involved a commitment to high spending, to producer-determined policies and to a 'top-down' and bureaucratic forcing down on to schools of what was seen by the central and local state as the 'good' of education that need not reflect the wishes of parents or, for that matter, their children. Indeed, the school was within the liberal tradition to seek actively to remove parental influence from children in the case of those parents who were too socially disadvantaged to know what was 'good' for their children.

The 'liberal dream's' collapse probably reflected a variety of factors. Many of the Local Education Authorities and central government reflected a belief that teachers were to be given substantial professional autonomy, both in the determination of the goals of education and the design of the organizational school means that were to deliver the goals. In such circumstances, variation from school to school became very large in terms of curriculum content, generating disillusionment among those parents whose children moved school (approximately 15 per cent of all children each year). Variation between schools in their quality and effectiveness in terms of their pupils' performance in their academic and social development was probably also a feature of the educational system in those years, since the respect for professional autonomy was related to the absence of any mechanisms for the maintenance of professional standards (such as a General Teaching Council) and to the absence of the routine monitoring of school performance that was already, for example, a feature of many US states and districts in the 1970s. The extraordinarily high public visibility accorded to the research findings showing British school differences and those factors which were apparently responsible for those differences is probably related to the widespread popular perception in England and Wales of high levels of school quality variation, and has no international parallel (see Reynolds, 1992).

Fourth, and related to the clear intellectual bankruptcy of the liberal policies that had been intended to generate at the same time both increased welfare for the individual and for the collectivity, the rise of the economic, political and social ideologies of the 'radical right' or 'neo-conservatives' itself had a powerful effect. In most accounts (e.g. Ball, 1990; Reynolds, 1989) it is clear that the radical right wishes to decentralize power to schools to avoid any effects of those local authorities (many of them in London) who were both interventionist and socialist (or at least social democratic) in terms of their ideology, on their perceived need for positive discrimination for children from deprived backgrounds, on their perceived need for equal opportunities strategies to eradicate continuing sexism and on their perceived need for policies of multiculturalism and antiracism. Decentralizing power to educational consumers – the parents – was also seen as a way of acting as a check on 'liberal' or 'radical' tendencies possessed by educational producers, given the historic tendency for parents to be less progressive in their educational thinking than the educational professionals. Decentralizing educational policymaking and power increasingly to school level might also have the added effects of refocusing the political discourse concerning education towards the level of the school rather than at the macro-societal level of national politics or the national 'state'. Crucially, educational malfunctioning, or the poor quality of school outcomes, could be seen as something requiring local, decentralized solutions rather than national macro-based remedies.

In summary, then, England and Wales have evidenced the practice of decentralization combined with centralization, although the practice has been clothed in the ideology of decentralization. Formerly individual schools were able to determine their goals as well as their means, for example, seeking to obtain social outcomes. This freedom is now taken away – the goals of education are centrally determined in terms of:

- the curriculum subjects;
- the knowledge content;
- the monitoring only of academic outcomes.

Schools now only have the freedom to determine the organizational *means* to achieve the state-determined *goals*, and even this freedom on means is restricted by the views of parents as consumers. The meso level – the Local Education Authorities – that might have posed a challenge to the intellectual and political hegemony of central, state-determined goals has also been severely weakened in their power.

In contemporary times in England and Wales, it is clear that the decentralization of power to schools, within a predetermined central state framework of evaluation and curricular control, is seemingly having quite considerable effects. There appears to be a considerable overload of new pressures and responsibilities at the level of the headteacher and the management of individual schools, where indeed the tensions between state policy, consumer preferences and organizational professional cultures seem to be being worked through.

There are hints of greater efficiency associated with schools' control of their own budgets, and hints of an increased variation in educational quality between schools, as schools differentiate themselves due both to the absence of the former constant presence of Local Education Authority influence and to the changes in the balance of pupils in terms of their distribution across the ability range that have been generated by the existence of the local educational markets that are consequent on the implementation of the 1988 Education Reform Act. Whether or not the reforms and the simultaneous decentralization/centralization initiatives truly improve educational standards, and for whom, remains to be seen.

NOTE

1 The National Education Goals Panel sponsors an informative electronic 'Daily Report Card', presenting news stories from across the USA relevant to progress towards the National Goals. Persons with access to the Internet can 'subscribe' to this free news service via e-mail by sending the following message (with a blank subject line) to LISTERV@GWUVM.GWU.EDU: sub rptcrd followed by your name (to end your subscription, send a message to the same address reading: signoff rptcrd).

REFERENCES

Arnman, G. and Jönsson, I. (1993) *Konskurrens för stimulans*, (Competition for stimulation), Stockholm: Skolverket.

Bäck, H. (1993) *Hur många och hurudana? Om organizationsförändringar, politikerantal och representativitet i kommunerna. Institutet för kommunal ekonomi, företagsekonomiska institutionen*, (How many and what kind: About organizational change, number of politicians, and political representativity in municipalities). Stockholm: Stockholms universitet.

Ball, S. (1990) *Politics and Policy making in Education*. London: Routledge & Kegan Paul.

Ball, S. and Larsson, S. (1989) *The Struggle for Democratic Education. Equality and Participation in Sweden*. London: Falmer Press.

Boyd, W.L. (1993) 'The politics of choice and market-oriented school reform in Britain and the United States: Explaining the differences', in G. Miron (ed.), *Free Choice and Market-oriented Schools: Problems and Prospects*. Stockholm: Institute of International Education, Stockholm University.

Chubb, J.E. and Moe, T.M. (1992) *A Lesson in School Reform from Great Britain*. Washington, DC: The Brookings Institution.

Economist (1991) 'Be bold, be British: A lesson for America's Schools'. **318** (7699) 23 March. 19–20.

Edström-Fors, E. and Gunnarsson, V. (1994) Skolans kostnader, effektivitet och resultat – en branschstudie, (School costs, effectivity and results – a branch study), Rapport till ESO. Finansdepartementet. Ds 1994:56.

Edwards, T. and Whitty, G. (1994) 'Choice in English secondary education: Lessons for America?' Paper presented at the annual meeting of the American Educational Research Association, April.

Ekholm, M., Fransson, A. and Lander, R. (1987) Skolreform och lokalt gensvar. Utvärdering av 35 grundskolor genom upprepade lägesbedömningar 1980–1985, (School reform and local response. Evaluation of 35 comprehensive schools 1980–1985), Publikation från institutionen för pedagogik, Göteborgs universitet 1987:3.

Gewirtz, S., Bowe, R. and Ball, S. (1994) 'Choice, competition and equity: Lessons from research in the U.K.' Paper presented at the annual meeting of the American Educational Research Association, April.

Hargreaves, A. and Reynolds, D. (eds) (1989) *Education Policies: Controversies and Critiques*. Lewes: Falmer Press.

Härnqvist, K. (1989) Comprehensiveness and Social Equality, in S. Ball and S. Larsson, *The Struggle for Democratic Education, Equality and Participation in Sweden*. London: The Falmer Press.

Katz, M.B. (1971) *Class, Bureaucracy and Schools*. New York: Praeger.

Lander, R. (1994) *The Assessment of School Performance: Background report to OECD/CERI – Sweden*. Department of Education and Educational Research, University of Göteborg.

Lane, J.E. (1995) Vi måste lära av Norge. *Dagens Nyheter* 18 januari 1995. (We must learn from Norway, *Daily News*, 18 January 1995).

Pettigrew, A., Schmuck, R.A. and Vormeland, O. (1982) International views on the Swedish school leader education. Report no. 6. Evaluation of the school leader education in Linköping.

Power, S., Halpin, D. and Fitz, J. (1994) 'The grant-maintained schools policy: The English experience of educational self-governance'. Paper presented at the annual meeting of the American Educational Research Association, April.

Pyddoke, R. (1994) Valfrihet inom skolan. Konsekvenser för kostnader, resultat och segregering (Choice within schools. Consequences for costs, results and segregation), Rapport till ESO. Finansdepartementet. Ds 1994:72.

Reynolds, D. (1989) 'Better Schools?', in A. Hargreaves and D. Reynolds (eds) *Education Policies: Controversies and Critiques*. Lewes: Falmer Press.

Reynolds, D. (1992) 'Doing Educational Research in Treliw', in G. Walford (ed.) *Doing Educational Research*. London: Routledge & Kegan Paul.

Skolverket (1993) *Beskrivande data om skolverksamheten 1993*. Rapport nr 8 (NAE: Descriptive data about schools in 1993).

The SIA-commission (1974) *SOU 1974–53. Skolans arbetsmiljö* (Working conditions and milieux of the school), Betänkande avgivet av Utredningen om skolans inre arbete – SIA. Stockholm: Utbildningsdepartementet.

Chapter 1

Forms of Decentralization and their Implications for Education

Jon Lauglo

INTRODUCTION

The object of this chapter is to construct and compare types of decentralization and their attendant rationales, and to point to their implications for the distribution of authority in education systems, and for ways of evaluating educational institutions. The task is broad, and only an intuitive sketch will be attempted. Like most efforts of this kind, the construction of this typology will be unevenly documented by reference to its recalled source material; and the format restricts the extent to which the types themselves can be elaborated. The resulting tentative conclusions about what the types imply will be summarized in a tabular form.

The scope of the chapter excludes the question of whether different organizational forms in fact serve the ends which are offered as justifications for them, nor does it examine the latent functions as well as the unintended consequences which the different forms of decentralization may have. Those questions are indeed important matters for empirical social research. The knowledge base is too weak for any internationally firm generalizations about the consequences of redistributing authority in education systems. Less ambitious tasks are feasible: empirically founded assessments of the consequences which occur when authority is redistributed in an education system at a particular place and time and in a particular context. But it remains beyond the ambitions of this chapter to review the findings which such national case studies have produced.

THE PROBLEMS IN DEFINING AN ALTERNATIVE TO CENTRALIZATION

In spatial terms, to decentralize means to disperse objects away from a central point. In current usage, the term decentralization refers not only to that process but also to the condition of objects being located remote from a centre – though it might have been useful to adopt 'decentralism' in order to denote structural condition as distinct from process. A centre can be defined precisely, for example, a point that has the greatest possible distance from all boundaries, or a point denoting the central tendency in a distribution. But 'decentralization' is not one location, and many different distributions of dispersed locations would have the same summary statistic as to degree of dispersal.

Thus, even in spatial terms, decentralization is a highly imprecise notion. It becomes even more imprecise when the concept is used to denote, as in the case of the present study, the distribution of authority in organizations such as national education systems. Here 'centre' may still have a spatial reference, for example, to decisions taken at the headquarters site, but it refers mainly to the apex in a hierarchical authority structure in an organization which may or may not be physically dispersed in a great number of sites.[1]

The concept of 'centralized' authority means concentrating in a central ('top') authority decision-making on a wide range of matters, leaving only tightly programmed routine implementation to lower levels in the organization. Thus, with regard to education, a ministry could make decisions in considerable detail as to aims and objectives, the structure and localization of provisions, curricula and teaching materials to be used, prescribed methods, appointments of staff and their job descriptions, admission of students, assessment and certification, finance and budgets, and inspection/evaluations to monitor performance. In practice, consistently 'strong' central control may be rare, because even when a central authority is keen to exercise strong and forceful direction and has the power to do so, different means of control may serve as substitutes for each other, for example, control of goals and objectives, of rules and regulations, of resources, training of staff, appointments and using information as a means of persuasion.[2] As an ideal type, the concept of bureaucratic centralism, which traditionally characterized much of the French public services, is reasonably unambiguous. In that pattern, public services are organized as separate *états*, for example, in education: separate *états* for primary and secondary school teaching. The bulk of employees are officials belonging to the civil service of the state. Once an official is recruited, trained and posted, mobility occurs by direct appointments which transfer or promote them – though account may be taken of their expressed preferences. Within each such *état*, co-ordination is achieved by centrally issued rules and regulations and by a clear hierarchy so that the chains of authority for each service radiate downwards from its ministerial headquarters in the capital. Military organizations typify most clearly this kind of centralism. Its degree of extension to 'civilian' public services has historically been part of efforts to build a strong modern state – whether by a monarchy (e.g., historical Prussia, tsarist Russia, France under Napoleon), or by modern forms of absolutism (Nazism, Stalinism), or by a democratically constituted national government with strong goals of centrally directed social improvement guided by technocratic and scientific expertise.

Bureaucratic centralism is also pervasive in many developing countries. There is the legacy of colonial rule with its needs both to control and to 'develop' in order to meet the needs of colonial rule itself; there is the statism implied by nation-building imperatives after independence. Many developing countries have, after independence, had policies for social and economic development (certainly in education) which have placed strong emphasis on central planning. Apart from such rationales, bureaucratic centralism is a pattern which tends to emerge when independently constituted local and regional government is weak to begin with – a condition common to many developing countries after independence.

Conceptually, 'decentralization' is far more problematic than 'centralized' authority. Indeed, in current usage 'decentralization' refers to a variety of organizational forms which differ in their rationales and in their implications for the distribution of authority on different agencies, groups and stakeholders. As will be later discussed and then further summarized in Table 1.1, the forms differ in what primacy they give to such different actors as intermediate and local political authorities, state officials at regional or local levels, institutional managers, the teaching profession, the larger group of 'inside' members of educational organizations (including students), parents, and non-government providers of education.

MOTIVES FOR REDISTRIBUTING AUTHORITY

The main present concern is with rationales – with publicly manifest justifications. But it is recognized that practical circumstances relating to the scale and complexity of a national education system also may play a major role in individual countries, as motives for decentralization. Among such circumstances may be the magnitude of the educational enterprise, the heterogeneity of the clientele for education, problems of communication, and the financial burden on the central government (UNESCO, 1982).

Other motives relate to the vested interests that ruling groups have in augmenting or defending their power and its legitimacy. Some groups will have more power than others to achieve authority shifts in their favour and to prevent shifts in their disfavour. Élites and bureaucratic establishments tend to protect their power and they may seek to enhance it. They will shed power only reluctantly – especially to their clear opponents and to other groups in which they have low confidence. They will be more ready to redistribute authority to groups whom they see as like-minded to themselves and whose competence they trust. Thus, a high degree of consensus about the ends and means of education among all concerned groups and stakeholders, mutual trust in goodwill and competence, may provide a climate which facilitates decentralization without much resistance by those who lose influence in the redistribution of authority. Under such conditions of relative consensus, the state may, for instance, devolve more authority over education to elective local government. The urge to defend power advantages will be greater when fractiousness prevails in the politics of education. Structural reforms of education (e.g. comprehensive reorganization of secondary schooling) tend to be politically controversial and meet with opposition from some of the professional groups affected. Therefore, governments bent on such reforms may become more willing to relax the reins of central control when the time comes that structural change seems securely achieved – as in the case of Nordic social democratic governments and the evolution of their policies on decentralization in recent years.

But authority distributions have great inertia and are not easily shifted, just because there is growth in 'mutual confidence and trust' among the various actors who would like to exert influence on education. Does it follow that decentralization only occurs under conditions of crisis or under radical change when new groups gain power against determined opposition from those whom they replace? Political expediency can be an important motive for redistributing authority – both for concentrating authority more or for distributing it more widely, and it can also be a motive for defence of the existing distribution. Polarized politics may induce a national government to retain tight control of education; and controlling the state apparatus tends to create more identification with it. Conversely, parties which long remain in opposition may become more convinced than they otherwise would have been, of the virtues of decentralization to those local bodies in which they are more influential. The evolution of British politics of education under Thatcher may be a case in point. The Conservatives stripped the power of the Local Education Authorities and the teaching profession, introduced stronger central control and gave more influence to parents (who are seen by Tories as more attuned to Conservative values in education). Conversely, Labour, which previously may have been the more 'centralist' party in its policies on educational reforms, has during its long years as an opposition party become more identified with the interests of local government and the teaching profession.

Under other circumstances, decentralization policies have resulted from political polarization. Faced with a secessionist movement a government may choose to use the means of control to 'keep the lid on' (e.g. Spain under Franco), or it may enter into a compromise by devolving more authority to regions in order to defuse dissent (Spain at present). A federal 'solution' to secessionist movements is not uncommon. The type of decentralization of education found in Papua New Guinea exemplifies such a constitutional compromise.[3] Though decentralization may be used to diffuse dissent when a dominant group hopes to remain in power, it can also be a means by which they seek to create buffers against central authority when they expect to lose power. For example, in its negotiations preceding majority rule in South Africa, the National party sought to reduce the power of the central state, and to devolve much power to provincial government.

While ruling groups and administrative or professional élites seek to protect and augment their power, they may also seek to avoid blame for social problems which they fail adequately to remedy. They may be inclined to diffuse responsibility more widely when faced with intractable policy problems. Thus, those with faith in a government's good intentions, and the cynics who believe that governments are driven only by self-interest, will have rather different interpretations of such decentralization measures as 'privatization' or 'community participation'[4] in providing finance for education when a central government lacks the resources with which to meet rising aggregate private demand for education. To what extent are such measures authentic practical attempts to cope better with a policy problem, and to what extent are they a means of escaping blame for failure? The answer which is given will tend to depend on the observer's trust in the government concerned.

Weiler (1990) argues that governments are driven by latent 'conflict management' motives when they adopt decentralization policies, and that recent decentralization trends reflect the ubiquity of conflict in modern society – a crisis of legitimacy, a proposition that also is a main theme in Lundgren's (1990) theorizing about decentralization. But this is at best a partial framework for explaining such policies. What is the empirical basis for concluding that the legitimacy of political authority is more weakly founded now than previously, or that conflicts are more ubiquitous? Here one will find much variation among contemporary societies. For example, the reconstructed governments of post-war Germany may have had a more uneasily founded legitimacy than countries with a long tradition of democratic government. Obviously, this applied to the DDR, but it is also likely that unease about legitimacy has been politically more important in the German

Federal Republic than in democratic countries with a less turbulent past. It is not accidental that theorizing about 'a crisis of legitimacy' has been important among social theorists in the German Federal Republic (notably Habermas), and especially among neo-Marxists whose theoretical assumptions have sensitized them to look hopefully for signs of erosion in the legitimacy of a state formation that they perceived to be an instrument of oppression under 'late capitalism'.

Do decentralization policies in fact characterize those societies in which political authority is more weakly established in contrast to other countries? Conflicts are not always successfully managed or contained by decentralization measures – concessions can be 'too little, too late'. In fact, centralist control is another common response to 'conflicts', for example, quite tight centralist control over education for Blacks in South Africa under apartheid, or the historical use of bureaucratic centralism in French education under the Third Republic to contain conservative clericalism – using state 'rationalist' education to drive back the forces of traditionalism. Motives relating to political expediency (including conflict management) will have varying force and expressions in different countries, as the 'real intentions' behind redistribution of authority. Sometimes they are of course publicly visible as stated intent, for example, as in 'necessary compromises' between groups that conflict and bargain. But when it is asserted that 'latent motives' are at work, imputed from the 'interests' which governments are said to have, the empirical substantiation behind such assertions is often weak and disputable. Even if consequences of policy can be reliably assessed and would match what is ascribed as a latent motive, they may not be the intended ones.

It is probably overambitious to attempt universalistic explanations, across time and place, about how latent political motives drive decentralization policies; for it is likely that the motive force of political expediency and the kinds of policies which such motives favour, will vary greatly among countries, depending on local circumstances. It is a theme which requires national case studies. Such investigations should at least make an attempt to get inside information about how decisions are made, and include an account of the motives and considerations acknowledged by the participants themselves. Motives cannot simply be imputed on the basis of theory, or even by observed consequences of policy.

FORMS OF DECENTRALIZATION

There are three main values invoked in rationales for decentralization: a politically legitimate dispersal of authority, quality of services rendered and efficient use of resources. The forms of decentralization differ as to which of these values they are primarily concerned with, though primacy on one value will tend to go with some regard for the others as well in the rationales which are offered. Arguments concerning political legitimacy, whether explicitly formulated as theories or ideologies or implicit in a country's political tradition, address the question: who has a legitimate right (and duty) to decide or to take part in decisions of different kinds? Efficiency rationales concern the extent to which optimal use is made of scarce resources in relation to goal realization.

The quality of education relates mainly to goal realization and to educational processes in which it is claimed that goal realization is implied. The norms by which 'quality in education' may be judged do not apply only to 'goal realization'

– or outcomes.[5] But in so far as education is deliberate activities designed to bring about learning, it is fundamentally a purposeful, goal-oriented activity to which the efficiency concept, with its instrumentalist assumption, in principle also applies. 'Efficiency' is a wider concept in that it denotes the quality of the system's operation – not only the quality of services rendered (in terms of goal realization and judged 'quality of process') to those who are reached by these services.

In delineating the types below, the starting point has been a search for ideas from which one may derive implications for a decentralized distribution of authority, and which at the same time have some salience in international public debate on education. These constraints restrict the range of ideas discussed in this typology. In particular, only a limited range of ideas concerned with quality of education is included, and most of these will turn out to be derived from forms of decentralization whose primacy is deemed to be 'political' – not surprising, given that in this instance the concern is limited to decentralization rationales which have different implications for the distribution of authority.

Education has a degree of autonomy. Over time, it may even be a source of change in the power relations among groups in society. It certainly has its own instrumentalities. But it is also socially embedded in a variety of ways; and thought about education is conditioned by more general ideas about society and its institutions. Thought and tradition relating to political legitimacy in a given society are likely to serve as a global framework which conditions ideas about how authority should be distributed in a wide range of institutions – including education. Similarly, concerns to improve efficiency will tend to relate to a larger range of institutions so that they are extended to also include education. However, ideas concerning the quality of education are rarely extended to apply to the efficient running of organizations other than schools, or to thought about a politically legitimate distribution of authority.

Given these considerations, the grouping of types under the two rubrics of 'political' and 'quality and efficiency' will necessarily be loose. The main purpose of the chapter is however to examine how different decentralization rationales differ in their implications both for the authority distribution and for ways in which educational institutions should be evaluated.

POLITICAL RATIONALES FOR DECENTRALIZATION

There are different rationales for decentralization depending on the answer that is given to the question: 'Who has the right to decide and by what ideas are such rights justified?'

Liberalism

Central to the liberal tradition is belief in the value of freedom from restraint, of individualist 'liberties' – values which historically were secured by struggle against state absolutism, against traditional social ascription and against the cultural hold of established religious orthodoxy. Thus, liberalism favours much individual freedom, and the main current of liberalism favours a generally wide dispersal of authority.[6] It is also characterized by much optimism about the value of education and the advancement of knowledge for the development of individuals and for social progress.

Liberalism has been an unusually pervasive social force. As such a broad current, it has diverse derivatives: strong local government, use of the market forces, strong professions and private provision of education are all types of decentralization rationales which can find justification in the liberal tradition. Thus, liberalism serves as an ideological umbrella for types among which conflicting claims may arise.

Liberalism militates against concentrating political power. It would rather contain it and divide it up among countervailing institutions and groups. As such, liberalism favours strong local government. But liberal views of local government are shaped by its urban cradle and by its historical struggle against traditionalism. Characteristically, the etymology of the English term 'municipal' government (even the American rural 'township') evokes the town with its greater variety of social life and its economic and cultural connections with a larger world, rather than the folk *Gemeinschaft* of a village or parish which in a liberal perspective tends to connote parochialism.

Faith in the 'invisible hand' of the market mechanism is a core ingredient of classical (and neo-classical) liberalism, not only as a means of efficient production for material 'progress' but also because the market was assumed to promote individual freedom.[7]

If liberalism becomes wedded to strong rationalist beliefs in unilinear progress and in the power of intellectual achievements to guide that progress, the emphasis on knowledge can provide arguments for centralist orchestration of education by an enlightened élite. Especially when pitted in a polarized struggle against traditionalism, rationalism can itself acquire traits akin to a secular religion, with a strong proselytizing mission using state schools as main agencies of its transmission, in opposition to the competition from religious 'traditionalist' education, as it did in the case of French education under the Third Republic (see Clifford-Vaughan, 1963). But in its mainstream liberalism tends to be wedded to a pragmatist view of knowledge that accords value to 'informed common sense', to inductionist empiricism, and which breeds scepticism against intellectually derived universally applicable 'solutions' to social problems.[8]

In contrast to socialist and populist views of education, which tend to prescribe for it the importance of not educating pupils away from respectively their working-class or 'folk community' roots, liberalism values education as a means to social mobility of individuals in a social structure which is thereby rendered more fluid and less culturally segmented. Individual mobility rather than the collective advancement of groups is the ideal.

Whether wedded to rationalism or to empiricist pragmatism, liberalism views the advancement and transmission of knowledge as a precondition for greater personal autonomy and for social advancement. Thus there is much general faith in the power of education. The concept of 'Liberal Education' – which in its classical Greek origins meant immersion in disciplined knowledge in order to free the mind from ignorance and error – has in the liberal tradition been the main concept of general education. Therein lies an emphasis on cognition, on developing the mind. Acquisition of disciplined bodies of knowledge are important for this purpose, but these are seen as evolving, not as static contents. The ideal is that learners actively engage with such evolving knowledge to 'make up their own mind'; knowledge is not simply to be handed down to passive receivers. It is an individualistic view of learning that stresses informed independent probing and reflection – critical thinking. It rejects the view that it is necessary for education to transmit beliefs, norms and values as preserves of 'received' culture that must not be questioned. It is a view of education which well accords with the culture of science. This is a view from which much respect for professional expertise may be derived, especially for professionalism that rests on mastery of cognitive knowledge.

A distinctly 'liberal' trend is individualist tolerance of social diversity – in keeping with the value of liberty in the sense of 'freedom from restraint'. Tolerance, even active support, for private provision of education is one derivative of liberalism, in accord with its tolerance of diversity, its historical association with promotion of the market mechanism in economic activity and, in classical Anglo-Saxon liberal tradition, the concern to contain the power of the state. The financial support offered to private schools in such countries as the Netherlands and Denmark is in the liberal tradition.

But private schools serve diverse aims.[9] The largest private systems of education are those associated with religious organizations which find public schools to be insufficiently attentive to their beliefs. When faced with claims of a private system which seeks to transmit orthodoxies, liberals face a dilemma, given their commitment to critical enquiry. It becomes for them, too, a question of how far to tolerate within education those values which they oppose. But compared to other ideologies, liberalism legitimates the further stretching of tolerance for 'that with which one disagrees'. Thus, liberalism is the stance which is most generally hospitable to private provision in education – regardless of the educational orientation of such provisions.

Federalism

At the time when the USA's Constitution was framed, federalism was philosophically articulated by Madison and Hamilton as a device to prevent tyrannical rule by decentralizing power – as part of a larger scheme of checks and balances against excessive concentration of power. Thus federalism can also find justification in the liberal tradition. But federalism also exists in many countries simply as a political compromise in the combination of 'member states' which have striven to ensure considerable self-government based on a degree of separate 'national identity'. It is a type of state formation that has been established either as a largely voluntary combination of member states or by devolution of power so that 'provinces' or 'regions' become member states in a country that was previously established within a more centralist framework. In the latter case, federalism has typically been a concession 'to preserve unity' in the face of strong separatist movements (e.g. Canada, Belgium at present). Thus, no uniform ideology legitimates federalism.

In a federation or a looser confederation in which 'sovereignty' formally is not conceded by the member states the constitution typically reserves for each state the powers not specifically delegated to the federal government.

Education is typically an area thus reserved for each member state, without direct federal control. Thus, each state has a constitutional right to fashion its own education system, which it may choose to run in a tightly centralized manner (at 'state' level) – or for which it may further delegate much responsibility to local bodies. The authority distribution may thus vary among the member states in a federation (as exemplified in the USA and Australia).

Though a federal government will have highly circumscribed authority over the education systems in member states, it can wield considerable influence by strings attached to offers of financial support to education – a mechanism which has been much used in the USA. Voluntary policy co-ordination among the states in order to ensure broad equivalence of credentials thereby facilitating the mobility of labour is also common. In the European Union, where the Maastricht Treaty is moving in the direction of a federation, both processes are now at work, serving to 'harmonize' to some extent the systems of secondary and higher education.

Much institutional homogeneity may develop within federations by a shared political culture and through professional networks. The institutions which emerge in some member states may provide models for others to adopt or modify. But since the distribution of authority rests on each state's right to fashion its own system of education, as it sees fit, not on a consideration of what level should make what decisions on 'efficiency' grounds, there will be scope for much variation. Recognition of equivalence of educational credentials, for occupational certification purposes, is not always ensured by federal authority or by voluntary agreements among member states (Switzerland and the USA are examples).

Harmonization in the interest of efficiency – to facilitate the mobility of labour – is thus only pursued to the extent that it suits the authorities in each state. This will vary among federations. Federations can break up (for example, the Soviet Union, the secession of Bangladesh from Pakistan), or they may remain uneasily unified (India, Canada, Belgium, Nigeria). They may contain states with a strongly separate cultural identity based on religion, language (Quebec, Swiss cantons, Belgium) and ethnicity (India). Historically, there are also monarchies which have had a 'federal' or 'confederal' character (Austria-Hungary, Sweden-Norway in the nineteenth century), within which strong movements of national separatism emerged. In such cases, the 'uneasy members' may pursue their own 'nationalist' education policies (Norway in the late nineteenth century), rather than harmonization with other members states or realms. Often this entails a relatively high concentration of authority at the level of the 'state'. Quebec is one example.

Thus, a federal form of government can coexist with a great variety of different distributions of authority over education within the member states. But in federations which achieve a securely established legitimacy, without separatist movements, convergence by mutual adjustments among member states as to educational structures is likely to occur. It is likely also that the growth of occupations which require some specialized prior schooling, and of federation-wide markets for goods, services, and labour will provide an impetus for such convergence in education structures.

Populist Localism

Populism is a challenge to the dominance of established élites which are conscious of their separation from and superiority to ordinary people. Thus, it is a form of social protest. In positive terms, a major political expression of populism is advocacy of direct and very local democracy. In present parlance the 'empowerment' of ordinary people in their local communities is a core value.[10]

Populist movements have diverse expressions, depending on the more specific values which imbue them and the élites which they react against. This diversity of expression makes it hard to fit populism within a 'conservative-radical' conceptualization of political groupings, for while it may be radical in its rejection of élite dominance, it tends towards conservatism in relation to the cultural values of ordinary folk.

It would be misleading to see populism as a spontaneous reaction of the populace. There is typically a 'counter-élite' which creates a role for itself as charismatic leaders and guides of 'the people'. Such counter-élites will actively seek to play down their own distinctions from ordinary folk and seek to cast themselves in the role of 'tribunes of the people'. In cultural populism they may actively work to reconstruct a new but more 'popularly derived' high culture. Language reconstruction movements (Gaelic in Ireland, New Norse in Norway, Finnish in Finland) are historical examples of this, as are 'low church' religious revival or contemporary Islamic fundamentalism. However, in spite of the nativism of their message, such cultural reconstructionists have typically also been much influenced by their own intellectual imports from abroad such as German national romanticism in the nineteenth century.

A populist view of education stresses the importance of learning arenas other than schools: the home, the community, the workplace. It supports the importance of learning from experience, of practical knowledge which is not formally structured (the kind which Polyani (1958; 1967) dubbed 'tacit knowledge'). Thus, a populist view of education values skills that can be applied to practical tasks and problems outside of school, in the home, the workplace and the local community. It is in this respect quite compatible with a pragmatist philosophy of education, which characteristically developed in the United States.

Populism harbours no great deference to formal schooling, but schooling may be valued as a cultural ornament. When schooling opens a window on to a larger world it must do so without alienating pupils from their origins. The 'high culture' which is valued is that which is 'close to the people' and which gives dignity to their condition – neither conservative exclusive culture nor the avant-garde cultural radicalism of an aloof élite. Thus, neither classical languages nor modern abstract art has any place among the ideals of general education associated with populism. Populism assumes that valued culture is already in place in the home, in the children's communities and in civic or cultural institutions with which people identify. Thus, school is to play a supplementary role; it is not a form of resocialization which would drive back the darkness of ignorance by providing enlightenment from high above.

Because populism holds up the rights to decide, and the good sense in making decisions, of the community of common people, it advocates – in keeping with Rousseau's theory of democracy – government by quite direct and frequent expression of 'popular will'. Distinctly populist forms of government include the plebiscites and the referendums, the town hall meetings and citizen assemblies. A populist view implies that public officials should be public servants, accountable to the local community which they serve. Thus, direct election of public officials is a populist trait. Populism implies that local government should be based on small 'community-like' population units – the village, the small town – and that such government, close to the people, should have extensive powers.

For education, populism means that schools should be local, community-based institutions, run by local government in small population units. Teachers are the servants of the community and of the parents whose children they teach. For teachers and school administrators populism may provide intrusive local taskmasters, though Norway is a case where teachers historically gained local status and much autonomy by their involvement as activists in populist movements.[11]

In general, a common denominator of populism is rejection of the authoritativeness of technocratic and professional expertise. To the extent that populism conditions mainstream politics of education today, it has important consequences for education, for it attacks the twin buffers which have sheltered educational professionals from localist intrusion upon their autonomy: deference to their professional expertise and their bureaucratic accountability to a centralist state.

Participatory Democracy

This form of decentralization rests on the assertion that those who have their daily work in an institution, the institution's 'participants', should have equal rights to take part in decisions affecting the work of the institution. It also asserts that the institution should have freedom from outside control. In its purest form, this mode of organization would be most clearly derived from a combination of the anarchist and syndicalist varieties of socialism. Anarchism assumes that all hierarchical organization is oppressive and that human beings are stunted in their self-realization when they are subjected to bureaucratic authority (Woodcock, 1962). Syndicalism maintains that work collectivities should be the building blocks for social organization. For all those who are part of the working collectivity of the institution, the coequal right to participate in decisions becomes both a condition for freedom and for avoiding alienation from their work.

The ideal social organization thus becomes a loose association of voluntarily co-operating institutions, each characterized by internally minimized hierarchy – a distinctly 'flat' organization structure. There should be much use of an institutional assembly of all 'participants' for making decisions. When authority is delegated by that assembly to committees or co-ordinators, there should be much and frequent rotation of persons in such positions of special responsibility. While decisions reached collectively would be binding upon the 'participants', the ideal way of resolving conflicts is by discussion, persuasion and mutual adjustments among equals. Voluntarism is a strongly nurtured norm, and rules and regulations are held to a 'minimum'.

Such anti-bureaucratic, anarchist ideas were generally important in the 'student movement' of the late 1960s and the early 1970s, conditioning the neo-Marxist thought connected with that movement, for example, the definition of Eastern European communism as a form of bureaucratic or state capitalism rather than as a form of 'true' socialism.

This anti-authoritarian movement had universities and schools as its base. It is here that the impact at the time was greatest. But in some countries the movement occasioned experimentation with new 'communalist' social forms outside of educational institutions – the hippie 'communes' and therapeutic communes for drug addicts. In some countries the ideological trend of the 1970s affected labour legislation by introducing new mechanisms for worker influence on management decisions; and some firms experimented with new forms of production as alternatives to the assembly line (e.g. at Volvo). In religious life, 'Liberation Theology' with its emphasis on social action and on 'empowering' the powerless in developing countries is arguably another legacy.

The 'deschooling' ideas in education bore much semblance to a fundamentally anarchist view of society. While schools were castigated as bureaucratic reproducers of oppressive inequality, the ideal held up by such writers as Illich and Reimers was voluntary participation in 'learning networks', persons offering themselves as 'skill models' rather than being officially appointed as teachers. Freire's concept of education as 'conscientization' (a precursor of the 'empowerment' concept) of impoverished adult persons so that they become aware of conditions which oppress them and are given a mindset to act collectively against those conditions can be seen as an adaptation of concepts associated with 'participatory democracy' – with an admixture of populist ideas.

Other examples from the 1970s include the wave of interest in 'dialogue pedagogy', and the idea that curriculum should evolve as 'negotiated knowledge' between teachers and pupils. The current of thought associated with all these concepts was strongly anti-authoritarian and anti-formal: a reaction against hierarchy in general and against bureaucracy in particular, against technocratic expertise, against subjects conceived as 'disciplines of knowledge'. A symbolic manifestation of this anti-authoritarianism was the reaction against conventions of formal dress, and against the use of titles and other formal modes of address. There was general scepticism against imposed 'requirements', against graded marking of submitted work and against individualistic competitive pursuit of credentials. Thus, in Norway, some junior academics started a campaign against the doctoral degree.

Some new 'alternative' institutions were established with the aim, *inter alia*, of practising very extensive participatory democracy in school governance and offering more scope for voluntarism in the style of learning. Examples are a scatter of 'alternative' schools both in the United States and in a number of Western European countries. An expression of anti-formalism in the definition of knowledge was more scope for cross-disciplinary 'social-activist-oriented' courses of study, and more recognition of 'group projects'. In education as a field of study an example is the development of 'social pedagogy' (e.g. Germany, Norway). Some new institutions of higher education (e.g. Roskilde in Denmark, Tromsø in Norway) combined an emphasis on inter-disciplinary 'problem-oriented' study with extensive participatory democracy.

What characterized the ideas of participatory democracy and the imprint they left on education was a more egalitarian distribution of authority among those who are internal participants in an institution. The 'rights' to such participation were emphasized along with arguments about how the exercise of such rights would promote both personal self-actualization and needed social activism.

The ideas associated with participatory democracy also affected prevailing thought about how schools improve. There was a reaction against centralist school reforms, against attempts to devise a 'one best system' by first trying out innovations in 'pilot schools', refining and adjusting, and then 'going to scale' with new structures in a centrally orchestrated manner. Rather, there was interest in improvement from below, for seeking to nurture a climate of open debate and shared problem-solving within schools with minimal imposition from outside.

At present the institution-communalist mood of the 1970s has receded as an active force of ideas. Perhaps more enduring than any institutional impact have been the attitudes of a generation of former university students whose formative ideas were influenced by the radicalism of the 1970s. Many of these found work as teachers in schools, in higher education, or in the service occupations of the welfare state. Further, the 'anti-professions' tenor of the decentralization concepts which at present are on the offensive (use of market mechanisms, management by objectives) may partly be nurtured by the suspicion among its advocates that too much prevails of the ideas from the 'student movement' among the social professions of the welfare state.

CONCERNS OF QUALITY OR EFFICIENCY

Systems of thought differ as to how far they have implications across a wide range of phenomena. In general, the systems of ideas which stand out in this respect will be those which have been most philosophically developed. The discussion above has already revealed that the 'political' rationales for decentralization (save federalism) all have implications for concepts of quality in education – not only for the distribution of authority – and that liberalism stands out as a 'parent ideology' of different rationales of more limited scope. Some of that varied brood will be considered below as separate types, among the forms of decentralization rationales that are mainly concerned with matters of quality and efficiency. As noted earlier, quality and efficiency concepts overlap, but they differ as to emphasis: goals and pedagogic process – or management and resource utilization.

Pedagogic Professionalism

'Professionalism' may be considered to be among the progeny of liberalism. In the history of British liberalism, professionalism probably also gained support from the evolutionary way that liberal ideas won through politically: as a gradual extension of 'liberties' in the sense of privilege to a widening network of different élites and establishments.

Autonomy for a profession is legitimated by its claim to specialized esoteric expertise, by the capacity of the profession to select, train and certify their members and to 'police' this membership when need arises so as to enforce norms of professional performance. Clients are assumed not to know what is in their own best interest when they receive the services which a profession provides; and lay authorities (whether political or lay-bureaucratic) are seen as insufficiently expert to direct and supervise the work of the profession. Thus professional autonomy implies distinctly weak evaluation of professional practice by outsiders. The skills and methods acquired during professional socialization, and the identification with a professional community which values quality performance, are supposed to obviate much of the need for such control.

For professions which work within the public services, the professional model implies that the administrative bureaucracy which regulates the profession's work should be staffed by professional cadres – by administrators who themselves initially were trained and certified as professionals.

Applied to education, the rationale of professionalism accords great autonomy to teachers; and it implies that their work should be regulated by others who themselves are within their profession. But the concession of professional autonomy presupposes that teachers succeed in establishing their credibility as professionals – that they not only have specialized expertise (so have farmers, shopkeepers, skilled workers), but that this expertise is esoteric – understood by the specially initiated alone, and that development of this expertise requires a long period of initiation which lays much stress on its theoretical foundations. The less strongly based the teachers' claim to esoteric expertise is, the more they will be directed and supervised by institutional managers, by more remote professional-bureaucratic authority (e.g. inspectors) or by political authority or governing bodies of non-educationists.

The professional expertise of teachers has two aspects – knowledge of the subject matter to be taught, and expertise in the process of teaching itself. In some countries, historical connections between education and religion may have sustained a special respect for school teaching among ordinary lay persons, for example, Confucianist and Buddhist traditions, Jewish traditions, the historical evolution of primary education out of preparation for religious confirmation in Lutheran countries (and of school teaching evolving as an extension of an office of the parish church, that of clergyman's assistant – the Lutheran deacon). Thus, sacred origins of school knowledge have historically served to build lay deference to the teacher. But general trends of societal modernization have undermined such religiously founded deference to teachers.

As to secular knowledge, the expertise with regards to 'contents' has historically been a firmer peg for claims of professional knowledge than has the expertise in how to teach. Autonomy is conceded most readily to those who teach a subject at its most 'advanced' level (e.g. university professors). Those who teach knowledge which is closer to what ordinary adults already know or who teach norms and values about which ordinary persons consider themselves to be 'equally expert', will tend to be accorded less autonomy by lay persons.

It is harder to gain external acceptance for the claim to esoteric expertise in how to teach. Obviously special expertise is involved, but that is also true for all manner of 'skilled' work in occupations which are not granted any special professional autonomy. Learning, and deliberate activities designed to make others learn, are universal human activities about which ordinary people have their own experiences and judgements, much more so than about the specialized contents which are taught.

It is through improving the traditional routines of whole-class teaching with recourse to a body of pedagogic theory that pedagogy has sought to base claims of professional autonomy. The varied strains within the progressive education tradition have been a common foundation for such claims. Of these strains, it is 'activity methods' which would seem to serve as a rationale for the most devolved professional autonomy, because this is the pedagogy of contingent responses to the needs and active interests of individual learners and to varied circumstances in their life and active concerns outside of school. Such a pedagogy may be guided by illustrative examples but it cannot be tightly programmed by manuals and regulations.

Organizing teaching by 'subjects' with their hierarchy of expertise extending to research and scholarship based at university buttresses the autonomy of university academics and it may strengthen their influence upon contents taught in school, but it sets limits to professionalism among schoolteachers. Nevertheless, the scope for schoolteachers' claims to professional autonomy is widened by an approach to curriculum which stresses the importance of themes and projects which cut across such subjects – another feature often associated with 'activity methods'.

The extent to which citizens and politicians are ready to accede autonomy to classroom teachers will reflect the views they have of such methods, not least based on their own school experience and upon the impression they gain from their own children when the latter are taught by such methods. Public opinion on the practical merits of 'progressive methods' is typically divided.

A more educated public will demand more education for the next generation, and this will add political importance to education. But when people are more educated, they will also more readily form their own confident judgements about the quality of pedagogy that they or their children receive, and they will assert their views with less deference to the teachers' professional expertise. Rising levels of education and the growth of other 'middle-class' occupations therefore tend to erode the special elevation which schoolteachers in some countries (e.g. France, Scotland) have previously enjoyed. In certain circumstances it then made them natural candidates for leadership roles during the formative period of broadly based civic life – as the most educated persons of popular origins, with scarce skills and ease of public speaking (e.g. Norway). Such skills have now become less scarce.

On the one hand, teachers now have a longer education and professional training than in previous times. Thus, the competence base for professionalism is likely to have increased. On the other hand, their public is much more educated than previously and less ready to defer to professional opinion. Lack of deference to professions is not confined to education. As the scale and cost of public services have grown, politicians have become more wary about accepting the judgements of professional 'insiders' about matters of quality and resource allocation in these services. Thus, the case for professional autonomy among schoolteachers is today uneasily founded in many countries.

Management by Objectives

Management by objectives is advocated by its supporters as a means to promote effectiveness and efficiency – to make operations more goal-directed and to use resources more optimally. It has been offered as a superior alternative to management by rules and regulations, proposing to give those at 'lower levels' in an organization more freedom in the choice of means and in allocating resources. In this respect it is offered as a form of decentralization of authority.

But this strategy also requires greater concreteness of what goals are to be reached by what time, and more shared planning of how these goals are to be realized. Each employee is to take part in setting timed objectives for his or her own work and work group. However, this planning is to occur with clear reference to the strategic goals for the organization as a whole and within the frames of more general objectives which are laid down by higher levels of management.[12] Thus, whether management by objectives enhances the autonomy for each sub-unit and each employee, rather than subjecting them to more exacting demands imposed from above, would then seem to depend on the nature of these objectives set at higher levels and on whether those at lower levels have a real participatory role in influencing them.

Management by objectives includes the establishment of performance indicators, as part of management information systems, that are used to monitor the extent to which objectives are reached. Institutionalization of quality assurance presupposes ongoing feedback from such indicators. Both the planning of objectives and the measurement of how well they are reached are means by which persons, units, and the organization as a whole are rendered more externally accountable.

The detractors of management by objectives tend to see it not as a form of decentralization but merely as a freedom to work under harder pressures of accountability on tasks which have become more binding because one has been induced to take part in setting them for oneself – and on terms strongly defined by central management.

Like scientific management, management by objectives stresses strong specification of tasks – but by goals, rather than by rules and regulations and a finely graded and stable division of labour. Like the human relations school of management, which once arose as a reaction to scientific management, management by objectives stresses the importance of group solidarity. But, while the human relations school gave special emphasis to meeting the personal needs of employees and to tapping the potential of informal networks, management by objectives gives more attention to explicit efforts to bind each employee to the organization's purposes.

Micro-level planning is more than an efficiency device, it is intended to build identification with the organization and collective engagement in its tasks – a strong 'institutional culture'. Observers sometimes point to historical antecedents for management by objectives in the programme budgeting techniques pioneered at the Ford Motor company and in the American Space Program. But a less immediately visible influence may derive from Western emulation of work organization in Japanese industry: involving each employee in groups which plan and critically assess their contribution to the organization, thereby building strong collective bonding to the organization's overall goals.

Management by objectives was a technique initially developed for business and industrial firms. Since the 1980s, it has influenced management of public services (including education) in a number of countries – at least in some modified form that stresses micro-level planning, specification of tangible objectives and management information systems. There is undoubtedly a case for better monitoring of the use of time and financial resources in education. Education is of course also a goal-directed activity. But management by objectives agrees more with certain strains of curriculum thought than with others.

Some educational goals are so formulated that they resist being broken down into a sequence of reachable targets whose attainment can be reliably gauged by quantitative indicators. Such specification tends to conflict with the humanistic concepts of general education which stress holistic 'understanding' and 'insight' and the development of 'critical thinking'. Such aims would be captured only very imperfectly by objective tests of goal attainment, and require an overall judgement of quality. Specified learning 'targets' would ill agree with the pedagogical ethos of 'activity methods' which tends to accord intrinsic educational value to certain pedagogic processes. Moreover, proponents of 'activity methods' often claim that objective tests and formal exams have undesirable backwash effects on the process of teaching and learning.

However, there is a strain of pedagogy which is quite hospitable to 'management by objectives' techniques, namely the curriculum tradition which favours specification of learning goals in the form of behavioural objectives. This approach is derived from behaviourist psychology. Benjamin Bloom's attempt to create a taxonomy of educational objectives is a well-known example. The more recent attempt to translate curriculum goals into quite concrete 'basic skills' is another example. These concepts may be seen as a manifestation of the 'hard' side of the American pragmatist tradition in education, as contrasted with the 'soft' side which, like European child-centred 'naturalism', has stressed less tangible process goals. It seems likely that the style of pedagogy which is most compatible with management by objectives tends to strengthen the authority of a cadre of pedagogic experts above the individual teacher – in the management structure of education and its allied curriculum experts.[13]

Regardless of pedagogic outlook, there is a conflict between the emphasis on external accountability and on group processes in planning, on the one hand, and the insistence on considerable personal autonomy which inheres in professionalism, on the other.

It remains to be seen how far management by objectives will penetrate and enduringly influence the running of educational institutions in different countries. But 'outside' demands for efficiency measures are unlikely to abate so long as there remains a tight squeeze on public finance for education. Thus, the cost consciousness side of management by objectives is especially likely to remain important for education.

The Market Mechanism

Use of the market mechanism in education is another form of decentralization which is justified by the desire to improve efficiency, though it may also be advocated to serve the classical liberal value of freedom from restraint for the individual person.

Advocates of the market mechanism assume that services of good quality and efficient use of resources are best achieved by competition. Educational institutions will compete for customers who are free to choose from the marketed supply of services. The flow of resources to each institution will then depend on the volume of their 'sale'. The customers may themselves pay for services received.

Alternatively, a quasi-market would be to tie funding from public coffers to the volume of services rendered, so that customers choose but do not pay themselves. Or a combination is used whereby the direct customers must pay for part of the cost. The contemporary euphemism for tuition fees is 'user charges'. The customers may be individual students or their families, or firms buying courses for their employees or public agencies buying education for their clients.

It is a type of rationale which implies that private providers should be free to establish schools and to compete with each other and with public provisions, and that families and individuals should be free to 'buy' such schooling. But no contemporary society relies on private fee-paying schooling as a main mode for organizing basic education. A major reason is that there is extremely unequal purchasing power among the 'customers'. And even economists in the neo-classical tradition argue that there are 'external benefits' of education which warrant a role for public subsidies – if not necessarily for public provision.

There are, however, numerous recent examples of how market forces may be adapted to public provisions and public finance. A main approach is to allow families a choice among institutions so that institutions are forced to compete with each other. Milton Friedman's (1963) concept of a 'voucher system' has been an influential proposal for how a publicly financed education market might operate. Each person would be given a non-transferable 'education voucher' to be used to buy education from among competing institutions which then would depend on these vouchers for their income. The voucher system has been much debated in some countries (especially in Britain under Thatcher, and in some states in the USA). No country has introduced a voucher system along the lines proposed by Friedman. But it has in a number of countries inspired change so that schools recruit students competitively rather than relying on catchment areas, with public finance being more tied to enrolments – or additionally, to the number of students who successfully complete their courses 'on time'. In return, schools may be given greater freedom to decide what to offer and to engage in sale of 'special' courses and services to institutional buyers. Recent policies in England and Wales, the United States, Denmark and Sweden exemplify to varying degrees moves in this direction.

When policies favour more use of market forces, much public regulation is usually still retained, for example, a minimum length of schooling required of all, some monitoring of performance and certification of institutions. But the rationale for the market mechanism assumes that customers will be induced to inform themselves adequately about the quality of services offered by different providers. It also assumes that the customers are themselves the rightful and best judges about what education to demand – in contrast to the assumptions in the rationale for professional autonomy.

The policies associated with increased use of the market mechanism in education may differ so much among countries that one should beware of firm generalizations about the likely effects. But research by Ball and his associates has highlighted some of the risks which in England may be associated with parental choice of school guided by publicized indicators of 'school performance': that schools compete to attract the most able pupils and are discouraged from enrolling the less motivated and less able, that schools may come to devote much attention to 'superficial' impression management, that competition undermines co-opera-tion among schools, and that it is 'middle-class' parents who disproportionately exploit the greater choice afforded them. Thus, increasing social class inequality in education may be a result, as well as greater inequality of opportunity between 'more able' and 'less able' students (Ball, 1993a; 1993b).

To ensure efficient production of quality services, the market mechanism relies on survival and expansion of those providers which are most competitive, and on the 'shaping up' or dwindling of those which fail to deliver the goods and break even. But if the most competitive schools have no surplus of places, or if they choose not to respond to demand by increasing their supply, the net result may be to reinforce inequalities in selectiveness among the existing schools, thus reinforcing status hierarchies among them. In culturally pluralistic countries, freer choice of which school to attend and what to study may also threaten cultural cohesion. In general, a major risk of releasing market forces in education is increased social divisiveness.

The rationale for competition and parental choice assumes that competing offerings will be available within reach of the customers. This assumption will be unrealistic for basic education in many localities with a small population base.

Deconcentration

When a system has been characterized by bureaucratic centralism, deconcentra-tion means greater geographical decentralization of state authority, transferring to regional and local officials more authority to take initiatives for new activity, to budget, and to recruit and deploy staff. Deconcentration is a structural change as distinct from the more easily revocable delegation of authority from superiors to staff who are directly responsible to them.

Deconcentration requires change in regulations, frequently also in legislative frameworks. But in contrast to other forms of decentralization, deconcentrated authority remains state authority with lines of accountability extending only upwards to the central government, even if non-officials are co-opted into local advisory councils. As such it is distinct from what is called 'devolution' – estab-lishing by constitutional change a federal system of government or transferring by law more autonomy to 'political' locally constituted government.

Deconcentration may occur within an existing *état* or branch of the state's civil service, without rearranging the division of responsibility among them, for example, so that regional or local education officers are given more responsibility while each remains accountable to the same chain of responsibility as before. A frequent goal for such change is to remedy clogged decision-making at higher levels – a problem which tends to grow as the scale of activity in a service expands – so that higher officials are given more time to concentrate on planning and more strategic decisions. A related rationale is the view that those officials who are closest to local operations know best what should be done, and should be given incentives to take initiatives rather than passing the buck to higher levels.

Deconcentration involves a relaxation of the network of rules which govern decisions at regional or local levels of officialdom. In this respect it resembles both management by objectives and professionalism, and it may subsume shifts in the direction of either of these other forms of decentralization, for example, more emphasis on professional training of intermediate administrators and introducing performance indicators in return for slacker constraint of rules and on budget allocations.

However, deconcentration frequently has aims which go beyond improved efficiency within a given *état*. It is often part of a strategy to improve local and regional co-ordination among previously separate public services and to strengthen regional planning (Conyers, 1982). For example, all levels and types of education operated in a region may be brought together under the office of a regional education director, rather than being separately accountable to different branches in the same ministry, or even to different ministries. Or education may be combined with other 'kindred' services (e.g. sports, culture, social services for youth) under a single administrative office at regional or local level. Typically, there are countervailing arguments about what is 'efficient' co-ordination when such change is proposed. The case for local co-ordination across branches is argued against the case for national co-ordination within a given branch of activity.

For schools, deconcentration means more accountability to closer bureaucratic superiors. This may imply more responsive and speedier decisions at the level above the school – if the intermediate officials develop the competence required to discharge their increased responsibility. There may be gains of better local co-ordination among services brought under the same administrative umbrella, but integration across previously distinct *états* will – like all such structural change – for a period to be resented by those most directly affected, as undermining values, identities and networks with which they have come to develop strong identification. The reconstruction of morale under such circumstances will in part depend on whether the change which is introduced has more resources in its train, and better training and career prospects, than the old order which it replaced.

THE FORMS COMPARED

Different Emphases and Relations

The forms discussed above are different alternatives to 'bureaucratic centralism' in a national education system. It has been shown that they would prescribe or legitimate quite different distributions of authority, thus sustaining the claim that 'decentralization' should not be thought of as a unitary concept.

Liberalism justifies a generally wide distribution of authority. Beyond that basic tenet, it tends to be a broad creed. Thus it may legitimate federalism (though federalism can also be based on other rationales). It can justify strong control by local government – although the localist *Gemeinschaft* ideal which populism has for small 'community-like' units of such government, will, in a liberal perspective, tend to be seen as 'parochialism'. It may also serve as a rationale for the use of the market mechanism to allocate resources for education. Further, liberalism is the one political rationale that most consistently supports private provisions in education in that it tolerates diversity of orientation among such provisions.

Compared to the anti-authoritarian socialist ideas which most clearly support 'participatory democracy', liberalism is less collectivist-egalitarian and would attach no particular exclusiveness to 'institutional participants' in its view of who should locally share in decision-making. But there is in liberal thought a distinctive emphasis on cognitive knowledge as a progressive force in society. Hence, it can legitimate institutional autonomy focused on strong professions.

All that federalism implies is distinctly weak power of the federal central bureaucracy and its political masters. It contains no clear prescription as to the further distribution of authority below the level of each member state of a federation. Thus, federalism may go with a high degree of bureaucratic centralism within each member state.

Populism would prescribe strong and distinctly 'local' political government of schools, and strong parental control. Current strains of anti-technocratic and anti-professional populist politics may also be compatible with management by objectives to 'keep professionals on their toes' and to facilitate accountability to local political masters.

Participatory democracy legitimates weak authority for all 'outside' bodies but strong codetermination for all those 'insiders' whose daily work is encompassed by the school. To the extent that parents of young students involve themselves in the daily activities of the school and become part of its 'working collectivity', parents may also be recognized as 'insiders', but in institutions with young learners the main participants will be the teachers. For mature learners (for example, university students) the students themselves will be important participants.

As a distinct form, professionalism means above all autonomy for each teacher. It implies distinctly weak influence for outsiders to the teacher's profession. But it may take the form of vertically organized professional establishments that extend from teachers to specialist offices within the education bureaucracy and to expertise based in universities. The autonomy which teachers have will depend on how far others concede special esoteric expertise in what is to be taught and in how to teach. In particular, the claims of professionals to autonomy will clash with populist scepticism against the expertise of culturally remote élites. A populist view would be that professions are simply occupations which, like the medieval guilds, have managed to achieve monopolistic control of certain occupational activities and that their autonomy is a shelter behind which much pursuit of self-interest thrives.

A case for professionalism that primarily is based on pedagogic rather than subject expertise can be stretched to accommodate some degree of participatory democracy. In schools the most influential insiders to participatory democracy will in any case tend to be the teachers, and 'participation' may be a means to socialize students to the role of politically active democratic citizens. But there are tensions between the emphasis on collective decisions in participatory democracy and the emphasis on personal autonomy that inheres in professionalism.

Management by objectives – in contrast to 'professionalism' and 'participatory democracy' – implies a management with strong capacity to plan and to mobilize involvement in planning at all levels in the education system. Like populism, but in a much more systematized manner, it is a style that lays bare the work of education to 'outside' scrutiny, serving as a means of control by those to whom institutions are externally accountable. Once objectives have been set, the greater flexibility to deploy resources would give management more room to manoeuvre but it also requires greater skills to resolve conflicts about resource allocation – as compared to administration by rules and regulations under 'bureaucratic centralism'. When management by objectives is imposed on staffs who have had aspirations to professionalism, management faces a difficult task: how to build committed participation in an approach which their staff often will perceive to thwart such aspirations. Management by objectives may be (but need not be) combined either with use of the market mechanism, or with a deconcentrated form of state authority.

The market mechanism relies on competition for customers, rather than on authority, as a means of externally regulating education. Like management by objectives it gives emphasis to management functions, but in this case especially to the need for management to 'market' the services offered.

Finally, deconcentration of a system that previously has been organized along lines of bureaucratic centralism means more authority to those agents of the state who have management responsibility for education at regional or local level. It seeks to 'off-load' routine matters from central offices, and to achieve more co-ordination among different public services at these levels – more regional planning.

The main implications that the different forms of decentralization have for the distribution of authority in education are summarized in Table 1.1, which also summarizes their implications for evaluating institutions.[14]

Implications for Evaluating Education

Comprehensive evaluation of education looks not only at learning outcomes but also at the processes and the rationales for practice. It is realized that theory-conscious practitioners of evaluation often find it useful to borrow evaluation ideas that derive from diverse theoretical rationales – and that the less theory-conscious are often similarly eclectic. Further, evaluation theory will draw on a larger body of thought than that which concerns decentralization of authority. However, the present concern is neither to map evaluation theory nor to describe evaluation practice. It is simply to explore those particular implications which the typal forms of decentralization may have for evaluating and monitoring educational institutions and practice.

Liberalism would rely on market forces or professional self-regulation, but would also generally justify much freedom for individual teachers and schools from intrusive forms of external evaluation. Federalism has no particular implications for how (and to what extent) the performance of schools should be evaluated.

Populist localism would lay bare the school to scrutiny by parents and local politicians. What is stressed is the external local transparency of small, community-based schools. Politicians and parents will be especially concerned to ensure that their views about the ends and means of education are reflected in the work of the school. Scrutiny may occur by personal visits, by each school reporting to its own board of parents and local politicians, and by schools organizing occasions for displaying their work. A populist view expects schools to contribute to 'community events' – for example, sporting events, festive or commemorative occasions, fund-raising drives. In agrarian communities, before mechanization, it also might entail the expectation that schools organize (or release) students to help out during harvesting or in reafforestation campaigns. Though formal proce-

Table 1.1   *Implications of Different Forms of Decentralization*

	Alternatives to Bureaucratic Centralism	Emphasis in the distribution of decision-making authority	Means of evaluating & monitoring institutions and educational practice
P O L I T I C A L R A T I O N A L E S	Liberalism	Wide dispersal, e.g: • strong local government in fairly 'large' units • private provision • market mechanism • professional autonomy	• market forces, or • professional self-regulation • weak state control
	Federalism	• the federal authority is weak • no further prescription	• no implications
	Populist Localism	• strong local government at 'community' level • parental control	• informal feedbacks through local transparency
	Participatory Democracy	• weak 'outside' control • collective 'inside' decisions • flat internal structure	• only 'inside' participation • collective process • control from 'below'
Q U A L I T Y & E F F I C I E N C Y	Pedagogic Professionalism	• individual teacher autonomy • weak 'non-professional' authority	• professional self-regulation • peer review
	Management by Objectives	• strong school management • outside scrutiny of results and expenditures	• performance indicators compared with objectives and budgets
	Market Mechanism	• competition • strong school management	• customer demand • accreditation of schools
	Deconcentration	• strong state agents at regional level • regionally unified sector planning	• management information systems

dures for evaluating the work of the school may be instituted when there is lack of trust in the school, much 'evaluation' may simply be the informal impressions which the work of the school leaves on local public opinion.

The concept of participatory democracy implies that evaluation should involve all inside 'participants' and be a collective process. In particular, it opens up 'evaluation from below': students evaluating their courses, staff (and students) evaluating management. These processes would be linked to collective decisions about what to teach and how teaching should be conducted, who should be responsible for teaching and management, and how the institution as a whole should be run. This style of operating implies frequent meetings to give critical feedback and to decide the course ahead.

Professional autonomy implies that the individual teacher should not be subjected to regularized scrutiny by others. But it does imply enforcement by the professional community of its own standards of professional conduct, and that procedures be activated when complaints are received. Beyond that, 'peer review' by panels of colleagues who are highly regarded for their special expertise would be the procedure to be followed for occasional evaluation of programmes or institutions.

Management by objectives would introduce quantitative indicators which would enable both 'insiders' and 'outsiders' to compare performance with the objectives which have been established for defined periods of activity. Use of objective tests to gauge improvements in knowledge, and the use of calculations of unit costs of schools and subjects typify such evaluation measures. As to learning outcomes, performance indicators tend to give primacy to mastery of fairly concrete skills and cognitive contents – since these are the objectives whose attainment can be measured most easily. A distinctive feature of the kind of quality assurance methods which often are used as part and parcel of management by objectives, is that regular meetings be held to review progress made (in the light of, *inter alia*, performance indicators) and to modify plans. Thus, the approach can entail a planned series of occasions whereby managers meet with their subordinates, individually or in groups, to evaluate the extent to which objectives are being attained.

The market mechanism relies on competition among institutions. Evaluation is implied in changing demand; students and their families 'vote' with their feet and with their payment of fees. By this way of thought, the direct customers will seek admission to those institutions which they think offer the best 'educational value'. But public authorities may use direct inspection and 'performance indicators' (test results, exam passes, unit cost data) for the purposes of certifying institutions or to determine the scale of public subsidies.

Under deconcentration the strengthened regional administration will typically 'inherit' and retain a system of school inspection to evaluate the performance of each school and its staff. But in so far as deconcentration is motivated by the desire to plan and co-ordinate in a better way the various public services in a region, it may provide an impetus for collecting more regional information about the demand for education, the patterns of student recruitment and flows between different levels of schooling, and about the labour market. Thus, deconcentration may stimulate the development of better management information systems for the purposes of regional planning.

The Imprints Left on National Education Systems

Education systems will rarely fit any one of the types in a clear-cut manner. With the exception of federalism, the types are proposed as ideal constructs that capture key features in systems of thought which have implications for the distribution of authority. As noted earlier, other forces (for example, political expediency, practical considerations) than publicly manifest systems of thought also shape the evolution of authority distributions.

The authority distribution may bear an enduring imprint of the forces of ideology, political expediency and other practical considerations which were actively at work in an education system's formative period (Scotford Archer, 1979). But that early structure may also have resulted from a compromise between opposed views, rather than by any single system of thought. In the later course of events the patterns of authority will be modified by a succession of different currents of thought with shifting thrusts.

For example, in Norway, there is a strong legacy of populist localism from the nineteenth century – the 'founding period' of basic schooling. Since the 1930s the further development of schools has been influenced by social democratic egalitarian goals and the associated view that the state had a strong role to play – though the degree of greater centralism which resulted was a far cry from archetypal bureaucratic centralism. From the late 1960s, there was a period in which the authority distribution in education was modified by ideas of participatory democracy. Following the successful campaign in 1972 of groups opposed to Norway joining the European Union, there was some reassertion of populist-localist ideas about curriculum and control of schools. Since the restrictions on public finance which emerged in the mid-1980s, there has been a series of decentralization moves designed to promote 'efficiency': local government being given more discretion over its own budget, the government seeking to introduce some adapted form of management by objectives (requiring schools to plan their activities in a more systematic fashion, and at present developing information systems for better monitoring the schools' goal attainment and resource allocation). There is also broader political interest than previously in adapting the use of the market mechanism to some limited parts of the education system. There has also been some 'deconcentration' of the remaining state authority at the county (intermediate) level, combining various branches of education within the same office and devolving a greater share of state authority to that office.

Other countries are similarly likely to evince a mix of traits in the way that education is governed, with 'founding conditions' having an especially enduring effect, and the system gradually being modified by a succession of different influences.

CURRENT TRENDS

In present 'avant-garde' intellectualism there is much concern with post-modernist ideas. Their common denominator is that they question the possibility of 'authoritative knowledge', and by implication, of authoritative visions of a 'one best society' to be developed by the application of such knowledge.[15] These ideas would seem to agree with much tolerance of pluralism in education – of the equal validity of different ways of understanding, of each person being free to explore his or her own preferences. In a broad sense, it would seem to provide a philosophical justification for 'voluntarism' and choice in education. It remains to be seen if these post-modernist ideas will prove to be more than a passing intellectual fad – a collapse of faith in rationalism analogous to the *fin de siècle* mood which characterized the last occasion when the Western calendar approached the end of a century. At present, it is even the end of a whole millennium which is imminent.

In the more mundane world of policy debate the collapse of Eastern European socialism has undermined the international credibility of those alternatives to the market mechanism which have relied heavily on state planning. It could be that more incrementalist concepts of social development, with more awareness than before of the limits to any social engineering based on 'science', and with more confidence in liberal values of widely dispersed authority, will for some foreseeable time remain the internationally dominant political ideas.[16]

The tight public finance which characterizes so many countries at present points in a similar direction. It is a context which raises questions about the future capacity of the state to finance and provide education. Giving more rein to local government, deconcentrating the operations of the state bureaucracy, managing by objectives rather than by rules and regulations, leaving more scope for private provision and exploring ways of making public institutions more efficient by subjecting them to competition, are all trends and proposals which arise out of loss of confidence in 'statist' bureaucratic centralism as a way of managing education.

Thus, it is likely that interest in some form of decentralization will continue for some time as an international policy trend for education. One may also predict that tensions will persist between egalitarian goals and decentralization policies, with attempts to find mechanisms to reconcile decentralization with these goals. Among the decentralization policies, one may also expect tensions to persist between 'external accountability' and 'market-driven' provisions on the one hand, and modes which emphasize participation in decisions by 'insiders' on the other.

It is often argued that 'professionalization' of occupational life is a general feature of contemporary society in that 'long' and specialized training, with mastery of more theoretical knowledge, is becoming a requirement for entry to a wider range of occupations. But deference to professional autonomy may at the same time be weakened by the greater confidence which citizens have in their own judgement about the quality of professional services which they receive – not least because more of them are themselves 'professionals' in this wide sense. Thus, recognition of the importance of expertise may go hand in hand with more impatience when weak performance is perceived, and with more support for making professionals accountable to lay persons. At present, the political concerns to improve 'efficiency' in labour-intensive and large-scale public services are other forces which would reduce or redefine the professional autonomy of, for example, teachers.

Education has never been a 'secret garden', privy to professional insiders alone. But it is becoming even less so. The power of expertise is not always weakened by increased transparency, for transparency also provides an opportunity to demonstrate competence to a wider audience. But a different form of competence is required for educators to assert a strong role under conditions of greater transparency, where there is more exchange with their clients and other groups who are external stakeholders in education. New forms of expertise and sensitivity are

43

required if that exchange is to be a genuine dialogue. Unless such expertise and sensitivities are strengthened, there are risks that teachers increasingly will be reduced to demoralized operatives controlled by strong management that either will be more accountable than previously to non-professional outside authorities, or whose decisions will be shaped more by market forces.

Such reconstructed 'new professionalism' requires skills in communicating professional judgements about educational quality to 'clients', political authorities and interest groups – skills that need to be tempered with openness and critical self-scrutiny about the foundations upon which professional judgements rest. Educators will also need to display more expert judgement about efficient allocation of scarce resources in education. Skills in resolving conflicts with outsiders are also required, for strength under conditions of 'new professional' openness is a tricky balancing act given the diverse views which assertive outside groups have about education.

ACKNOWLEDGEMENT

This chapter is reprinted from *Comparative Education*, **31** (1), 1995 with permission from Carfax publishers.

NOTES

1   But geography and authority structures are intertwined in a national system of education, and geographical remoteness has implications for authority; for example, remoteness may perforce breed a degree of autonomy from distant bureaucratic superiors. There will be a need to act on unforeseen contingencies. The freedom to manoeuvre within a space defined by rules may be greater when one's taskmasters are geographically remote.

2   That governments can relax some reins of control (for example, rules and regulations) while tightening others (e.g. objectives, performance indicators), and that less central direction of individual schools can be replaced by tighter controls by local government, is one of the theses in Gustav Karlsen's study of recent parallel processes of centralization and decentralization in Norwegian education. Gustav Karlsen (1991) *Desentralisert skoleutvikling. En utdanningspolitisk studie av norsk grunnskole med vekt på 70 – og 80 – tallet* (Decentralized development of education. A policy study of the Norwegian basic school with special reference to 1970–90). PhD dissertation. Department of Education, University of Trondheim.

3   For a study of how this system works see Mark Bray (1984) *Educational Planning in a Decentralised System: The Papua New Guinea Experience*. Port Moresby: University of Papua New Guinea Press/Sydney: Sydney University Press.

4   On the practicalities of justifications and implementation, see Mark Bray with Kevin Lillis (eds) (1988) *Community Finance for Education: Issues and Policy Implications in Less Developed Countries*. Oxford: Pergamon Press.

5   As Robert E. Stake has reminded me, in comments on an earlier draft of this chapter.

6   An early classic on the educational ideas inherent in the great ideological and religious traditions is: Nicholas Hans (1949) *Comparative Education. A Study of Educational Factors and Traditions*. London: Routledge & Kegan Paul.

7   Liberalism has become divided on faith in the market forces versus the need to

regulate them – especially in those countries which historically have given market forces the freest reins – the liberal heartland countries of Britain and the USA. Social liberals have sought to regulate the market and have given much support to welfare state provisions in order to protect individual freedom from concentrated corporate power, to promote a greater degree of equality than what unchecked market forces would produce and in order to counter the vagaries of business cycles.

8   A far-ranging recent contribution on the relation between science and kindred forms of social inquiry on the one hand, and social improvement on the other is Charles E. Lindblom (1990) *Inquiry and Change*. New Haven: Yale University Press. In many respects the book is within the Anglo-Saxon Pragmatist Liberal tradition, with a strong admixture of (populist?) scepticism against the authoritativeness of social science as a basis for 'solving' social problems.

9   This diversity makes 'privatization' ill-suited as a 'form of decentralization' in its own right. Consider the management heterogeneity among, for example, the large-scale education systems run by the Catholic Church in many countries, the proprietary 'secretarial courses' run for profit-making, the élite private schools run as private foundations, and 'community based' Harambee schools which exist as poorly resourced second-choice alternatives to public secondary schools in Kenya.

10 A more detailed discussion of populism and an attempt to trace its influence in the Norwegian education tradition is given in J. Lauglo (1995) 'Populism and education in Norway', *Comparative Education Review*, **39** (3).

11 For a comparison of Norway with Denmark, France, the USA, England and Scotland, see: J. Lauglo (1982) 'Rural Primary School Teachers as Potential Community Leaders. Contrasting Historical Examples in Western Countries', *Comparative Education*, **18** (3).

12 An adaptation of management by objectives to the planning of education programmes and projects in developing countries is exemplified by the Logical Framework Analysis which has been adopted as a major planning technique by the World Bank.

13 Advocates of management by objectives in education may find it hard to build such alliances because many curriculum experts, especially in university education departments, are loath to impose upon others a style of work which ill agrees with their own professional culture.

14 Ms Unni Hagen, currently a doctoral student at the University of London Institute of Education, working on a comparative study of school management under conditions of tight squeeze on public finance, has assisted in summarizing these conclusions in a tabular form.

15 For an interpretation of its implications for education see Rust, Val D. (1991) 'Postmodernism and its comparative education implications,' *Comparative Education Review*, **35** (4).

16 If so, the ideas of Charles E. Lindblom, *op. cit.*, are highly pertinent. Otherwise, a study that is much quoted both by its adherents and by its detractors is Francis Fukuyama (1992) *The End of History and the Last Man*. London: Hamish Hamilton. He argues that the collapse of its authoritarian alternatives, both to the left and to the right, has left liberal democracy as the end state of world history.

REFERENCES

Ball, S.J. (1993a, 1993b) *Market Forces in Education*. Paper presented at IPPR-Goldsmiths' Seminar, 25–26 March. See also Ball, S.J., 'Education markets, choice and social class: The market as a class strategy in the UK and the USA', *British Journal of Sociology of Education*, **14** (1).

Clifford-Vaughan, M. (1963) 'Enlightenment and education', *British Journal of Sociology*, **14**.

Conyers, D. (1982) *Introduction to Social Planning in the Third World*. New York: Wiley.

Friedman, M. (1963) *Capitalism and Freedom*. Chicago: University of Chicago Press.

Lauglo, J. (1985) 'Educational change and the control question: Scandinavian perspectives', in Lauglo, J. and McLean, M. (eds) *The Control of Education. International Perspectives on the Centralization-Decentralization*. London: Heinemann Educational Books/Institute of Education, University of London, Studies in Education, No. 17

Lundgren, U.P. (1990) 'Educational policymaking, decentralization and evaluation', in M. Granheim, M. Kogan and U.P. Lundgren (eds) *Evaluation as Policymaking. Introducing Evaluation into a National Decentralized Educational System*. London: Jessica Kingsley.

Polyani, M. (1958) *Personal Knowledge*. New York: Harper & Row.

Polvani, M. (1967) *The Tacit Dimension*. London: Routledge.

Scotford Archer, M. (1979) *The Social Origins of Educational Systems*. London: Sage.

UNESCO Regional Office for Education in Asia and the Pacific (1982) *Three Training Modules on the Decentralization of Educational Administration*. Bangkok: UNESCO.

Weiler, H.N. (1990) 'Decentralization in educational governance: An exercise in contradiction', in M. Granheim, M. Kogan and U.P. Lundgren (eds) *Evaluation as Policymaking. Introducing Evaluation into a National Decentralized Educational System*. London: Jessica Kingsley.

Woodcock, G. (1962) *Anarchism*. London: World Publishing Company.

Chapter 2

The Liberal Paradox

David N. Apsin

'Quality' and 'equality' have long been regarded as one of the fundamental antin-
omies in education. The different values attached to, and the effects generated by,
each of them are set up by their proponents and critics in such a way that the
pursuit of one is almost universally accepted as militating against the achievement
of the other. Much less have they been seen as values both of which could be
equally promoted without damage to the other; much more have they been
regarded as a pair of opposites, between which, as Heraclitus remarked, no equi-
librium is possible but only a continuing tension.

This has been particularly true recently of questions about the proper control
and direction of educational institutions. Here, because of the importance of the
civil and social outcomes attached to them by proponents of the two values who
take sides in a debate about quality, efficiency and effectiveness in the administration and funding of schools and other educational institutions, the tension
between advocates of central control, on the one hand, and devolution to local
community management, on the other, might well be seen as a function of two
different political ideologies as to the preferred direction of development, lifestyle
and optimum future of a society.

On one side of this divide would stand those who believe that it is only
through central planning, direction and assessment that the best in quality of
schooling for a society's young may be achieved and, at the same time, the needs
and interests of a whole system may be equitably addressed, co-ordinated and
provided for, given that resources to service these needs are not infinite. In turn,
those limited resources have to be seen as only part of a number of calls upon the
common wealth of a whole society. All of these must therefore be clearly ranked
in some kind of order of priority, in the determination of which all constituencies
may have a say but central government must have the final power.

Against this view would stand those who believe that the interference of
central government in local affairs has increased, is increasing and ought to be
diminished; the local community may be counted on to know its own needs best
and should be accorded the independence and right to determine, without interference from elsewhere, the uses to which its own resources are put. On this view,
individuals by themselves and individual members of any particular constituency
or fortuitous aggregation, acting as individuals and deciding freely for themselves,
should have the right and power to prefer, choose and obtain access to those

things they believe to be the best for their young, through the availability of a diverse range of possibilities and opportunities from among which they will have the right to select and to which they may differentially devote their own resources. In this way, proponents of this view would hold, quality will be achieved through local control and the exercise of individual choice from a range of options.

The difference between the ideologies represented by these two views may thus be characterized as that between *dirigisme* and 'free marketism' – a difference that I shall characterize, for reasons that I hope will become clear, as that subsisting between 'centralist conservatives' and 'radical liberals'. The way in which these differences are expressed may be looked for in the various policies adopted by each tendency relating, *inter alia*, to welfare, housing, health and education. I use the word 'tendency' advisedly, for certainly, as far as the politics of the USA and the UK are concerned, one can find devotees of the centralist *dirigisme* that I see as basically conservative, and of the desire for individual autonomy and choice that I call 'radical liberal', present in both main political parties.

Such differences would not be hard to find, at least in Australia. It would not be too much to say that those tendencies, and their underlying political ideologies, may be most clearly discerned in the educational thinking as between the current Australian Labor Government and its coalition Opposition – manifested and evidenced in the policies and pronouncements of the previous Federal Minister, the Secretary for Employment, Education and Training, John Dawkins, who was essentially a centralist, and those of his then Opposition shadow, Dr David Kemp – the 'advocate of choice, as opposed to edict from the centre'. The same contra-position may also be discerned at the level of the states, where the bearers of the ideologies in question would be found in the work of present and previous Ministries of Education, where recent developments bear all the hallmarks of centralist conservatism and radical liberalism.

On a wide range of matters of cardinal educational importance – the content of the curriculum, the relationship of schools with the centre, admission policies, zoning, public examinations and testing, the pursuit of excellence and equity – some of the states appear to be in sharp opposition, this opposition being a function of two diametrically opposed political and educational philosophies, those of the *dirigiste* Left and those of the New Right.

It is an initial paradox, therefore, to note that in Australia, at commonwealth level and elsewhere in the states (formerly in Victoria, for example, and recently in Queensland), what I have termed 'conservative' policies for education have been espoused by governments of a Labor persuasion – that party which is historically more closely associated with the pursuit and adoption of radical and liberal policies; while what I have termed the 'radical liberal' education policies of the Australian Opposition at the commonwealth level and past and present governments in New South Wales, Victoria and Western Australia, are products of a 'Liberal' party that is historically most closely associated with what might be called the old High Tory philosophy emanating from the direction of the Tamworth Manifesto of the British Conservative and Unionist Party. In Britain and the USA, by contrast, those two tendencies may be found in one and the same party – even, at certain times and on certain issues, in one and the same government.

This suggests a profound paradox. I shall argue that there is indeed such a paradox at work in the education policies of the Australian Labor Government and that behind this is an even greater paradox, in that marked similarities may be observed between the educational policy and practices of the Australian and the UK governments – the latter, until recently at any rate, purporting to be one, all of whose endeavours over the last ten years have rested on and sprung from an underlying philosophy that may be seen as not only radically liberal but even, in some respects, radically anarchistic.

The inherent paradox has, I argue, transferred itself to Australasia and been at least a part of the causes of problems, inconsistencies and incoherences in recent education policies adopted and implemented there, at least so far as the questions of funding, management and control have been concerned. The understanding of such paradoxes must therefore be part and parcel of any attempt to understand the complexities of relations and the accompanying tensions between central and local government in the management of schools and school systems and is a necessary precursor to any attempt to unravel or dissolve them and so ameliorate that management.

SOME PRELIMINARIES ON DEFINITION

I should perhaps begin with one or two definitions: I certainly need to make clear what I mean by 'paradox' and 'liberal', since they provide the framework of what follows.

By the word 'paradox' I do not mean something like 'fanciful', 'curious', 'strange' or 'unusual', such as 'a paradoxical opinion', for instance or 'a paradoxical attitude', in the sense of quizzical appearance. I use the term rather in the following two senses:

1 A paradox arises in an argument, especially that of a syllogistic kind, in reasoning in which the premises and the conclusion drawn from them appear to be in direct contradiction. This can be a paradox resulting from a formal fallacy or from the content of the premises. The end result produces an argument that is incoherent rather than merely inconsistent or unintelligible; the string of reasons – premises and conclusion – end in being just mutually opposed, and so are self-contradictory.

2 The other sense of paradox would be the Wittgensteinian one, where a word is used in one and the same sentence in different senses and in such a way as to produce confusion or even unintelligibility.

An example of the first case use might be: 'The weaker a state makes itself, the stronger it becomes' or the classical Roman one: '*Si pacem vis, bellum para*' ('If you wish for peace, prepare for war'). An example of the second case would be: 'He curried favour with the King with the same vigour as he curried chicken'. Here one sees the conflation of two senses of quite disparate uses of the word 'to curry', neither of which would have anything to do with another activity – that of currying *horses*. By paradox, then, I mean a developing string of argument, thought, organizational system or whatever, in which the end result leads either to contradiction or confusion.

By the term 'liberal' I mean not the Liberal Party of Australia; I do not wish to refer to any one particular political party or creed. I have in mind here the liberal principle – the ethical notion that people are presumed to be free from external interference until good reason can be given for interfering with that freedom. This principle goes back to Aristotle's *Politics* and *Ethics*, where the notion of the 'free man', of the 'free citizen', was the one feature of a person's relations with the world outside him that was held to be a characteristic constituent of the preferred optimum form of democratic life, typified by the free citizen of the Athenian state, for instance, as opposed to the life of constraint lived by slaves and barbarians (i.e., by all those who were *not* Greek-speaking, adult, *or* male – hence, by women and children too).

I take that particular definition of 'liberal' in order to oppose it to the idea of 'anarchy', a word of Greek root. 'An-archy' comes from the Greek 'AN-APXH' (meaning 'without head', 'without beginning', or 'without principle', and so 'ANAPXIA' – 'without rule or government'). The idea behind this term is perhaps better summed up, from a political point of view, in that well-known humorous aphorism regarding the so-called Anarchist's Charter: 'Rule one: "There shall be no rules"; Rule two: "Not even Rule one!"'

The idea that I have in mind here is well connoted by the notion of 'licence', as opposed to 'liberty', where licence has the sense of 'anything being allowed, anything going', of there being any possible phenomenon, event, or behaviour, that conforms to no rules. Of course, as soon as I say that, I show the illogicality of the idea. For even to frame the concept of 'anarchism' itself requires me to follow the rules of the language game within which the idea of anarchism is conceived and articulated. Semantically speaking, 'anarchism' itself is a contradiction in terms, because its very articulation requires one to engage in a rule-following activity. And the rule-following thereby carries its own constraints with it. The concept 'Anarchism' is thus a prime example of a semantic and conceptual paradox.

I now come to the idea of liberty or to that of the 'liberal attitude' which might be preferred in its stead. I refer first to the work of John Stuart Mill, *On Liberty*. Mill's notion is that liberty, in the sense in which I have defined it, is one of the preferred values and the prime presupposition of any tolerable democratic or acceptable form of life. The minimum interference of any outside agency, be it individual or governmental, with the private life of the individual is the ideal, in so far as the preferred activities of that private life do not interfere with the rights of others to the same kind of liberty or enjoyment. Mill's formulation is that the minimum necessary interference with an individual's freedom to do exactly as he or she likes is only justified in so far as it is intended to prevent or punish infractions of the rule allowing the same freedom to other people with minimal possible interference on the same basis.

Mill qualifies this by noting that not everybody has the advantages of education, insight and upbringing that will enable him or her to accept this; consequently on occasion we have to '*force* individuals to be free'. That is to say, we have to interfere with their normal pattern of rights in order to open up to them the greater advantages that membership of society conferred by education and by training will subsequently confer upon them, once they have been made aware of the benefits of that kind of participation in a public form of life.

Hence comes the basic presupposition of the 'liberal' value: it is the *a priori* presumption of the complete freedom of any individual to be or behave unconstrained by outside interference of any kind, the onus of justification for any such interference being thrown upon those who would seek to impose a constraint upon freedom. That is to say, in any action, policy or situation, individuals shall be presumed to be free to do as they like until cause can be shown why that freedom should be curtailed; those who seek to curtail it, the external agents, have to produce a moral justification for doing so. It is in pursuit of just such a principle (e.g. the *prima facie* infraction of freedom involved in setting up compulsory schooling) that, in order to get individuals to see the range of life options from which they can work out a preferred pattern of acceptability for themselves, we have to subject them to some compulsion – in this case to a compulsory system of education – in which these options can be set out before them.

Eventually, then, the liberal paradox comes to be seen as two sides of one and the same coin: freedom on the one side, constraint upon the other. As it has been remarked, 'We have to set the constraint to catch the freedom'. That is the paradox; the resolution of the paradox comes at the point at which individuals are sufficiently free from ignorance, prejudice or malice that they can go on, so to speak, 'on their own', once the necessity for the constraint has disappeared.

THE 'REVOLUTION' OF RECENT CHANGES

Perhaps only so much is needed in the way of rudimentary philosophical groundwork before I begin talking about the 'revolution' (for it is nothing less) that has taken place recently in the politics and practices of some governments, notably those in Australasia since the mid-1980s, which I want to suggest parallel, are illuminated by and in some sense spring from those of the current UK Government since its election in 1979. I do not want to postulate any necessary causal relation between the two; the development of policies espoused by governments in this part of the world, in economics, housing, health, social welfare and education, on similarities which I wish to indicate, seem to me, at any rate, all to be part of the same *Zeitgeist* that can be observed to have been at work more widely in the world during the last decade, and nowhere perhaps more than in the United States in the Republican administration, which might in some senses (not least in view of the increasing budget deficits its own policies caused over the rest of the world) be regarded as the *fons et origo mali*. All I believe I can do is to point out some parallels and some illuminations of policies, and hazard the tentative hypothesis that their adoption in one country has not been without its echoes in the other.

In what follows I wish to pick out some particular developments in the education and welfare policies of the UK Government, try to show what seem to me to be remarkable parallels with what is happening in Australasia and suggest that all of these constitute paradoxes. In this I have a substantial sense of *déjà vu* when I look around the political economy at what is happening with respect to education in Australasia, having seen many of these developments in the UK already – not least with respect to the tension between the reality of what I believe to be the increasing centralism and *dirigisme* of central government, and the rhetoric of their professed desire to vest management and control of schools within the local community.

There are two paradoxes here to which I want to point. I start by mentioning that which seems to come about particularly in the UK. The Conservative and Unionist Party seemed, in its manifestos for the three elections in 1979, 1983 and 1987, to embrace a policy that had all the hallmarks of justifying the minimization of government interference in the life and the welfare of individual citizens of the country. The Conservative Manifesto in 1979 was predicated upon two bases. First, the notion that an increasing reliance upon what is called 'welfarism' since the close of the Second World War had increasingly enfeebled the political economy of the UK and had given its citizens a welfare mentality, to the point at which their reliance on being able to count on the state's patronage and support was assuming a larger and larger proportion of the major concerns for and means of the promotion of their own welfare on the part of the UK citizens. Autonomy, it was alleged, was decreasing; independence and self-sufficiency were also decreasing as a function of people's becoming increasingly dependency-minded; in consequence the financial burden upon the state was correspondingly growing larger and heavier. This phenomenon was clearly to be deplored – and overcome.

The second predicate in that policy was the 'revolution' in the economies of Western-developed countries since the great oil crisis of 1973–74, and the sea change that had been brought about in world economics since that time.

The Thatcher Government, elected in 1979 and subsequently in 1983 and 1987, therefore set itself the targets of:

1 Lessening by every means in its power the extent of state interference in individual citizens' rights, its credo being: 'We want to minimalize the interference of central government and maximize individual independence.'

2 Turning that independence to the economic purpose of making the UK increasingly competitive in a world economy that is assuming all the fierce competition of the marketplace.

3 Showing that its own productivity can make the UK increasingly self-sufficient.

I should perhaps add that there are obvious parallels to be drawn here between the UK and the Australian and New Zealand economic and political situations; I suggest that the reasoning to support the instituting of such policies based upon such premises, notwithstanding supposed political differences, has been similar in all three cases. At all events the principles adumbrated above set out what can be regarded as the three bases of the UK Government's 'official' policy. It is quite clear that, in relation to a number of areas of government activity, policy and legal enactment, based on those predicates, have been driven home with increasing urgency and resolution. Two fields will provide examples: health and social welfare, and economic policy.

Health and Social Welfare

The idea of 'the dole' and of unemployment benefits has been increasingly restricted in the UK, to the point at which the Government has been long considering introducing means-tested and work-related employment benefits, substantially oriented to getting people to look positively for work. That has been one way of attempting to reduce state dependence. With regard to health and other forms of welfare, the UK National Health Service, because of the increasing costs of treatments and number of people drawing upon it, has been increasingly short of the funds that are allocated to it by the Treasury through the Department of Health. It is therefore felt that private enterprise welfare agencies and medical services of all kinds ought to be brought in (much on the American model) so as to introduce the kind of private medical system with which people in Australia are familiar and thus to induce people to pay for them themselves: 'User pays!'

This emphasis on the idea of non-state-funded, and the privatization of, welfare and community service provision has even extended to the notion of private security firms running public prisons. Certainly, one of the main growth areas in both the UK and the USA in recent years has been that of private police and security firms, whose uniforms, areas of operation and behaviour lend to them the aura of paramilitary organizations. Both these developments are symptomatic of a privatizing approach to the management and funding of welfare and security systems that now very much informs the UK agenda.

Economic Policy

Entrepreneurialism has become so marked a feature of UK economic life that, until relatively recently, the growth of the UK economy appeared to be strengthening and Gross Domestic Product increased beyond what was expected. Here, of course, I refer only to that part of the UK in the economically productive South-East, roughly in a line from the Wash to Bristol: I am *not* referring to the rest of the country to the north-east and north-west of that line, where a different and quite tragic economic landscape can be easily observed. Indeed the rich South-East has more recently been feeling some of the chill winds of adverse economic change, with an increase in interest rates, inflation and unemployment, as the world recession has begun to bite. Nor need I mention that much of the economic growth has been based upon the income derived from the glut of North Sea oil and the sale or privatization of national assets, agencies and utilities, ranging from British Telecom to the water authorities.

Despite all this, however, UK economic policy is still based on a preference for *laissez-faire* of the most extreme kind and this is the operating motto and motivating machine of the UK approach – at least so far, that is, as the employers and the Government are concerned. Nothing that the UK Prime Minister, John Major, has said suggests any cause for thinking that this shibboleth of Reagan-, Thatcher-, or Roger-nomics is about to be even modified, much less abandoned, in spite of the powerful and debilitating remarks made of it by such critics as Sir Ian Gilmour, who have trenchantly made observations about its real effects.

THE PRINCIPAL PARADOX OBSERVABLE IN GOVERNMENT PRACTICES

Here, however, we encounter the paradox. For the policy of *laissez-faire* does not operate with respect to all the policies of the UK Government; quite the reverse. Here we come to the other side of the coin. For while the *laissez-faire* principle has been elevated to the status of a government credo in economics, health and welfare, in three other areas, at least, there has been an increasing emphasis upon interference, dominance and an authoritarianism in the policies of the UK Government that amounts to autocracy. The areas in which the UK Government has exercised an increasing degree of *dirigisme* are in law and order (especially with respect to industrial relations), public communications in and through the media and, crucially for this work, the whole field of education, especially as regards its management and control.

The evidence of increasing authoritarianism and centralism in *law and order* can be found, *inter alia*, in the fact that the mechanisms for total community control are already in place in the UK. For some years now it has been possible to link up all the computers operated by the police, the Drivers and Vehicle Licensing Agency, the tax offices, the Department for Education and Employment, the Department of Health and the Department of Social Security, to a central register in London. These powers are already being used by national forces of police and of security, at the UK Government's behest, in pursuit of its policies of full disclosure and control. The need for such a policy in Northern Ireland was, of course, obvious; the justification for its use to prevent the spread of a strike, however – as was done in 1984–85 during the national miners' strike – rather less so. It is a paradox that a government that was elected, albeit with only 40-odd per cent of a 70+ per cent turnout at the last election, on a mandate for minimalization of state interference, should be erecting a panoply of public control and be pre-occupied with the control of what it regards as secret matters, given the rhetoric of its predilection for 'open' government.

In the field of *public communication and the media* – another of the current UK Government's centralizing concerns – it will be widely known that it was only the Supreme Courts of New Zealand and New South Wales that overturned the desire of the UK Government to maintain secrecy in the Peter Wright case. It is noteworthy that the verdict of the New South Wales Supreme Court could not be reported at the time in the public press of Great Britain because of government control applied there by the imposition of 'D' notices. One of the UK Government's own backbenchers who tried to introduce a Private Member's Bill in March 1988 to tidy up Section Two of the notorious Official Secrets Act, was subverted and disciplined by having it 'talked out' on official government authority, because the legislative initiative for reform simply did not come from the Cabinet. Freedom of action in such matters evidently extends only to members of an inner circle.

The third example of paradox is found in education, the area with which we are most deeply concerned. The educational policies that have suggested to me a major paradox in the politics of the UK Government, which has purported to espouse minimalization of state interference in public institutions of all kinds, of which private individuals are supposed to be considered the electing members, cover a number of areas of concern. I pick out three of them here – two concerning schools and one relating to teacher education – to furnish us with examples that indicate the centralizing tendency of the Department for Education and Employment, the arm of the UK Government particularly concerned with the funding and control, the management, the direction, the shaping of policy for public education.

On matters relating to schools, first I refer to the Education Act 1988, the legislation that now most profoundly affects the educational and curricular freedom previously held to be one of the most valued features of the English state school and its programmes of instruction. Following the Education Act 1944 the only curriculum areas under centralized curriculum control in state-maintained schools in the UK used to be physical education and religious instruction, as well as a daily act of worship. The rest of the curriculum was a matter to be left to the judgement of the individual headteacher of the school concerned, advised, of course, by the local authority and its advisers and inspectors, and by a governing body.

Since the Education Act 1988 all that has now changed. There is in its stead a state-dictated curriculum made up of three 'core' subjects: English, mathematics and science; a further set of 'foundation' subjects, such as a modern foreign language, history/geography, music or art, physical education and some element of religious studies, subjects which, taken together, shall constitute 70 per cent of the available curriculum time; the other 30 per cent to be distributed among a range of options (options in the sense that one may choose between them, not options in the sense that one is free to choose or not to choose) devoted to such a range of subjects as a second foreign language, classical studies, another science, health education, some more games and so on. A number of subjects, such as personal and social education, peace studies and sociology, will now therefore struggle to find space on the timetable. They are clearly *not* on the agenda, and it is not hard to imagine why not.

In the actions of the UK Government here we see for the first time the imposition of a national system of education in Britain. And there has been a further imposition to ensure that a curriculum constructed along these lines is not only to be available but actually delivered in schools. Progress and achievement in all these subjects are to be monitored and assessed at regular intervals: at the ages of 7, 11, 14 and, finally, with a General Certificate of Secondary Education leaving qualification, at the age of 16 when compulsory schooling ends. This regular testing is to be conducted on a national criterial basis, the criteria being those drawn up by working groups on which Her Majesty's Inspectors (HMI) are leading figures, but also working with teacher advice and so on.

Talk of a national curriculum has been increasingly prominent in the language of Australian Federal Ministers of Employment, Education and Training since Dawkins's time, and particularly strong since the so-called 'Hobart' Declaration made at the meeting of the Australian Education Council (AEC) in Hobart in April 1989. Minister Dawkins and subsequent Federal Ministers believe there are good reasons for supporting the idea: there is much to be said for greater uniformity in assessing the performance of school-leavers; there ought to be basic standards of literacy and numeracy that could be tested nationally; in some matters of curriculum delivery, such as styles of handwriting, there is a case for some national uniformity; while parents' mobility of employment across Australia and between the states ought not to disadvantage their children as much as it does at the moment. There is also thought to be a strong case for a national approach to and standards of teacher education and training, so that qualifications obtained in one state can be recognized and accepted in another, and arrangements facilitated for the portability of credit for professional development activities, leave entitlements and pension rights between states, areas that cause real difficulties at the moment.

Dawkins's view on all these matters was that the current state of affairs militates against the freedom of movement that he saw as so much a part of economic regeneration and growth, a necessary precondition for the government's economic objectives. A subsidiary motive may, of course, have been to attenuate, if not entirely to eliminate, the large-scale ideological differences obtaining between and observable in the public education systems of some states having governments of fundamentally different persuasion, informed as they are by radically different political philosophies, as a part of encouraging such mobility.

For these reasons and others an attack on the subject was put up for discussion by the Federal Minister for Education, Employment and Training at the meeting of state Premiers in Brisbane in October 1990, notwithstanding the fact that the provision and funding of education in all but the tertiary sector is constitutionally the preserve of the states. The proposals put forward by Minister Dawkins at that meeting represented a change in policy from which the state Premiers turned away, a view reiterated firmly by the state Ministers at the meeting of the AEC in Perth in July 1993. Perhaps they recalled the view taken by the then Shadow Minister of Education, Dr Kemp, to the effect that the history of federal forays into curriculum was not encouraging: in the 1970s either platitudes or partisan theory prevailed. I do not doubt, however, that we shall have to live with and continue to look at the idea of a national (centrally imposed) curriculum in Australia. Certainly, once the Canberra bureaucracy has got hold of such an idea, its centralizing tendencies will tend to give accelerated impetus to the irresistible progress of the state juggernaut.

That is the first of the paradoxes of educational freedom: we are all free to set up what curricula we like, 'provided', as one Premier is alleged to have said, 'it is ours!'

The second point relating to schools arises from the UK Government's dictating of teachers' terms and conditions of service, which occurred in April 1987. There had been a long, wearying and drawn-out battle between the teachers' unions and the representatives of the local authorities concerning salaries, increases and working conditions. It was known that the teachers wanted their salaries to be upgraded in real terms, to keep pace with inflation instead of falling behind, as they were progressively doing, given the small rates of salary increases there had been in the order of 2, 3 or 4 per cent, with inflation running higher. Teachers' salaries had fallen a long way behind those for jobs of comparable responsibility since the Hoghton award of 1974, and teachers wanted this matter to be redressed and were prepared to engage in industrial action to get it. Sir Keith Joseph, during his period of office as Minister for Education, wanted salary negotiation to take place with reference to the idea of teachers accepting a contract of service in which certain duties would be stipulated and certain engagements entered into; Joseph sought to negotiate that contract. The negotiations were tortuous and long-lasting. When Sir Keith was ousted from the portfolio of the education service and Kenneth Baker was put in his place, the latter, within a few months of coming into office as Secretary of State, simply stopped the negotiations that had been taking place between the teachers' unions and the metropolitan authorities and, at Easter 1987, unilaterally imposed a settlement, without the possibility of any further recourse to teachers, unions or employers. The settlement was to be a salary rise in the order of 7.8 per cent; teachers were obliged to accept a contract of service; and the contract of service was to be predicated upon the basis of 1,365 contract hours of teaching time per year. UK teachers now have to account for all those hours: anything in excess of them will not be paid for and anything short of them will be required to be made up.

This kind of financial control and oversight was made much easier by the innovations introduced in the 1988 Education Act relating to the funding of schools. From now on, schools could opt to have their funding directly from central government, without interference from any intermediary authority, and devote the funds they received to principles, purposes and practices they chose for themselves; they could also, if they chose, look after their organization and administration themselves. This principle of local school management (LSM) could be, and was, extended to all matters of governance, the hiring and firing of staff, the provision of resources from internal and external sources, and payment for the professional and curriculum development needs of the school and its staff.

In this set of practices we see the paradox of centralization versus decentralization exemplified. For one of the phenomena associated with this development has been described by Aspin and Chapman in *Quality Schooling* (1994). Setting up LSM has had the effect of reinforcing the government's centralization of educational purposes, curricula and assessment, while at the same time achieving the decentralization of blame for poor educational performance.

It is easy to imagine what has been happening since that time. Teachers' willingness to look after parents' evenings, school games, extra-curricula activities, school visits abroad, ceased at a stroke. Teachers' willingness to take courses in their own time, even for professional purposes, much less for personal or wider academic development, could no longer be automatically relied upon (Baker's imposed contracts gave teachers six days per annum, immediately known as 'Baker days', for any professional improvement – a ludicrous allowance of time, given all the major changes in curriculum, teaching style and assessment teachers were now being called upon to implement – and for which no additional resources were granted). Furthermore, teachers' access to such courses was now confined to those programmes of which the school council approved and for which it was willing to pay (in whole or in part). Many of these were more likely to be related to such directly applicable professional requirements as increased expertise in evaluation and assessment, catering for children with exceptional needs of various kinds, and the management of programmes and budgeting. Deeper and broader professional courses, involving history, philosophy and sociology would, in spite of their obvious potential for strengthening teachers' academic qualifications as well as making their understanding of their professional roles, responsibilities and opportunities much more informed and sophisticated, were hardly likely to be looked on with favour by school councils operating now with much more meagre resources to devote to professional improvement and teacher growth.

As a way of politicizing the teacher force, this authoritarian *Diktat* – like similar policies instituted by Dr Terry Metherell, the former Minister for Education in New South Wales – could hardly have been more likely to succeed. UK teachers quickly came to believe they were now regarded not so much as educators but rather as economic functionaries acting with the rule book and the stopwatch – and many in consequence began to behave in like manner. In many schools those extra-curricular educating elements in the government school service arising from school plays, school visits, school games, the debating society and other such activities, began to disappear.

Because of this imposition of central control, and also because of the move to the LSM approach to funding, direction and organization, very many schools are now run on the Manpower Services model. It is hardly surprising that, according to recent reports, over 40 per cent of the teaching force in the UK is now actively seeking to leave the profession, nor that over 25 per cent of teachers are alleged to be experiencing forms of illness, the main symptoms of which would qualify them for admission to an out-patients clinic in a hospital.

I come now to the second set of considerations demonstrating a preoccupation with the central control of education. These relate to one of the functions of tertiary education institutions. The *dirigiste* and centralizing tendency of the educational policies of the UK Government bite particularly hard with respect to teacher education and training. For an ominous innovation was introduced in the mid-1980s. Instead of the plethora of courses and models of teacher education one could find previously, there was instituted at that time one government-appointed central licensing body for teacher education operation – the Council for the Accreditation of Teacher Education (CATE). This body was made up of a Vice-Chancellor in the Chair, representatives from teachers' unions, parents' organizations, and the world of business, industry and commerce, all of whom were given equal say in the determination of policies, and met for the accreditation of courses and programmes in teacher education and training. Any institution that wished to train teachers had to subject itself to the advice of a local professional committee, both being subject to HMI review and, finally, to visitation by a panel from CATE, to see if it met the criteria laid down for acceptance and the granting of permanent Qualified Teacher Status by the Secretary of State, who was given over 400 new powers, along these lines, in the Education Act 1988. Mr Baker sought to disarm criticism at the time by claiming he would 'never use them'.

On the contrary, his successors have used them still further. The most recent UK enactment has established an even more centralized government agency, that shall be responsible for all teacher education and training, to be funded out of the monies formerly granted to the universities through the Universities Funding Council. Universities which maintain Departments or Faculties of Education, other professional training agencies, and schools themselves (operating now under the freedoms granted to them by LSM schemes) must bid to this agency for funds to conduct training and education courses for teachers both pre-service and in-service. Bids shall also be made to this agency by all those institutions wishing to engage in educational research, curriculum and/or professional development.

Another of the Minister's new powers has been to make a move to improve teacher supply, that effectively bypasses (and bids fair to render redundant) the activities of teacher education and training institutions altogether by arranging for academically qualified but non-professionally trained and educated persons to join the staffs of schools and to receive 'on the job' training and recognition by the

Ministry in due course. This of course devalues still further the idea of a fully professional and properly trained and qualified teaching force. It reduces the status of pre-service training to the apprenticeship model that prevailed after the passing of the Education Act 1870 – that of 'sitting next to Nellie'.

To judge by this set of examples the UK Government appears to have arrogated to itself powers of such a centralist tendency as to make one suspect that the plea for election in 1979 on the ground of the *minimalization* of interference on the part of central government in individual citizens' lives was a cynical plea for excuses – specious rhetoric. Certainly, very many of those most affected in the new order of industrial relations in education – teachers in schools, lecturers and research students in universities, students in schools doing public examinations and/or seeking admission to tertiary education institutions, and parents receiving notice of the closure of their local schools – would unhesitatingly affirm their direct experience of what a former Conservative Prime Minister saw as the need for 'The smack of firm government'. They are not alone in this experience; there are states in Australia now where a similar authoritarianism and similar outcomes are being encountered.

Yet everything other than the imposition of these stringent centralist and *dirigiste* tendencies, in the case of such areas as the foregoing, would appear, on the contrary, to be the ruling emphasis in matters of economics, in health, in social welfare, and in the acquisition, possession and control of such items of major public importance and concern as the media – for the appraisal and potential criticism of which we need, above all, an educated, widely informed, critical and independent-minded populace. Such a populace might then find it easier to see why the UK National Curriculum includes, as one of its major requirements, a study of 'the economic roots of a free society'.

In these circumstances it is instructive to go back to read the manifesto of the 1979 Conservative Party, to examine the elucidation of its principal beliefs and values in the work of one or two of its main academic apologists, Professor Roger Scruton and Professor Antony Flew (see Flew, 1989; Scruton, 1980), and to compare with these the writings of Milton Friedman in *Capitalism and Freedom* (1962) and Friedrich von Hayek in *Law, Legislation and Liberty* (1976 and 1979), and then to compare the ideology espoused in that manifesto and these writings, and look at what has actually happened in the various fields referred to. For there are, on the one hand, policies and programmes advocated in such writings that are of the most minimal, 'radical anarchist' kind; on the other, placed directly side by side with them, are the experiences had and the observations it is now possible to make, of the effects of highly autocratic, bureaucratic, centralizing powers of government in action – powers that one used to associate with states on the other side of the former Iron Curtain.

This is an internal paradox of a government's policies in operation that, though masquerading under the name of the Conservative and Unionist Party, purports to espouse a 'radical liberal' philosophy, and it is one that is hard to reconcile or even to make sense of. Indeed, so far from uniting constituencies (an aim articulated by Mrs Thatcher when she uttered the famous prayer of St Francis of Assisi on entering Downing Street on the morning of her victory in 1979), recent UK Conservative Government has estranged, divided and fragmented them (an outcome graphically illustrated by the riots associated with the imposition of the so-called 'poll tax'); and it has done so by adopting and enforcing centralism and autocracy in some matters close to the heart of the populace, while allowing and encouraging a liberty amounting to licence (to judge, for example, by recent cases of fraud and immorality not only in the City of London but even within its own politicians' ranks) in others.

As a parallel to the above, the policies of central government in Australia and New Zealand exhibit not only the paradox I describe with respect to the situation obtaining in the UK but the larger paradox of having similar policies enacted and put to work under the aegis of what purported in both countries to be government of a *labour* persuasion.

A similar case of the operation of two tendencies referred to, anarchism and centralism, can be observed to be at work in Australia and New Zealand. A similar list of examples could be drawn up, on the side of the 'radical anarchist' tendency, under the heading of economic policy in business in New Zealand; in Australia the list on that side would again include economic policy, and certainly the media. On the side of the centralist tendency, one could count the strong government control of health and welfare in New Zealand, in line with the previous socialist predilections of the Lange Government, and with an even stronger centralizing tendency with respect to education. In Australia this is amply illustrated by the Curriculum Guidelines exercise of 1987 (cf. NBEET 1992; Marsh, 1988 and 1994; Skilbeck, 1990), and the Hobart Declaration of 1989, the Dawkins White Paper, and the outcome of the deliberations of the Wilson Committee on Quality in Higher Education, with respect to institutions of tertiary education (see Aspin and Chapman, 1994).

The working of that same tendency and tension in public policy matters may also be observed with respect to Australia, too, perhaps in even starker form than that obtaining in the UK. A similar force can also be observed to be at work in many aspects of Australian government policy: in political and industrial economy, where one can easily discern the dominance of central government control, with less concern for industrial relations, yet *pari passu* with government policies and actions that suggest a clear commitment to an apparent embracing of *laissez-faire* economics on the one hand along with a remarkable degree of centralist interventionism on the part of the Treasurer on the other. In other matters, however, such as possession and control of the media and transport and the deregulation of the banks and lending there has been an adoption of radical libertarian policies amounting almost to a degree of licence, of which one suspects both Adam Smith and Milton Friedman would have heartily approved.

Most obviously, however, the kind of interventionist centralism set in train in Australia became increasingly evident in the kind of pronouncement one saw coming out of the Department of Employment, Education and Training (DEET). The Green Paper 1987 and its successor the White Paper 1988, together with other official government publications since (especially the plethora of publications concerned with 'quality'), bear all the marks of the UK 'Manpower Services' model of educational planning, along with the stress on the need for the development of a 'vocational education'-driven engine of economic recovery as being first in the imperatives of *all* education policy in the Australian commonwealth. Only after the elevation and achievement of this prime desideratum do other purposes, such as the social, ethical and cultural, receive any attention in official documents. Even then such mention as one finds is very much a function of, and can be subsumed under the heading of, 'economic purposes'; look at the justifications for learning languages other than English now, for instance.

This dichotomy was neatly encapsulated in the events of 1988. There we had the paradox that, within three months of the publication of the Green Paper in 1987, with all its ideals of equality, access, participation, emancipation, the enfranchising of disadvantaged minorities so as to increase their freedom, and so on, another document was issued. The report and recommendations of the Wran Commission on students' contributions to the funding of higher education were published and subsequently adopted by the Federal Government, enacted in its policy of a Higher Education Contribution Scheme (HECS). The conclusions of the Wran Report already ran directly counter to many of the high moral ideals so firmly espoused as the credo of the motivating thrust of government education policy as set out in the Green and White Papers; the effects of their adoption and implementation in HECS, however, have manifestly so worked as to exclude or disadvantage some classes of student, and especially single women, and to advantage others – especially those who could afford to pay university HECS fees 'up front' (for which a 15 per cent reduction was granted).

Certainly, as applied to institutions of higher education, since the time when the Australian Government took over the power of funding from the states to the Federal Government, Dawkins's reforming zeal went much further than even Baker's in the UK. Since 1988 Australian government policies initiated and led by Minister Dawkins have wrought changes to the national higher education scene that are now regarded as nothing short of revolutionary.

With respect to one matter – that of funding – there is of course considerable similarity with the UK; the difference between the UK and Australia is one of degree only. Governments in both countries, to judge from the evidence, have implied that education has been overfunded and have reduced resources accordingly. In an OECD comparative analysis of 1986 Australia came only tenth in a list of 13 OECD countries that reported an education budget as a percentage of its GDP (the UK was not the first in that league table either), the same figures suggesting a declining commitment to education over the years both before and after that benchmark. In 1980–81, for instance, the share of the budget assigned by the Australian Government to education was 8.1 per cent (2.24 per cent of GDP); of this higher education received 4.6 per cent (1.24 per cent of GDP). In 1989–90, by contrast, this proportion had been reduced to 7.75 per cent of budget (1.78 per cent of GDP); higher education's figures had come down to 3.5 per cent (0.82 per cent of GDP).

The figure for higher education is actually much worse than it appears, since, as a direct result of government policies, student numbers have increased in the same ten-year period by 34 per cent; universities have become seriously overcrowded and staff–student ratios have risen alarmingly, some believe to the point at which quality of teaching and learning is seriously affected. At the same time the numbers of those qualified for admission to tertiary education institutions but for whom there are no places available ('unmet demand'), lies well in excess of

50,000 (sufficient to fill three or four medium-sized universities).

This latter feature is in line with Dawkins's insistence on the vocational preparation of a workforce to make Australia a 'clever country', that can employ its intellectual resources in the pursuit of economic growth and competitiveness, and the consequent application to the tertiary sector of a Relative Funding Model, in which engineering and science subjects are massively privileged over arts, humanities and social science ones. The former feature – the introduction of HECS and the granting to the universities of the power to charge fees for students coming from overseas and those doing post-graduate courses – is obviously a function of the same kind of a government-driven orientation towards lessening subsidy and increased profitability that has marked the UK Government's approach towards public utilities generally, where the value of 'service' counts for less than the value of 'paying one's own way' in the world. The railways in the UK are a case in point.

Yet to suggest that the differences between the working out of education funding policies in the UK and in Australia have been merely matters of degree, only as a part of emphasizing the similarities between these features of the reorganization of education in the UK and Australia, risks falling into the fallacy of oversimplification. There are as many differences as similarities in the groundwork of the education policies, at least so far as the basic justifications for changes in the organization and funding of higher education go, and these make the issue much more complex for anyone concerned to understand and untangle the tensions between centralism and devolution in the debate about the purposes, proper management and funding of educational institutions generally.

As was ably pointed out in a leading article, entitled 'Dawkins' way' in the *Times Higher Education Supplement* (13 April 1990), there are at least five areas of difference. The first lies in the political context in which the policies were being articulated and promulgated; the main purpose of the Australian government education policy is a conscious push to modernize Australia's economy and institutions to adjust both to the demands of a knowledge-led post-industrial world, and it has placed the state at the centre of this process of modernization. This is contrasted with the UK Government's piecemeal approach of 'politicized tinkering and destructive privatization'.

The second contrast is to be found in the origins and character of Australian university institutions where, first, the older of which were constructed to follow a Scottish model of tertiary education and the newer along the lines bearing close similarities to those of some key American institutions, and where, secondly, research priorities and external earning policies are increasingly targeted to Australia's increasing awareness of itself as part of the patterns of growth, demand and interrelationships of all the constituent elements of the Asia-Pacific region.

That is certainly one reason for the third difference: 'a sustained expansion both of student numbers and institutional budgets', in which there is a deliberate attempt to get an increasing number of Australia's younger generation and its various previously disadvantaged minorities – women, Aborigines, ethnic groups and rural dwellers – to have the chance to make a contribution to the development of the country's culture, community and economy by securing access to and then following courses in tertiary education institutions of all kinds.

A fourth difference lies in the plain fact that the Australian Government has been quite open about its aim to impose direct control from the centre upon the future direction and development of tertiary institutions. It does this on the basis of advice it receives from the National Board for Employment Education and Training (NBEET) and its various constituent councils – those for Higher Education (HEC), Schools, and Technical and Further Education. It is through this body, NBEET, that the Australian Research Council (ARC) also provides advice to the Minister – but it is he who makes the decisions and imposes them directly.

Nowhere is this more evident than in the annual funding exercise in which a team of officials from DEET visits each tertiary institution and negotiates its 'educational profile', on the basis of which the institution then receives funds direct from Canberra. This part of the process is open and admitted; and it becomes quite clear that, through various mechanisms such as the 'claw-back' in which DEET takes back a certain amount from each institution for specifically targeted research purposes, the Government is determined to impose its view of the appropriate level of growth and the proper direction of development in tertiary institutions.

Here there is clear central dominance. At the same time the Government is uncomfortably aware of how much this process impinges upon and erodes traditional ideas of academic freedom; to which end the Government itself commissioned one of its former employees, a former counsellor for the HEC, then turned Professor of Education and later Deputy Vice-Chancellor of a university, to work out the proper terms and operating procedures to be enshrined in a 'Charter for Academic Freedom'. Whether this will do anything more than make an obeisance to outside critical appraisal and public accountability, and make the Government really amenable to the possible reversal of any of its higher education policies, remains to be seen.

The fifth difference is found in the extent to which the Dawkins revolution was pushed. In the attempt 'to rationalize the higher education system to produce viable institutions to compete internationally' (as the THES remarked), Dawkins established a Unified National System (UNS) of higher education in which the previous binary line between universities and other forms of tertiary institution, such as institutes of technology and colleges of advanced education, was abolished. At his diktat all institutions above a certain minimum size and desirous of participating in the UNS and of obtaining access to its funding formulas (not least with respect to research) merged into a much smaller number of universities. In this policy Dawkins was later followed by the Government of the UK – *plus ça change* . . .

There were, let it be agreed, some advantages to this proposal: economies of scale, easier (if initially more costly) management, greater ranges of courses, easier credit transfer, increased access to a greater constituency of students, institutional flexibility, course rationalization, and so on. But there are obvious disadvantages, too: the inertia and resistance to change of existing institutions; the additional complexity and tortuousness of decision-making; the protracted timelines caused by the inevitable increase in the bureaucracy of management and control; the necessity for devolution while still being governed by a strongly imposed central plan; the difficulty of marrying together institutions of previously widely disparate character, ethos, values, interests and experience into one overarching corporate identity and plan – above all, perhaps, the clear implication of an acceptable and appropriate movement in and between institutions towards a 'league-table' mentality with respect to research and research excellence. Either there will be, as has already been well observed, most recently in the recommendations of the Wilson Committee with its setting of institutions into six different 'bands', an emphasis upon devoting a greater proportion of research funds to targeted research excellence in institutions of greatest productivity (so that what are actual league tables operative in the UK become operative *de facto* in Australia) – though without the necessary supporting funds for research infrastructure that were previously part of core fund granting processes. Or there will be a levelling down effect as research funds are diverted away from those who have demonstrated research excellence and productivity, and towards those institutions where research has previously been very limited or non-existent.

Where the resources for research grants are scarce, one or the other of the above is bound to happen. The universities fear that in due course both will happen, at the behest of the government, in the name and on the basis of a policy of commitment to 'quality', research excellence and the concomitant requirement for 'selectivity' and 'concentration' in resources and courses; or, in the name of 'equal access' and 'fairness', there will have to be wider and 'more equitable' distribution of resources. Both substantially erode the freedom such institutions have to plan for their own futures and for contributing to the development of the Australian economy and the expansion of its culture in areas where they have already established powerful presence and productivity.

It is such fears that have led to the debate about the nature, direction and control of higher education in Australia being as sharp and pointed as it has been these last years – a debate that the recommendations of the Wilson Committee published in 1994 will only serve to exacerbate. For where two of the largest, most productive and most internationally known and respected of the country's universities are effectively demoted to 'second division' status, there must either be something wrong with the model and/or its criteria – or there must plainly be some sort of (centralist) political agenda at work. The latter suspicion is not diminished when one observes one university, which had not previously enjoyed such prominence but which had a number of very powerful connections with Canberra, being elevated to a status of equality in the second banding with those two. The message as regards government central control and its importance could not have been made more clear.

The contrast in all this with the UK is that no one has suggested the Australian Minister is animated by a desire to 'bring universities to heel' or to erode or even to emasculate their powers of independence and criticism. It was perhaps one of the worst effects of Thatcherite policies generally in the UK that people honestly felt that that right had been progressively taken away – not only in education but in so much else besides. (See Arnold, 1989, and the 1988 issue of the influential journal *Index on Censorship*, referred to in an article by Rothwell, 1988.) Consultation still remains a central feature of public debate about education in both Australia and New Zealand; there is still a strong feeling that the public's right to speak and be heard is respected. That was indeed the principal basis of the 1986 Curriculum Guidelines document put out by the New Zealand Education Department.

There is an impression that Minister Dawkins and his successors have tried to preserve that right in Australia, even in areas of marked contentiousness, where their views on schooling, the curriculum and testing run counter to those strongly held in some of the states. In his speech at the Premiers' Conference in Brisbane in October 1990 Dawkins, for example, tried to persuade Premiers and their Education Ministers that there was much to be said for the co-ordination of states' policies on such matters as curriculum, testing, the portability of teachers' pension rights and service conditions – even on such detailed matters as styles of handwriting.

Yet, given this beginning, that attempt at 'friendly persuasion', and the lengths to which Canberra public servants will go in order to secure acceptance and implementation of their Minister's policy objectives, it is not unreasonable to suppose that similar pressures, programmes and procedures to those that have already been exercised with respect to higher education are going to come into play with respect to the public schools, a national curriculum, and the training and employment of teachers. It is deeply worrying, for instance, that on more than one occasion Minister Dawkins was quoted as saying that he never heard any counter-arguments to positions he put forward on a number of contentious matters in education. This is odd, seeing that such arguments were mounted and printed almost weekly in the columns of the press, professional journals and at conferences, where officials of his department stayed on after his departure and had to face numerous criticisms of government thinking and approaches to such matters. One suspects that the only arguments to which he would have allowed credibility were those that he wanted to hear on matters that were close to his heart, that he saw as national priorities, and on which he wanted academic and professional support: a set of nationally co-ordinated priorities in producing a high-standard education for economic development and competitiveness; a better quality of life for Australia's citizens generated by targeted research and development programmes in tertiary education institutions; increased commitment and contribution to regional economic development, defence involvement, and cultural understanding; and increased social justice accepted and extended through and in all the nation's schools.

Minister Dawkins's reasons for wanting to require such aims of Australia's educating institutions are set out in two sources. One is Dawkins's speech as Chairman to the Inter-Governmental Conference on 'Education and the Economy in a Changing Society' held at the OECD in Paris on 16 March 1988; the other is the philosophy enshrined in the DEET publication *Strengthening Australia's Schools*, put out at the same time (May 1988). From these documents it is clear that Dawkins was concerned with increasing quality in Australian education, as a means of increasing scientific and technological economic power and economic competitiveness in the nation. Clearly he believed schools, as well as the tertiary sector, have a vital and indispensable role in bringing this about. For the effect of centralist tendencies to promote these aims in schools as well as the tertiary sector may be observed in the impact of such measures as award restructuring and the extending of promotion possibilities to a new category of teacher – ASTs (those with advanced skills).

The Australian Government desires – and nowhere more than in education – a highly competent and better-paid workforce in order that Australians shall enjoy a better range of choices and employment opportunities and thus be less of a burden on the state and enjoy a better standard of living. Australians cannot, according to the view of those in leading positions, in both government and academe: 'preserve their quality of life, protect the environment and enhance the nation's economic competitiveness without a strong education system and a serious scientific research and development effort'. The push towards creating a 'clever country' will rest upon and thus requires a first-class education system, 'especially in areas linked to wealth-generating industries', as an absolute priority (DEET, *Strengthening Australia's Schools*).

There are unfortunately two obstacles to the achievement of this end: one is the realization that, as Frank Larkins in *The Higher Education Supplement* of *The Australian* newspaper (1988) has maintained: 'The slow pace of change in community attitudes to recognize education, innovation and hard work as the cornerstones of national prosperity is perhaps the greatest impediment to Australia becoming a "clever society" . . .' The other is that Australia must achieve this, as Dawkins avers, on the bedrock of a sound economy – and here is where the underlying paradox begins to strike home.

To promote and secure the twin goals of increasing international market competitiveness, while at the same time extending social justice at home so that more can participate in the goods laid open by an empowering high-quality education, will commit the government to two policies, the requirements of which do not always sit easily together: running a first-rate higher education system of real quality and excellence and one aiming for increased access and participation; *and at the same time* trying to operate it as a public business, subjected to the business norms of profit and loss budgeting and accountancy, quality in product and service delivery, and customer satisfaction.

The former features of government education policy are manifestations of a concern to provide a high-quality education to all the state's citizens because, simply put, education is in itself a good thing; that knowledge is worth having and pursuing, and that the community's identity is secured and its future welfare promoted by increasing the number of those able to take advantage of this particular form of social good. The latter desiderata are the requirements that animate the economic and educational vision of those whose thinking on these matters is informed by a kind of a grocer's shop mentality and by selective reliance upon certain of the so-called Victorian virtues, such as economic independence, thrift, hard work, humility, 'family values', frugality and 'living within our means', but with much less reference to such other cardinal virtues as caring for other people, compassion, support and assistance to the needy, and the elevation of the ideal of service to the needs of the poor, disenfranchised and uneducated.

Those virtues would be hard put to gain a point of purchase in a political economy where the power and control of the government had grown to the point at which the then Australian Treasurer (the same one who deregulated the financial markets in 1984 and so opened the door to those whose philosophy and practice in business matters bore greater resemblance to the views of Gordon Gekko than St Francis of Assisi) could freely and without embarrassment confess to having 'engineered' a recession as an instrument of a supposedly entrepreneurial and competitivist economic policy (the inconsistency between which two policies is plain). Where there is simply no work and dependence upon unemployment benefit is rapidly increasing, where bankruptcies, failures of major private undertakings and even public institutions such as banks and building societies have been features of the economic landscape of recent years, and when, in the attempt to recover from both world trade recession and financial mismanagement, the severest and most savage cutbacks have been imposed on such basic public service utilities and Ministries as education, health and social welfare, any conspectus of Victorian virtues inevitably moves to the growing visibility of other parts of the Victorian landscape with which the writings of Dickens long ago made us familiar. *Hard Times* has become a real metaphor for our present condition.

The move towards centralism in education is thus a function of what Hunt (1987) has termed the 'incorporation of education' as a public and social institution into the political and economic realm at governmental level. An example may be found in the increasing corporatism of such bodies as the teacher unions, the Federated Association of University Staff Associations (FAUSA) (now the National Tertiary Education Union (NTEU), the Australian Vice-Chancellors' Committee (AVCC) and perhaps especially the Australian Research Council (ARC). They have buildings and large staffs, infrastructure and research arms, media consultants and political lobbyists – all the necessary features of that kind of enterprise that throbs, hums and produces, the model for which is clearly drawn from large American commercial and industrial undertakings. Education and its provision has, it is argued, been similarly incorporated; it has become another part of the industrial-economic arena, simply because, like freedom itself, it has come to be viewed as a part of, or a commodity produced by, a corporate enterprise having a strictly limited number of purposes, the chief of these being economic. On this kind of thinking education and liberty are simply commodities that have their price. They are no longer taken to be the prime presuppositions and indispensable conditions for the development of any form of rationale, tolerable and civilized form of life: like social welfare itself, they are seen by the New Right as luxuries that we can only obtain at a cost and that we might in certain circumstances have to think of giving up. Even the work of the Good Samaritan himself, so it was argued by one of the principal proponents of this tendency, required a minimum capital power and adequate financial resources to provide the services of mercy, compassion and practical help.

There are two problems with such an approach, unfortunately: one is the sheer logical fallacy of postulating an analogy between the nature and purposes of public service institutions such as those of education, health and welfare, and those of independent and private firms or agencies in the world of business, commerce and industry. Education is regarded by some of those who hold the second of the two views adumbrated above – though not all – either as a commodity or as a set of skills and a repertoire of knowledge appropriate for utilitarian purposes.

Now certainly one function of education is a preparation for the world of work (or, in these days, of non-work); it is also, however, much more than that, as has been argued from the days of Plato to the present. As Mary Warnock (1978) showed, education is also at least as much if not more about inducting the young into the values of getting on with and relating well to other people, and of developing the capacities for and exercising imagination and developing creativity, the better to understand the past, monitor and evaluate the present, and plan for and direct their future. All this requires their being inducted into the cognitive and affective worlds; for only thus will they be able to understand and operate according to the norms and conventions of those modes of discourse, forms of theory and patterns of action that human beings have progressively developed, in order to conceive, comprehend and communicate about their experience of the world they share, and in that way make it manageable and malleable.

This process requires a lifetime of experience and dynamic and ongoing transformations of the human organism. Education, so Edward Bond remarked, 'cannot be put on like a coat of paint' (Bond, 1976). It means coming to see the world in a different way and as a bearer of the human traditions of critical and creative thought, not as a consumer of packages of pabulum pre-prepared and easily digestible for immediate regurgitation and solely economic purposes.

The other problem with the managerialist approach referred to above arises from the fact that, when people are taken on to 'manage' such corporatized bodies, they very often begin to lose all the skills and qualities that secured them election in the first place. Nowhere, perhaps, is this more obvious than in the new managerialism that has overtaken schools, colleges and universities, where all the talk of and stress on the importance of 'middle' or 'senior management teams' and the distinction of these from the 'workers' – talk readily engaged in by some employers and employees – has led to a situation in which people come to positions for which their previous professional experience has provided them with only the minimal necessary training and for competence in which they therefore have to be trained anew.

In these circumstances it is understandable that lecturers, teachers, students and parents are increasingly beginning to ask some disturbing questions: how far can it be ensured that all the primary functions of educating institutions will be preserved; how well are arrangements for professional development and appraisal possible, conceivable and in place; and how far is the necessity for multi-skilling and ongoing, diversifying training and education going to be a part of the future of the teaching profession – above and beyond the level of those advanced skills required to establish and secure excellence in teaching, for which the teacher chose to be trained in the first place? For there is a professional paradox in that, as things currently stand in Australia, teachers in training can expect to spend no more than a maximum of about 15 years in the classroom.

But this is only one of a number of paradoxes to which I have been pointing. The larger one – that between *laissez-faire* minimalism on the one hand and authoritarian centralism on the other hand – seems to me to be at work in many parts of the education systems in the UK, in Australia and New Zealand. When one reads the Australian Government White Paper and the Wran Report of 1988, for example; when one hears talk of a national curriculum and reads the Hobart Declaration of 1989; when one examines the various reviews of teacher education, teacher quality and teacher effectiveness that have either just been completed or are now being proposed; when one reads of the efforts of the Australian Minister of Employment Education and Training to get the Premiers of the various states to embark on the 'co-ordination' of their education policies, one will, I suggest, quickly discern the imprint of the same footprints that have already been trodden firmly into the concrete in the UK and elsewhere, and become hardened and coercive.

I can only hope that the concrete in Australia will stay moist enough for long enough for some of us to be able to mount the argumentative brush that will enable some of the rougher edges to be smoothed down, so that people who follow us down these paths will not trip and stumble, as those people in the UK who are having to tread them now, have found. For I wish to suggest that the paradox that arises in the interplay between liberal values such as autonomy and independence at the local school level and the interventionism that seeks the subordination of the local enterprise to some overarching requirements of central governmental systemic control and direction, needs to be resolved or dissolved if the manifest dysfunctions, abrasions and wastage that can be clearly observed in the workings-out of some countries' and systems' education policies are not to be carried forward into the future, to the gradual attenuation and elimination of many of their worthier goals.

This is perhaps the conclusive reason for insisting upon the cardinal importance of a wider conception of education than that with which managerialists work. I should therefore like to conclude by suggesting that the function of educating institutions is more appropriately predicated upon a Popperian view of the provisional nature of knowledge and the ephemeral and changeable status of all public institutions, including government, in the objective world.

I see the work of educating institutions as more properly embodying a dynamic and organic conception of education of the kind argued for above. This is exhibited in the critical and scientific approaches and achievements of minds trained in and bearers of the value of that version of Popper's philosophy (1943) that treats no theory or practice as 'established' truth, that rejects outright the view that 'there is no alternative' to the government's view of the right way of doing things, that views every policy proposal as nothing more than a hypothesis put up for test and by all possible means to be knocked down. A citizen body educated along these lines and armed with this approach to theory-construction and the tentative solution of problems will be able and committed to subject the theoretic bases and axiomatic pronouncements of the *dirigiste* tendencies of governments of the centralist hue to a serious, sustained and positive critique that looks only to the short-term solving of what are recognized as immediately tractable problems, conducing to a minimal social amelioration, and not to some long-term millennium or ideological paradise.

The aim of educating institutions in Australia must therefore be to show that the role of public and educating institutions in any modern 'open' society, such as the one Popper apostrophized, has to be, *inter alia*, to produce a well-informed citizenry aware of all the various ramifications of policy and practice in a complex and sophisticated society such as ours is today. This, we may hope, will help them become aware of the dangers of the centralizing tendencies on the part of governments of both Left and Right persuasions. But it will also sensitize them to the risks inherent in allowing credence to those who would, in policy matters and decision-making at the local level, allow a 'hundred ideas to flourish and a thousand schools of thought contend', in an aim of the anarchic liberation of all possible voices concerned to have a say in the direction and control of all those institutions in which they, for one reason or another, have a direct interest. Such an education will enable citizens to criticize the thinking of both totalitarians and anarchists to judge the best and the worst between them.

In such societies citizens will need to be committed, informed and knowledgeable participants in the processes of democratizing their political and social arrangements. They will need a basic understanding of, and the associated power of critical scrutiny in, all the diverse kinds of thinking and appraisal called for in the exercise of their franchise for communitarian purposes. Along with this will be needed the ability to establish for themselves what counts as the appropriate knowledge requisite for the development and articulation of such judgements, and the settled and steady disposition to deploy it.

In this endeavour it will be vital that citizens be oriented towards the emancipation that the decentralization of all the key functions of those institutions that enshrine democratic beliefs and values, and the critico-creative mode of thinking embodied and exemplified in the hypothetico-deductive approach to acquiring and appraising knowledge, can confer. This will require a sound education – but one much wider and much more iconoclastic than that encapsulating the economic approach to community living and social values. For such an education, I claim, is to the ultimate benefit of all the denizens of those countries, cultures and communities in which the forms and procedures of open, critical and sceptical approaches to knowledge-getting are instantiated and applied.

The effect of the adoption and tenure of such an approach in Australasia and the UK would lie in the creation and provision of a set of skills and competences available and ready to be applied as a positive and progressive heuristic method in the tentative solution of problems that immediately beset us. With such an approach we could seek to capitalize upon the beneficial effects of the destabilizations that the critical scrutiny, comparison and tentative correction of such really centralizing (while rhetorically decentralizing) theories, powers, structures, systems and regimes might ultimately be able to achieve. In this way we might hope to dissolve or remove the paradoxes that the coalescence of both liberal and conservative tendencies in our political and educational arrangements is currently and negatively causing.

These are the outcomes of what may be regarded as a really liberating approach to education, based upon the Popperian predicates of a critical and evolutionary educational epistemology. They have much more to do with the ability of future generations of citizens critically to assess, support or amend policies claimed to be directed towards economic, social or individual ends, than with the production of a properly trained workforce meet to do the work that their government controllers assign to them in pursuit of what are, after all, narrowly sectarian and nationalist interests, without the necessary broadening a wider world vision would give them.

In this undertaking, perhaps the voice of one of Australia's recent citizens –

and one who loves it 'warts and all' – will help to set these matters in a new light by pointing to the paradoxes that can result from the driving home of those public policies that are concerned to set a constraint in order to promote freedom – only to end up by enforcing the one and destroying the other.

REFERENCES

Ackerman, B. (1980) *Social Justice and the Liberal State*. New Haven Conn: Yale University Press.

Arnold, G. (1989) *Britain Since 1945: Choice, Conflict and Change*. London: Blandford.

Aspin, D.N. and Chapman, J.D. (1994) *Quality Schooling*. London: Cassell.

Aulich Report, (1990) *A Fair Chance for All*. Report of the Senate Standing Committee on Employment, Education and Training. Canberra: AGPS.

Berlin, I. (1969) *Four Essays on Liberty*. London: OUP.

Bond, E. (1976) 'An Introduction to '"The Fool"'. *Theatre Quarterly*. Spring.

Cranston, M. (1954) *Freedom – A New Analysis*, (2nd edn). London: Longmans, Green.

Dawkins, J.S. (1988) Speech to Inter-government Conference on *Education and the Economy in a Changing Society*. OECD Conference, Paris, 16 March.

DEET (Australian Government Department of Employment, Education and Training) (1987) *Higher Education: A Policy Discussion Paper*, (The Green Paper), December. Canberra: AGPS.

DEET (Australian Government Department of Employment, Education and Training) (1987) *Skills for Australia*, September. Canberra: AGPS.

DEET (Australian Government Department of Employment, Education and Training) (1988) *A Changing Workforce*, May. Canberra: AGPS.

DEET (Australian Government Department of Employment, Education and Training) (1988) *Strengthening Australia's Schools – a Consideration of the Focus and Content of Schooling*, 23 May. Canberra: AGPS.

DEET (Australian Government Department of Employment, Education and Training) (1988) *Higher Education – a Policy Statement* (The White Paper), July. Canberra: AGPS.

Flew, A. (1989) *Equality in Liberty and Justice*. London: Routledge.

Friedmann, M. (1962) *Capitalism and Freedom*. Chicago: Chicago University Press.

Friedmann, M. (1976) *Price Theory*. Chicago: Aldine.

Gewirth, A. (1978) *Reason and Morality*. Chicago: Chicago University Press.

von Hayek, F.A. (1960) *The Constitution of Liberty*. Chicago: Chicago University Press.

von Hayek, F.A. (1976 and 1979) *Law, Legislation and Liberty* [Collected Works] **1–3**. London: Routledge & Kegan Paul.

The Hobart Declaration: National Goals for Schooling (1989). Department of

Education, Employment and Training – Australian Education Council. Canberra: AGPS.

Hunt, F.J. (1987) *The Incorporation of Education: An International Study in the Transformation of Educational Priorities.* London and New York: Routledge & Kegan Paul.

Marsh, C.J. (1988) *Curriculum: Practices and Issues* (2nd edn). Sydney: McGraw-Hill.

Marsh, C.J. (1994) *Producing a National Curriculum: Plans and Paranoia.* St Leonards NSW: Allen & Unwin.

Mill, J.S. (1962) *On Liberty* (ed. M. Warnock). London: Fontana.

NBEET (National Board of Employment, Education and Training) (1992) *Curriculum Initiatives.* NBEET-commissioned Report No 12. Canberra: AGPS.

Nozick, R.S. (1974) *Anarchy, State and Utopia.* Oxford: Blackwell.

Popper, K.R. (1943) *The Open Society and its Enemies.* London: Routledge & Kegan Paul.

Raz, J. (1986) *The Morality of Freedom.* Oxford: Clarendon Press.

Rawls, J. (1973) *A Theory of Justice.* Oxford: Clarendon Press.

Rothwell, N. (1988) 'Democracy fettered in Land of the Magna Carta', *The Australian*, 14 September.

Scruton, R. (1980) *The Meaning of Conservatism.* London: Macmillan.

Scruton, R. (1982) *A Dictionary of Political Thought.* London: Macmillan.

Skilbeck, M. (1990) *Curriculum Reform: an overview of trends.* Paris: OECD.

Times Higher Education Supplement (1990) 'Dawkins' way'. 13 April.

Warnock, M. (1978) *Schools of Thought.* London: Faber.

Wilson, B.G. (1993) *Committee for Quality Assurance in Higher Education: Guidelines for Preparation of Institutional Portfolios.* Canberra: Department of Education, Employment and Training (Higher Education Division).

Wran Report (1988) *Report of the Committee on Higher Education Funding.* Presented to the Minister for Employment, Education and Training in 1989. Canberra: AGPS.

Chapter 3

The Politics of Choice and Market-oriented School Reform in Britain and the United States: Explaining the Differences

William Lowe Boyd

Since 1980 most English-speaking nations have experienced a remarkable transformation in how people think about educational policy and the management of schools (Ball, 1990; Clark and Astuto, 1986; Harman *et al.*, 1991; Wirt and Harman, 1986). Despite substantial differences in political traditions and social contexts, striking parallels exist between these nations (especially Australia, New Zealand, the United Kingdom, and the United States) in the policies and reforms that have been adopted (Beare, 1991; Beare and Boyd, 1993). These developments, of course, are part of a larger international pattern. Worldwide social, economic and technological trends have generated pressures (particularly in economic competitiveness and the character of the workforce) that few existing school systems can satisfy (Coombs, 1985; Plank and Adams, 1989). Consequently, the reform and restructuring of school systems is an international phenomenon.

In many countries, especially in the English-speaking world, education reform is driven by a conviction that market-oriented reforms (i.e. measures that would unleash market forces in education, as opposed to education systems run as centrally controlled, government monopolies) are the key to more effective and efficient education systems. This conviction represents the triumph of neo-conservative critiques of the welfare state, a success fuelled in part, ironically, by the 'contradictions of capitalism' reflected in the worldwide economic problems (i.e. recession, 'stagflation') beginning with the OPEC oil embargo in the mid-1970s. The strong parallels between the United States and Britain in this triumphal critique in the education policy domain can be seen by comparing the very similar analyses by Ball (1990, p. 35) for the UK and by Clark and Astuto (1986, p. 5) for the USA. Each of these analyses highlights the dramatic shift in policy goals from an emphasis on equality, access and the common school to an emphasis on excellence, selectivity and school choice. Truly, the politics of excellence and choice have reconfigured the education policy debate (Boyd and Kerchner, 1988).

After outlining the striking similarities in education reform between Britain and the USA (well described in Whitty and Edwards, 1992), this chapter explores the differences between Britain and the USA in the politics of choice and market-oriented school reform, and considers the policy implications of recent develop-ments. The chapter is based upon recent research conducted in both countries as part of a Fulbright research project comparing the Thatcher and Reagan educa-tion reform efforts and their continuation under their successors.

HANDS ACROSS THE SEA?

The parallels between the school reform efforts of the Thatcher and Major govern-ments and those of the Reagan and Bush governments are indeed extensive. Some of these similarities come from conscious transatlantic borrowing of policies. For example, Kenneth Baker (Secretary of State for Education) made a whirlwind visit to the United States, saw some of our magnet schools, and this led to the idea for the creation of city technology colleges (CTCs). Similarly, the idea of school–busi-ness compacts or partnerships, especially the example of the Boston Compact, got a lot of attention in Britain. More recently, aspects of the British Education Reform Act (ERA) 1988 are strongly echoed in 'America 2000'.

In contrast to the piecemeal, decentralized approach to reform in the USA, education reform in Britain has been centrally directed and, with the passage of the 1988 Education Reform Act, comprehensive and systematic. Many commen-tators have noted that market-oriented competition was the central theme of the ERA, with the notable exception of the (somewhat counter-balancing) National Curriculum component. The key competitive components are

1   what Hywel Thomas calls the 'pupil as voucher scheme' (open enrolment with funds following students)

2   provisions for state schools to 'opt out' of their Local Education Authority (LEA) through a vote of parents and become 'grant-maintained' schools directly funded by the national government.

Both components expose the LEAs to competitive pressures.

Some highlights of the parallels that have developed between Britain and the USA are the following:

1   In both countries, reform efforts are driven, and largely justified, by the claim that a better-educated workforce is needed to enhance economic competitiveness.

2   In both countries reforms are simultaneously increasing both the degree of centralization and the degree of decentralization of school governance. Thus, in both nations more decision-making authority is being shifted to the school level – 'school based management' (SBM) in the USA; 'local management of schools' (LMS) in Britain. But, at the same time, there are new centralizing forces: the National Curriculum in Britain and the new National Goals in the USA (a surprising and totally unprecedented development, given the strong American tradition of local control of education).

3   Both countries have magnet schools, programmes for school choice, and school–business partnerships. In a strange turn of events, the city technology colleges in Britain, which were

patterned after American magnet schools, may have been the inspiration for the Bush administration's proposal asking private industries to contribute to the funding for its proposed 'New American Schools'.

4   Similarly, the 'Assisted Places' scheme in Britain has had a counterpart in unsuccessful proposals for federal vouchers for disadvantaged urban youngsters to attend private schools. But this idea has in fact been adopted in one city – Milwaukee, Wisconsin.[1]

Although the idea of market-oriented reforms has been imported to Australia and New Zealand, and crops up now even in such unlikely spots as Sweden (long the bastion of the ideal welfare state), the natural habitat of the market model is the United States. But, if the Thatcherites have their way, Britain also will be its home. Indeed, something like a race is under way to see which of these two nations can outdo the other in the pace of its market-oriented education reforms. Thus, in March 1991, *The Economist* magazine challenged the United States to 'Be bold, Be British' in an editorial extolling the virtues of the more radical and comprehensive reforms in education under way there. Then, in February 1992, the darlings of American market-oriented reform, John Chubb and Terry Moe, published an article in Britain's *Sunday Times* magazine (essentially reprinted in Chubb and Moe, 1992) acknowledging the British lead in radical reforms but arguing, as they do for the United States as well (Chubb and Moe, 1990), that these reforms do not go nearly far enough, that all schools should 'opt out' (i.e., be made independent) so Local Education Authorities (LEAs) cannot interfere with their operation. Although Chubb and Moe's rhetoric has not been matched by public policies in the United States, President Bush's 'America 2000' education strategy to 'reinvent the American school' (by creating at least 535 'New American Schools' with a combination of public and private funding) has produced a typically American and, to some, bizarre offshoot. A private corporation, Whittle Communications, has launched a vast plan to build at least 200 *private, for-profit* schools around the country by 1996, a proposal dubbed by some 'McSchools' (i.e., schools akin to McDonald's franchised hamburger restaurants).

But this is no joke; it is a serious venture. Some key leaders of market-oriented education reform, notably John Chubb and Chester Finn, have quit their jobs and gone to work full-time for the Whittle Communications project, a commitment which entails, not least, moving from the corridors of power in Washington, DC, to Knoxville, Tennessee, the headquarters of Whittle Communications. In *Big Business Goes to School* J.S. Friedman (1992, p. 188) described the magnitude of this private undertaking: 'Whittle estimates that $2.5 billion to $3 billion will be required to put his first 200 schools into operation. By the year 2010, there could be 1,000 campuses, according to Whittle executives, each with day care facilities and elementary, middle and high schools.'

Significantly, President Bush shifted his position from being initially only in favour of parental choice among public (state) schools to espousing government-financed choice among both public and private schools. This position is included as part of the 'America 2000' education strategy and was also demonstrated in the public support given by Bush's Vice-President, Dan Quayle, and his Secretary of

Education, Lamar Alexander, to an unsuccessful bill for a private school voucher plan in the state of Pennsylvania in late 1991.

DIVIDED BY A COMMON LANGUAGE?

Despite all the parallels and a common language, some of the key words and concepts in market-oriented education reform do not mean quite the same thing to 'Brits' and 'Yanks'. We are, as Winston Churchill liked to say, 'divided by a common language'. The major overarching factors shaping reform that vary among nations seem to be:

- the historical social context;
- political culture;
- ideology and paradigms;
- governance structures.

Obviously, despite a common heritage (up to a point), Britain and the United States vary greatly along these dimensions. And because of these differences, especially the first three, choice and market-oriented reforms connote rather different meanings and implications in the two nations. As a consequence, one of the most striking differences between the two countries is how much more politicized and ideologically charged these reforms have been in Britain.[2] By contrast, they have commanded substantial bipartisan support in the United States, especially from both Democratic and Republican state governors. One of the interesting things about this is that the very thing that is at the heart of the ideological dispute in Britain – the shift towards market forces and consumerism – is present in the United States but with relatively little rancour so far. Still, and this is important, it has been present in a more muted form (until recently) and has not been at the heart of everything being done, as in the case in the ERA (with, of course, the notable exception of the National Curriculum).

Commenting on the origins and implications of the Education Reform Act 1988, Brian Simon concluded by stressing:

> the ideological struggle surrounding the whole initiative. This relates
> to the Government's reliance on market forces and competition as
> main motivations for change – frequently stressed by Kenneth Baker
> – as opposed to the concept of equal provision of a public good
> (education) which must inevitably power local authority provision,
> and which, therefore, relies on cooperation. These two principles
> now stand opposed. Outcomes will be very different according to
> who gains the victory.
>
> (Simon, 1989, p. 29)

Similarly, Hywel Thomas captures the tension between co-operation and competition when he asks, regarding the dynamics unleashed by ERA, 'Will heads and principals be entrepreneurs or pirates?' (Thomas, forthcoming, p. 26). And, in a masterpiece of British understatement, Brian Simon, again speaking of the 1988 Education Reform Act, says:

A 'radical' measure, strongly and almost unanimously opposed in its passage through Parliament by all parties but the one in office, as well as by those most directly concerned (local authorities, teachers, parents' organizations and others), is likely to lead to a degree of confrontation when it comes to implementation.

(Simon, 1989, p. 24)

So, why so much difference in this regard? To begin with, the tendency toward politicization in Britain, maximized by abrasive Thatcherite 'conviction' (as opposed to 'consensus') politics, is encouraged by the greater class distinctions and class-consciousness there than one finds in the United States. Thus, in assessing the context of American politics, the British political scientist David McKay emphasizes the lack of a working-class or socialist political tradition in the United States. This, in turn, relates to the American belief in equality and social mobility and 'absence of a feudal and aristocratic past, with all the deeply rooted social cleavages which such arrangements imply' (McKay, 1989, p. 20).

In Britain, market choice in education tends to be associated with privilege; with private, independent schools; with the tradition of selective grammar schools; and with 'decomprehensivization' of state high schools and re-establishment of selective schools. (In the UK, the commitment to comprehensive high schools is precarious and quite recent, that is, dating from 1965.) By contrast, in the absence of an aristocratic past, and with a long history of comprehensive, non-selective high schools and few élite private schools, choice of schools has a less élitist connotation in the United States. Reflecting this reality, Frank Dobson, the Labour MP for Holborn and St Pancras, stated, in a talk to American Fulbrighters in January 1991, that he felt British education policy has been shaped by what might be called the 'National Exclusionist Front', that is, a *de facto*, but none the less real, effort to keep the populace divided along inegalitarian lines.

Beyond class-consciousness, another important distinction between the nations lies in their orientation toward collectivist or individualist approaches. McKay contended that 'Nothing more accurately seems to represent Americanism than a stress on individual rather than collective action' (McKay, 1989, p. 27). For Americans generally, the least government is the best government and 'rugged individualism' is a great virtue. In turn, this individualism links up with capitalism and entrepreneurship. The American political scientist, Walter Dean Burnham, observed that: 'In a society and political culture saturated by the values of free enterprise, welfare policy occupies an ambiguous position. Policies that are, in effect, "welfare for business" are rarely so regarded by the public, much less subjected to large-scale political controversy. Welfare for the poor has always occupied a very different position' (Burnham, 1983, p. 480). The American inclination to trust business more than government was also exemplified recently by the surge of support for the independent candidacy of billionaire H. Ross Perot for president. This phenomenon was emblematic of both the widespread disaffection with US politics and the willingness to turn to tough-minded business leaders for solutions to *public* policy problems.

Taken together, these considerations help explain the greater acceptance in the United States of market forces and competition in education policy. A

Thatcherite campaign to 'create an enterprise culture' was clearly unnecessary in the United States. Liz Bondi made a similar point:

> Despite the similarities between 'Reaganism' and 'Thatcherism' there remain profound differences in the political cultures of the USA and the UK, which go some way to explaining contrasts in policies concerned with choice and diversity. The absence of a strong collectivist tradition in American politics probably accounts for the lack of partisan opposition to these policies: the emphasis on individual freedoms in the rhetoric of the New Right in Britain is simply unnecessary in the USA because opposition to the idea lacks any substantial organization or ideological basis. This in turn has allowed the emergence of policy initiatives from a variety of political quarters and policy initiatives that are more pragmatic than proselytizing.
>
> (Bondi, 1991, p. 132)

Another important difference, associated with the centralized and comprehensive education reform effort in Britain, as contrasted with the decentralized and diffuse approach to reform in the United States, revolves around the system and structure of government. The British parliamentary system permits a government with a strong majority to ramrod things through that usually would require very substantial compromises in the more fragmented USA political system. Clearly, strong ideology and 'conviction politics' were contributing forces in the comprehensive reforms embodied in the ERA. But the parliamentary system and centralist tendencies (particularly under the Thatcher Government) stand in sharp contrast to America's strong federal system, constitutional and complicated governmental check-and-balances, and tradition of state and local control of education. Rather than a comprehensive Education Reform Act, American reform has relied on a melange of commission reports, diverse state legislation and home-grown initiative and innovation in (some) local school districts. Of course, the decentralization and diverse nature of the US reform movement is not very surprising, given 50 states and a tradition of decentralized, local control of schools. (Education is traditionally 'a state function, locally administered'.)

As Bruce Cooper (1990) has noted, America's decentralization has impeded a sweeping enactment of market-oriented reforms, which were more readily enacted in Britain's highly centralized political system. But, at the same time, the decentralization of the US system has helped experimentation with choice in education. If decisions were centralized at the federal level nothing would have happened due to the frequent stand-off between the Republican-controlled executive branch and the Democratic-controlled Congress. This is the reality that stymied the passage of Bush's 'America 2000' legislative package. Nevertheless, it remains alive because it also rests upon state and local community initiatives which have been rather enthusiastically taken up in many places, and a cleverly designed private-sector initiative, the New American School Development Corporation.

A final important difference between the two nations is that, although teachers and schools have also come in for almost as much criticism in the United States as in Britain, Americans have been making a big effort since 1986 to substantially increase the pay and professionalism of teachers. This sort of thing is conspicuous by its absence in Britain. When it comes time to look at how reforms are implemented, this difference in the treatment of teachers is likely to make an important difference. Guthrie and Pierce observed that:

> Not only is the Thatcher government expecting to accomplish educational changes with precious little by way of additional financial resources; it is also attempting to accomplish these radical goals without much professional assistance. Given the low levels of additional resources, the long-run success of the Thatcher agenda in education will depend crucially upon the cooperation of professional educators. However, little has been done systematically at a policy level to curry their favor or induce their cooperation. Conflict between the national government and teachers has increased, and Thatcher critics, and some teacher representatives, assert that they have been asked to bear the blame for the failings of the English education system.
>
> (Guthrie and Pierce, 1990, p. 202)

If the ERA is eventually found wanting, if it is unable to meet the human capital imperative, unwillingness to seek the productive co-operation of teachers may be the single most important dimension to which future critics will ascribe its failure.

By contrast, Guthrie and Pierce noted in the United States 'where reform is widespread but far less fundamental,' the co-operation of teachers has been sought repeatedly and many of the 'second wave' reforms 'are deliberately aimed at enhancing the professional status of teachers' (ibid., p. 202).

NO RENAISSANCE WITHOUT REVOLUTION? DEVELOPMENTS SINCE 1990

By the end of 1990, there was a growing sense in the United States that, despite undeniable progress, the school reform movement was falling well short of the level of improvements needed to protect and advance the national interest. Thus, despite the second wave's call for fundamental restructuring of schools, progress in 'restructuring' seemed slow and ambiguous, in part because of a lack of agreement about exactly how schools should be restructured. In this context, calls for more revolutionary reforms began to be heard with increasing frequency.

A number of developments suggested that we might have been moving into a time of more fundamental and radical reforms. President Bush's appointment of a new Secretary of Education, Lamar Alexander, brought a much more dynamic thrust to federal education policy (see Gigot, 1991). As Governor of Tennessee, Alexander gained a national reputation as a leading educational reformer. Upon becoming Secretary of Education, he surrounded himself with market-oriented reformers and critics of the *status quo* (David Kearns, the former Xerox chairman; Diane Ravich, neo-conservative historian of education) and like-minded informal advisers (Denis Doyle, Saul Cooperman and Chester Finn).

Alexander remarked that, 'One of the lessons of education reform in the 1980s is that we've been too slow and too timid. What we need is a populist uprising'

79

(quoted in Gigot, 1991, p. 6). Consistent with this view, in unveiling the 'America 2000' education plan developed by Alexander, President Bush said, 'To those who want to see real improvement in American education, I say: "There will be no renaissance without revolution"' (quoted in Norris, 1991, p. 11). Yet, as Norris observed, Bush aspired to revolutionize American education with an expenditure of no more than $820 million over five years, less than the cost of one Stealth bomber. Moreover, no new money was involved since the funds would be drawn from the Education Department's existing budget.

The new plan proposed $550 million to build 535 new schools – presumably one for each Congressional district – designed to be 'national models of excellence'. In a proposal reminiscent of the city technology colleges in Britain, American industry was asked to contribute $150 million toward the construction of these schools and, in turn, would have a voice in their design and curriculum. This new school scheme, Norris (1991) suggested, might be a 'sweetener' to help gain acceptance of companion proposals to increase parental choice. (As it turned out, Congress rejected both schemes.) Here, Bush proposed to spend $230 million to encourage school districts to adopt choice schemes and again advanced the controversial idea that federal Chapter 1 moneys for disadvantaged students should be allowed to follow them to private and even parochial schools.

Republicans had proposed this idea for Chapter 1 before, but continue to be beaten back by liberal Democrats in Congress, who fear, as do many urban educators, that an exodus to private schools might ensue and further jeopardize the already precarious finances and standing of embattled urban schools. Indeed, one of the most surprising developments in early 1991 was the revival of interest in public funding for private school choice. *Education Week* carried a front-page story (Olson, 1991) proclaiming that 'proposals for private school choice [were] reviving at all levels of government'. It highlighted:

1 President Bush's proposal for financial incentives for school districts adopting choice policies for public and private schools;

2 a proposal before the Detroit Board of Education, to permit some private schools to become public schools eligible for public funding;

3 a decision by officials in Epsom, New Hampshire to provide tax abatements for property owners who sponsor a high school student's private education;

4 Milwaukee's much publicized experiment with a publicly funded voucher plan enabling low-income students to attend private non-sectarian schools (in effect, a local version of the Chapter 1 voucher idea).

Together with campaigns for similar ventures in Pennsylvannia and Michigan, these developments suggested an unexpected breakdown of the recent political consensus that publicly funded choice plans should be restricted to public schools.

This shift in opinion seemed attributable mainly to a combination of impatience with the pace of reform and the effects of Chubb and Moe's (1990) influential book and Polly Williams's leadership in the Milwaukee venture (Olson,

1991). Ms Williams is a black, inner-city leader and former welfare mother who has become a state representative in Wisconsin. She is an articulate and dynamic speaker and her advocacy for private school choice for inner-city families has brought a legitimacy to the concept outside of right-wing circles. With black, inner-city leaders in Detroit as well as Milwaukee supporting private school choice, and some liberal Democrats beginning to re-examine their positions on the subject, there could be a sea change in the making.

However, since parochial schools comprise by far the largest portion of our private schools, the future of private school choice in the United States really depends on the Supreme Court's position on the Constitution's First Amendment 'wall of separation between church and state'. Always in the past, the Court has held that the First Amendment prohibits any public funds going to church-related activities. But the Court now has a conservative majority as a result of appointments during the Reagan era. As happened in Australia in a similar situation (Boyd, 1987), the Court might in the future interpret the First Amendment to permit public moneys going to religious organizations, so long as all faiths are treated equally and none are favoured. If this should eventually happen, there will indeed be a sea change in education policy. For the present, however, the organized political opposition, as well as legal barriers, to private school choice still remain imposing. So the future is still very much in doubt.

'BE BOLD, BE BRITISH'

As noted earlier, as Secretary of Education Lamar Alexander was preparing to unveil the new federal education policy, *The Economist* (23 March 1991) published an editorial challenging him to learn from the English experience, to 'be bold, be British'. Clearly, British school reform under the Conservative Government is bold. But, from a mainstream American point of view, it also seems unbalanced. Mainstream Americans have to be concerned about *equality* as well as excellence and efficiency. Equity concerns are built into our system through the legal guarantees embodied in the Bill of Rights and the Fourteenth Amendment to the US Constitution, which guarantees all citizens 'equal protection of the laws' and 'due process of the laws'. Our policy-makers have to think about these things as they craft legislation. No similar provisions distract Conservative politicians from their goal of efficiency in Britain. With a strong majority in Parliament, Tory ministers pursue their objectives with an unhampered zeal that American congressmen can only envy.

Although the Conservative Government is more moderate under John Major than it was under Margaret Thatcher, it nevertheless continues to pursue a market-oriented, Thatcherite education policy largely unadulterated by concerns for equity.[3] In the United States, even advocates of choice systems, such as Coons and Sugarman (1978) and Chubb and Moe (1990), tend to wrestle with, and try to build in, safeguards against the obvious inegalitarian consequences of completely unregulated systems. The same does not seem to be the case in Britain.

As noted earlier, Britain's 1988 Education Reform Act (ERA) emphasized market-oriented competition between schools. Again, the key competitive components are the 'pupil as voucher scheme' (open enrolment with funds following students), and provisions for state schools to opt out of their Local Education

Authority (LEA) through a vote of parents and become 'grant-maintained' schools directly funded by the national government.

Although the United States has nothing quite like the grant-maintained scheme, Chubb and Moe (1990) are, in effect, advocating a gigantic 'opting out' scheme for American schools. In contrast to Britain, however, their proposal would have our state-level policy-makers opting their schools out of existing state systems of democratically controlled, school-district governance in favour of a market-driven system of state-funded public and private schools. Still, the likely effects of Chubb and Moe's scheme and of the British 'grant-maintained' scheme are similar. In both cases, schools are removed from democratic, community governance and community-wide planning is replaced by the 'invisible hand' of the marketplace. What is especially worrying in the British context is a possible revival of the inegalitarian, two-tiered system of selective grammar schools and secondary modern schools. During 1991, the then Secretary of State for Education, Kenneth Clarke, not only urged all schools to opt out (and offered attractive financial incentives to do so), but also decided to relax the earlier regulation preventing newly opted out schools from changing their character (most likely from comprehensive to selective grammar school) for five years. The fear among egalitarians is that this is creeping privatization of state schools and a possible reintroduction of selection and élitism. The response from defenders of government policy is that opting out is a key means for freeing schools and making them more efficient, effective and responsive.

Policy-makers on both sides of the Atlantic would be well advised to look closely at the empirical studies of school choice that are beginning to accumulate in Britain. They give us, for the first time, some systematic, large-scale data on what happens when choice schemes with particular features are implemented. Parental choice policies similar to those in the ERA for England and Wales have been in effect in Scotland since 1982. Studies there (Adler et al., 1989; Echols et al., 1990) provide an important test of the assumptions undergirding the ERA. Some of Adler et al.'s main findings challenge these assumptions:

1 For a majority of these parents, choice involved finding a satisfactory alternative to the district school rather than making an optimal choice from a wide range of possible schools.

2 In requesting schools for their children, parents have been influenced much more by geographical and social factors, for example, proximity and discipline, and by the general reputation of the school, than by educational considerations.

3 On the whole, the schools that have gained the most pupils have been the formerly selective schools in middle-class areas, while the schools that have lost most pupils have been those that serve local authority housing schemes in deprived peripheral areas.

4 There is considerable evidence of 'band-wagon' effects, and little evidence of the market functioning as a self-correcting mechanism.

(Adler et al., 1990, pp. 4–5)

Although Adler et al. concluded that the outcomes of parental choice in Scotland have also included less efficient use of resources, a widening of inequalities between schools and the re-emergence of a two-tier system of secondary schooling in the big cities, he nevertheless argues that parental choice of schools should not be abandoned but, rather, the policy should be modified as needed to ameliorate these undesirable outcomes.

CONCLUSION

Despite their important differences, both Britain and the United States are experimenting with similar market-oriented policies as means to fundamentally restructure and improve their schools. Sentiment in the United States is becoming more supportive for bold and even revolutionary measures for school improvement. But the array of forces and checks-and-balances in the American political system favour incremental rather than radical change. However, the Supreme Court holds the 'wild card' with the possibility of a reinterpretation of the First Amendment separation of church and state. Should this card ever be played, it will redefine the game and American education policy might begin to look 'bold and British'.

ACKNOWLEDGEMENT

Previously published in German translation in *Zeitschrift für Pädagogik*, January 1993, Heft 1/93, 53–69.

NOTES

1 For an evaluation of the Assisted Places Scheme, see Edwards, Fitz and Whitty (1989).

2 Most of the British school reform literature is combative. Contrast, for example, the description of British reform in Ball and Whitty (1990) and Francis (1990) with that of American reform in Murphy (1990) or Boyd and Kerchner (1988).

3 For support of this statement, see Ball (1990), Ball and Whitty (1990) and Whitty and Menter (1989).

REFERENCES

Adler, M. (1990) 'Parental choice and the enhancement of children's interests'. Paper presented at seminar on *Public and Private Choice in Education*, Centre for Educational Sociology, University of Edinburgh, 4 March.

Adler, M., Petch, A. and Tweedie, J. (1989) *Parental Choice and Educational Policy*. Edinburgh: Edinburgh University Press.

Alves, M.J. and Willie, C.V. (1987) 'Controlled choice assignments: A new approach to desegregation', *Urban Review*, **19**, 67–86.

Bacon, K.H. (1990) 'Liberals are joining conservatives in urging use of free-market philosophy to reform schools', *Wall Street Journal*, 5 June, A24.

Ball, S.J. (1990) *Politics and Policy Making in Education: Explorations in Policy Sociology*. London: Routledge.

Ball, S.J. and Whitty, G. (eds) (1990) 'English education in a new ERA: Urban schooling after the Education Reform Act', Special issue of the *Urban Review*, **22** (2), June.

Bastian, A. (1990) 'School choice: Unwrapping the package', in *Choice in Education: Potential and Problems*, W.L. Boyd and H.J. Walberg (eds). Berkeley, CA: McCutchan.

Beare, H. (1991) Chapter 1 in G. Harman, H. Beare and G.F. Berkeley (eds) *Restructuring School Management: Administrative Reorganization of Public School Governance in Australia*. Canberra: Australian College of Education Press.

Beare, H. and Boyd, W.L. (eds) (1993) *Restructuring Schools: An International Perspective on the Movement to Transform the Control and Performance of Schools*. London: Falmer Press.

Blank, R.K. (1989) 'Educational effects of magnet high schools'. Paper presented at conference on *Choice and Control in American Education*, University of Wisconsin-Madison, May 17–19.

Bondi, E. (1991) 'Choice and diversity in school education: Comparing developments in the United Kingdom and the USA', *Comparative Education*, **27** (2), 125–34.

Boyd, W.L. (1987) 'Balancing public and private schools: The Australian approach and American implications', *Educational Evaluation and Policy Analysis*, **9** (3), 183–98.

Boyd, W.L. (1992) 'The Local Role in Education', in M. Alkin (ed.) *Encyclopedia of Educational Research*, 6th edn. New York: Macmillan.

Boyd, W.L. and Kerchner, C.T. (1988) *The Politics of Excellence and Choice in Education*. London: Falmer Press.

Boyd, W.L. and Walberg, H. (eds) (1990) *Choice in Education: Potential and Problems*. Berkeley, CA: McCutchan.

Brimelow, P. (1990) 'American perestroika?' *Forbes*, 14 May, 82–6.

Bryk, A.S., Lee, V.E. and Smith, J.B. (1990) 'High school organization and its effects on teachers and students: An interpretive summary of the research', in W.H. Clune and J.F. Witte (eds), *Choice and Control in American Education*, vol. 1. New York: Falmer Press, 135–226.

Burnham, W.D. (1983) *Democracy in the Making*. Englewood Cliffs, NJ: Prentice-Hall.

Caldwell, B.J. (1989) 'Paradox and uncertainty in the governance of education'. Paper presented at the annual meeting of the American Educational Research Association, San Francisco, 29 March.

Chubb, J.E. and Moe, T.M. (1990) *Politics, Markets, and America's Schools*. Washington, DC: The Brookings Institution.

Chubb, J.E. and Moe, T.M. (1992) *A Lesson in School Reform From Great Britain*. Washington, DC: The Brookings Institution.

Clark, D.L. and Astuto, T.A. (1986) 'The significance and permanence of changes in federal education policy', *Educational Researcher*, October, 4–13.

Coombs, P.H. (1985) *The World Crisis in Education: The View From the Eighties*. New York: Oxford University Press.

Coons, J.E. and Sugarman, S.D. (1978) *Education by Choice: The Case for Family Control*. Berkeley, CA: University of California Press.

Cooper, B. (1990) 'Local school reform in Great Britain and the United States: Points of comparison – points of departure', *Education Review*, **42** (2), 133–49.

Cuban, L. (1979) 'Determinants of curriculum change and stability, 1870–1970', in J. Schaffarzick and G. Sykes (eds), *Value Conflicts and Curriculum Issues*. Berkeley, CA: McCutchan.

Doyle, D.P. (1988) 'The excellence movement, academic standards, a core curriculum, and choice: How do they connect?' in W.L. Boyd and C.T. Kerchner (eds), *The Politics of Excellence and Choice in Education*. New York: Falmer Press.

Echols, F., McPherson, A. and Willms, J.D. (1990) 'Parental choice in Scotland', *Journal of Education Policy*, **5** (3), 207–22.

Economist (1991) 'Be bold, be British: A lesson for America's schools', **318** (7699), 23 March, 19–20.

Edwards, T., Fitz, J. and Whitty, G. (1989) *The State and Private Education: An Evaluation of the Assisted Places Scheme*. London: Falmer Press.

Elmore, R.F. (1988) 'Choice in public education', in W.L. Boyd and C.T. Kerchner (eds), *The Politics of Excellence and Choice in Education*. New York: Falmer Press.

Fliegel, S. (1990) 'Creative non-compliance', in W.H. Clune and J.F. Witte (eds), *Choice and Control in American Education*, vol. 1. London: Falmer Press.

Francis, M. (1990) 'Race and the education reform act', *The Urban Review*, **22** (2), June, 115–29.

Friedman, J.S. (1992) 'Big business goes to school', *The Nation*, 17 February, 188–92.

Friedman, M. (1955) 'The role of government in education', in R.A. Solo (ed.), *Economics and the Public Interest*. New Brunswick, NJ: Rutgers University Press.

Gigot, P.A. (1990) 'Bush team fails the test on school choice', *Wall Street Journal*, 8 June, A12.

Gigot, P.A. (1991) 'School reform now turns to revolution', *Wall Street Journal*, 8 April, 6.

Glass, G.V. and Matthews, D.A. (1991) 'Are data enough?', *Educational Researcher*, **20** (3), April, 24–7.

Guthrie, J.W. and Pierce, L.C. (1990) 'The international economy and national education reform: A comparison of education reforms in the United States and Great Britain', *Oxford Review of Education*, **16** (2), 179–205.

Harman, G., Beare, H. and Berkeley, G.F. (eds) (1991) *Restructuring School Management: Administrative Reorganization of Public School Governance in Australia*. Canberra: Australian College of Education Press.

Hawley, W.D. (1988) 'Missing pieces of the educational reform agenda', *Educational Administration Quarterly*, **24** (4), 416–37.

Jencks, C. (1966) 'Is the public school obsolete?', *The Public Interest*, **2**, Winter, 18–27.

Kearns, D. and Doyle, D. (1988) *Winning the Brain Race: A Bold New Plan to Make Our Schools Competitive*. San Francisco: Institute for Contemporary Studies.

Kirst, M.W. (1989) 'Who should control the schools? Reassessing current policies', in T. Sergiovanni and J. Moore (eds), *Schooling for Tomorrow*. Boston: Allyn & Bacon, 62–89.

Mazzoni, T. and Sullivan, B. (1990) 'Legislating educational choice in Minnesota: Politics and prospects', in W.L. Boyd and H.J. Walberg (eds), *Choice in Education: Potential and Problems*. Berkeley, CA: McCutchan.

McKay, D. (1989) *American Politics & Society*, 2nd edn. Oxford: Basil Blackwell.

McNeil, L.M. (1986) *Contradictions of Control: School Structure and School Knowledge*. New York and London: Routledge & Kegan Paul/Methuen.

McNeil, L.M. (1988) 'The politics of Texas school reform', in W.L. Boyd and C.T. Kerchner (eds), *The Politics of Excellence and Choice in Education*. New York: Falmer Press.

Moore, D. and Davenport, S. (1990) 'School choice: The new improved sorting machine', in W.L. Boyd and H.J. Walberg (eds), *Choice in Education: Potential and Problems*. Berkeley, CA: McCutchan.

Murphy, J. (ed.) (1990) *The Education Reform Movement of the 1980s*. Berkeley, CA: McCutchan.

Nathan, J. (1990) 'Progress, problems, and prospects of state educational choice plans', in W.L. Boyd and H.J. Walberg (eds), *Choice in Education: Potential and Problems*. Berkeley, CA: McCutchan.

National Commission of Excellence in Education (1983) *A Nation at Risk: The Imperative for Educational Reform*. Washington, DC: US Government Printing Office.

Norris, B. (1991) 'A revolution starts with small change', *Times Educational Supplement*, **3**, 11 May.

Olson, L. (1991) 'Proposals for private-school choice reviving at all levels of government', *Education Week*, **10** (22), 20 February, 1, 10–11.

Parkinson, M. (1989) 'The Thatcher government's urban policy, 1979–1989'. *Town Planning Review*, **60** (4), 421–40.

Plank, D. and Adams, D. (1989) 'Death, taxes, and school reform', *Administrator's Notebook*, **33**, 1–4.

Raywid, M.A. (1989) *The Case for Public Schools of Choice*. Bloomington, IN: Phi Delta Kappa.

Rothman, R. (1990) 'Paper launches academic attack on Chubb-Moe book on education', *Education Week*, **10** (11), 14 November, 1, 20.

Simon, B. (1989) 'The Education Act, 1988: Origins and implementation', *The Welsh Journal of Education*, **1** (1), 24–9.

Thomas, H. (forthcoming). 'The education reform movement in England and Wales', in H. Beare and W. L. Boyd (eds), *Restructuring Schools: An International Perspective on the Movement to Transform the Control and Performance of Schools*. London and New York: Falmer Press.

Tyack, D. (1974) *The One Best System*. Cambridge, MA: Harvard University Press.

Walker, R. (1989) 'Bush to appoint group to proffer education ideas', *Education Week*, 14 June, 1, 17.

Wall Street Journal (1990) 'Review & outlook: Teachers vs. kids', 6 June, A16.

Weisman, J. (1992) 'Skills and schools: is education reform just a business excuse?', *Washington Post*, 29 March.

Whitty, G. and Edwards, T. (1992) 'School choice policies in Britain and the USA: their origins and significance'. Paper presented at the annual meeting of the American Educational Research Association, San Francisco, 20 April.

Whitty, G. and Menter, I. (1989) 'The progress of restructuring', in D. Coulby and L. Bash (eds), *The 1988 Education Reform Act: Conflict and Contradiction*. London: Cassell.

Wirt, F. and Harman, G. (eds) (1986) *Education, Recession and the World Village*. London: Falmer Press.

Wong, K.K. (1989) 'Choice in public schools: Their institutional functions and distributive consequences'. Paper presented at annual meeting of the American Political Science Association, Atlanta, August 31–September 3.

Chapter 4

Educational Decentralization as a Policy Strategy in an Era of Fiscal Stress

Leslie C. Eliason

A comparison of US and Swedish education policy during the post-war era quickly reveals two very different approaches to the public provision of schooling. In many respects, the Swedish and American systems fall at opposite ends of the spectrum of central versus local control of educational policy-making. Swedish education has been among the most centralized and standardized across geographical units, while the American system is among the most decentralized with a wide range of variation from one local administrative unit to the next. Nevertheless, in both countries reorganization of the administrative relations governing the educational system has involved decentralization. While decentralization takes on different meanings in these two contexts, one important question this convergence of reform rhetoric raises is why two such different contexts should give rise to somewhat similar reform initiatives. The answer offered here emphasizes the political utility of decentralization as a policy strategy that stresses changes in decision-making structures rather than reform of classroom practices including pedagogy, curriculum, and learning methods and objectives.

The motives for educational reform today, as in earlier periods, arise from the political and economic context within which the educational system is situated, even though many of the perceived problems of the educational system are endogenous to the system. Seen from the perspective of authors such as Kingdon (1984) and March and Olsen (1989), the stream of policy solutions that rose to prominence during the 1980s emphasizing neo-liberal solutions to the problems of the fiscal crisis of the state collided with ongoing reform of relations between national (federal), regional (state) and local authorities. The drive to make government more efficient through cutbacks and economizing measures came together with the continuing demand for greater response to citizen demands by the public sector. Within the broader international setting of intensified global competition for markets and dependence on trade as one source of national income, the educational system has (again) become a highly politicized object of reform initiatives.

Decentralization's popularity derives from its promise of bringing about change in administrative or governance relations. Politicians from across the political spectrum find decentralization palpable or even desirable for a variety of reasons. It gives the appearance of rather dramatic change without requiring politicians and policy-makers to specify precisely how schools and schooling should change. Ideally this should result in better schools, but empirically the evidence has not yet demonstrated that this is the case. Because decentralization focuses on process rather than outcome, it allows central authorities to appear to be doing something without having to contribute to what kinds of changes need to be made at the school or even classroom level.

Furthermore, since decentralization coincides with an extended period of fiscal stress at all levels of government in both Sweden and the United States, it is part of the ideological as well as pragmatic political solution to the questions concerning how to manage cutbacks and impose fiscal restraint. In both Sweden and the United States, decentralization has moved some authority to lower levels within the system of jurisdictional hierarchy in education, but revenue-raising authority remains concentrated in the hands of elected officials. Moving spending decisions to lower levels has tended to concentrate power at a lower level, but still within the hands of administrators and politicians rather than teachers or site-based management groups.

This chapter offers at least a preliminary answer to the rather intriguing question of why politicians in two such different contexts would choose the same policy strategy, especially when it requires central politicians and policy-makers to cede their authority to other less powerful units of decision-making.

Looking across countries and across time, an interested observer of educational reform movements notices that major reform efforts arise only partly as a response to the expressed needs and interests of those most directly affected – students and teachers. Major educational reforms give expression to changing societal definitions of the role and function of education. In particular, since education is closely tied to upward socio-economic mobility and the allocation of élite positions in democratic societies (meritocracy), the most fundamental of social values are often contested in educational policy-making. Among the justifications for state provision and control of educational institutions, the economic imperative of an educated and well-trained workforce capable of fulfilling the demands of industry and business and producing the technological innovations necessary to fuel the engine of economic growth reigns supreme.

Since the early 1980s, educational reform has been on the political agenda of most advanced industrial democracies. The recurrent nature of educational reform movements points to the cyclical nature of public concern with the quality of education, performance issues, access to education, and the role that educational attainment plays in determining life chances. The strongly held belief that the performance of educational institutions is directly related to international economic competitiveness has been with us at least since the 1930s. However, the intensification of global economic interdependence and concern with trade as a source of national wealth over the last two decades has further stimulated concern in many countries about the adequacy of contemporary public educational systems.

The ongoing educational reform period that has stretched over the last decade corresponds to, and indeed is in part one expression of, the broader assault on the viability of the contemporary nation state to finance and perform adequately a wide range of social welfare functions acquired and expanded over the past century. As consistent economic growth has become more and more elusive, governments of advanced industrial states have run into serious problems financing their public sectors. The common response throughout the 1980s has been to undertake restructuring of public functions, particularly those involving social welfare benefits and large public bureaucracies. It is no accident, therefore, that education and health care have emerged as the twin crises of public management. Education and health care rank as the two largest sectors of public sector investment in social services. Thus budget cuts and efforts to restructure the public sector to increase efficiency and respond to consumer concerns about the adequacy of service provision have been an important part of the reform movements in education and health care. And conversely, education and health care have become popular targets of those calling for major reforms of the public sector.

While concern about the performance of the educational systems of many Western European and Anglo-American countries runs high in public opinion polls, the solutions offered in most states have focused less on changes in the classroom, curriculum and teacher training than they have taken up the issue of administrative reform. Restructuring the administrative structure and rethinking how schools are governed have been the principal dimensions of educational reform over the past decade. While each country has taken a slightly different approach to redefining control and authority in the decision-making and administrative apparatus of its educational system, the striking similarity across national contexts is the omnipresence of decentralization as the central project of educational reform in the 1980s and 1990s.

Decentralization means different things in different contexts. But the central feature of this policy reform strategy involves moving the locus of decision-making authority away from the *status quo ante* to another position, either closer to the local community, lower in the hierarchy of intergovernmental relations, or even from the local school system's central administrative bureaucracy out to the individual schools. The fascinating conundrum in these reforms is posed by the fact that most decentralization initiatives are launched and supervised from the so-called centre of the existing system of educational governance. Why should politicians and bureaucrats in the central administration advocate decentralization?

An unwritten law of politics holds that once acquired, power is rarely conceded willingly. This tenet finds one contemporary expression among public-choice models of bureaucratic behaviour. According to Wagner's Law, public spending is destined to outstrip the overall growth of the economy (Bendor and Moe, 1985; Bendor et al., 1985; Buchanan, 1967; Kristensen, 1987; Lindbeck, 1993; Lindbeck et al., 1993; Niksanen, 1971). Bureaucrats will try to increase their budgets and staff resources while resisting attempts by others to control their behaviour. Similarly, agencies are easier to create than to eliminate. Reasoning along these lines, bureaucrats in national agencies are generally reluctant to relinquish their decision-making authority and budgetary control to regional or local governments.

So why has decentralization become so popular and progressed at such a rapid pace during the 1980s in so many countries? Did voters demand it? While one might be inclined to herald the triumph of the democratic process and government responsiveness to the will of the people, decentralization has not been the product of a discernible ground swell of public sentiment or organized grass roots movements demanding greater participation in public decision-making. While it is true that taxpayers have become increasingly sensitive to how public funds are spent and the overall burden created by what the media have presented as government out of control, these have not been specifically linked to demands for decentralization. Greater efficiency and limits on excessive spending in areas of public procurement have been recurrent themes. But responsiveness was linked to decentralization principally by politicians rather than organized interests or community groups. The principal exponents of decentralization as a policy strategy have been national politicians.

What motivation do politicians have for advocating moves along the continuum between local and central administration in education? This question can be answered in at least two ways. The first set of answers flows from the reasons given in public pronouncements by reform advocates, many of whom sincerely believe that decentralization is the key to unlocking the innovative potential at the school level. The problems of the education system – both in the United States and Scandinavia – lie not in lack of funding or personnel, they argue, but rather in the administration and governance of schools. This view has gained considerable currency over the last decade with the result that the relationship between national, state or regional, and local authorities in education has been overhauled. Under the banner of decentralization, national policy-makers in countries with such widely divergent bureaucratic structures, traditions and educational systems as those of the United States, Sweden, Australia and the United Kingdom have divested central authorities of their responsibility for overseeing specific policies and programmes. Instead, what administrative responsibilities remain at the national level involve developing and promulgating national performance standards, framework budgets, and some (but now much more limited) research and development work.

The term decentralization conjures up images of greater citizen participation and influence as well as greater local autonomy to respond to local needs and demands. Strong normative arguments support the notion of decentralization, which can take many forms. Distributing power can serve as a built-in protection against abuse of power. Giving some functions to local government and others to national authorities allows for the most appropriate allocation of responsibilities to take advantage of economies of scale while also bringing important decisions closer to those most directly affected, allowing for greater 'voice'. Geographical decentralization allows citizens the 'exit' option, since they can move to those communities with the policies they prefer (Hirschman, 1970; Weimer and Vining, 1989, p. 119).

In practice, however, decentralization has its drawbacks. Along with increasing the complexity of the policy system and thereby complicating policy analysis and implementation (Bardach, 1977), decentralization increases the number of sites at which political conflict can take place (Smith, 1985). Decentralization also produces an incentive for jurisdictions to impose fiscal externalities on each other as they compete to attract wealthier residents and discourage poorer ones from migrating into the community (Weimer and Vining, 1989, p. 122).

Aside from these pitfalls, decentralization as a policy response to calls for educational reform creates expectations of change leading to improved educational performance which decentralization in and of itself cannot ensure. Indeed, decentralization in the United States has failed to produce anywhere near the level of change its advocates predicted. In Sweden, decentralization has led to the dismantling of the National Board of Education and with it some of the advantages that originally led to creation and expansion of a central policy-making agency. But the results of decentralization have been mixed at best. Changing where and how decisions are made does not guarantee that better, more efficient, or more effective school practice will result. As Elmore observed:

> The politics of structural reform in education has increasingly
> become a politics about the authority and legitimacy of various
> institutional arrangements, disconnected from any serious treatment
> of whether these arrangements can be expected to have any impact
> on what students learn in school. The stakes of structural reform are
> largely reckoned in terms of who gains and who loses influence
> within the governance structure, not in terms of whether structural
> change leads to changes in the conditions of teaching and learning.
>
> (Elmore, 1993, p. 39)

Furthermore, recent research on decentralization efforts in the United States (Tyack, 1993) shows that the current reform movements in education, while touted as decentralization, often involve a mixture of moves that increases the power of central authorities through fiscal framework legislation and standardized, centrally determined performance criteria while devolving other decisions about how to carry out these mandates. As Cohen (1990) has argued, decentralization often increases the complexity and number of bureaucratic agencies involved in education since new agencies are added not as replacements for existing ones, but in addition to them. So while decentralization is supposed to be an antidote for overbureaucratization, it may actually exacerbate administrative complexity. In Sweden as in many USA school districts, decentralization and site-based management strategies have been implemented through a top-down approach in which the national agency, in the case of Sweden, or the central district administration, in the case of many USA localities, hires or appoints 'oversight teams' to supervise decentralization.

Examining the recent record of decentralization reforms in two systems as different as the United States and Sweden, the evidence suggests that decentralization has been a common strategy for addressing the problems of many different public sector organizations and that it has been applied to education in response to a more general critique of public sector management. Furthermore, decentralization's appeal lies in the fact that it does not prescribe a particular set of results or expectations about the outcome of decision-making processes. Instead, decentralization emphasizes a more general approach to educational administration.

The common term in the American debate – educational governance – reflects the core attitudinal component of recent reforms: that the crisis in the schools is related to the problems of governing *per se*. This suggests that an ideological fusion has occurred between decentralization reforms and the resurgence of classical economic liberalism favouring deregulation, decentralization, flirtations with privatization, and other forms of market-based incentive structures during the last decade in Sweden and the United States.

During an era of intense scepticism about the ability of government intervention to produce any kind of desirable social change, reforms drawing on the logic of market mechanisms (vouchers, privatization, business involvement in schools, etc.) have proved capable of mobilizing considerable support among a highly cynical public. At least since the publication of *Free to Choose* (Friedman and Friedman, 1980), classical liberalism has made a powerful comeback in the public debate in the United States and the United Kingdom where it has always enjoyed broader popularity than in most other advanced industrial democracies. The political movements that captured this revival found their expression in the Reagan and Thatcher governments. While public policy during their tenures in office may not always have reflected the purest of *laissez-faire* approaches, the rhetoric of both administrations tapped in to a strong current among the voting public. The upsurge in decentralization reforms has coincided with the broader public sector reforms emphasizing less government and more market.

Classical liberalism holds that markets are, by definition, the most desirable allocation mechanism. They decentralize social decision-making by allowing individual preferences expressed through transactions between buyers and sellers, consumers and producers to determine the allocation of goods and services. From the perspective of classical liberalism, markets are by definition efficient except when market failure occurs. The debate about whether the state should be involved in welfare provision at all has become the central battleground of academic researchers as well as political advocates of almost every persuasion (Marmor, 1993). What seems clear is that how one answers the question of the appropriate limits of the welfare state depends on whether one defines welfare programmes as public goods and in general, whether one takes an economistic perspective on the concept of welfare itself (cf. Demsetz, 1993; Miller, 1993; Prychitko, 1993; Schmidtz, 1993; Varian, 1993).

Decentralization as a conceptual approach to the problems of governing democracies has been part of the American political tradition since its founding. Indeed the federal structure itself reflects the deep scepticism held by drafters of the Constitution about putting too much power in the hands of central governmental authorities. Conversely, the Swedish tradition has relied much more heavily on a strong central state capable of administering and implementing legislation throughout the country. During the expansionary period of the welfare state in Sweden (1950s and 1960s), central authority was exercised as a means of equalizing resources across geographical regions and socio-economic classes. The strong central agency in the field of education policy, the National Board of Education (*Skolöverstyrelsen*, SÖ) not only oversaw monitoring of the educational system, it also provided the expertise and evaluative capacity to guide educational reform including the introduction of the comprehensive school (Eliason, 1988).

The idea of moving decision-making authority away from the centre and top of the administrative hierarchy (Stockholm, the central state, the peak administrative agencies) became part of the political debate in Sweden during the late 1960s and early 1970s (Hemerén, 1988, pp. 232–3). This also corresponded to a

period of municipal and county government reform in which the number of enti-
ties was dramatically consolidated to make the individual units more efficient
through economies of scale and greater resources to secure administrative competence (Strömberg and Westerståhl, 1983). Decentralization meant different things
to different actors. Thus, for some decentralization implied greater autonomy for
local governments, for others it was intended to generate greater efficiency. Still
others expected that decentralized decision-making would mean greater citizen
influence over the allocation of resources and the design and implementation of
public policy.

During the 1980s, the power and influence of neo-liberal ideas and their advocates increased in both the United States and Sweden. The Reagan presidency
signalled a redefinition of the appropriate role of the federal government in education. Since 1980, policy debates in the United States have been coloured by a
general scepticism about the desirability of any large-scale national programme
and about whether government can, through public policy, achieve broad social
goals such as equality and individual achievement. Cynicism plays a role, particularly in policy areas such as education where earlier reform efforts have been
deemed failures. Even progressive-minded reformers in the United States and
Social Democrats in Sweden during the 1980s began to question whether government action or state intervention was desirable. Despite explicit policies to
promote educational equity, the overall performance of the American educational
system as reflected in various measures including test scores, drop-out rates and
teacher assessments has not shown clear improvement. Similarly, even though (or
some would argue, because) the Swedish educational system's capacity was
expanded considerably while its structure was reformed to provide for a single
comprehensive school for all children, socio-economic background factors
continue to be strong predictors of student achievement and participation in
higher education. Parents seem to fear that the drive toward equity has diluted
the quality of education in the public school systems of both the United States and
Sweden. Increasingly, then, equity and excellence are seen as competing, if not
mutually exclusive, goals (Boyd, 1988, p. 302; Clark and Astuto, 1986). Strikingly,
US federal education policy continues to emphasize achievement rather than
equity, despite the change in political control of the White House. In Sweden the
Social Democrats have actively participated in raising these issues at least since
the party congress in 1986. Together the Social Democratic party and the LO, the
peak organization of the labour movement, launched a public debate about the
future of the welfare state within which education became an important topic of
concern (Socialdemokraterna, 1989a; 1989b).

In the United States decentralization, it is hoped, will stimulate greater
parental interest and involvement in their children's education. Together, parents,
teachers, students and administrators along with community and business leaders
are supposed to find creative cost-effective ways to improve the learning environment. Through school-based management councils, these interests meet and
discuss initiatives. In Sweden local school authorities are now responsible for
generating their own plans for implementing the general guidelines, goals, and
objectives established by national policy-makers. However, in both contexts, the
struggle over who gets to decide has been intensified by the nature of the issues

to be decided. Either local decision-makers are left with less important imple-mentation details, or they are called upon to work out the details about how to implement fiscal austerity measures. Nevertheless, school-based management continues to gain ground in the United States, with initiatives in over half of the states.

Decentralization by implication means greater variation in educational provi-sion. This is a basic assumption of the market-based model in which schools are freed from central direction in order to respond to the demands of their clien-teles. Schools are encouraged to develop 'profiles' or act as 'magnets' to attract students and parental interest. Voucher plans, by extension, further promote the general goals associated with decentralization by allowing parents and students to vote with their feet and choose to spend their educational allotment on the school of their choice. Competition for students should produce better schools. But whether the logic of the market works in education, particularly if educating all school age children is a high priority, remains to be seen. Studies extolling the virtues of increased school autonomy (Chubb and Moe, 1986; 1990) have received more public attention than other studies that take a more cautious stance on the mixed evaluations of voucher experiments to date (e.g. Corwin and Dianda, 1993; Parker, 1989; Rist, 1991).

While American politics has a long tradition of favouring markets over state intervention, Swedish public attitudes toward government involvement in social and economic relations have generally been more positive. The Social Democratic party, having formed the government for most of the post-war era (except 1976–81 and 1991–94) generally favoured state action to promote social and economic equality. During the 1980s, however, decentralization efforts have been part of a larger debate about the appropriate role, function, and size of the public sector. Social Democrats have been at least as much a part of leading this concern as have more conservatively minded public figures. Calling for 'renewal' of the public sector, Swedish Social Democrats hoped to steal the thunder of their non-social-ist opposition (e.g. Gunnar Heckscher, former Swedish Conservative party leader and an economist; see Heckscher, 1984). On the Social Democratic side, Casten von Otter (1986), a researcher on social issues and a vocal member of the Social Democratic party, has advocated various reforms that would introduce market-like incentives into the public sector. The symptoms they hope to treat are common to many advanced industrial democracies: unchecked public sector growth in terms of both spending and personnel (Peters, 1985), unmanageable deficits and a crowding out of private sector initiative by public spending. Decentralization is one element in a broader plan to overturn entrenched interests and practices in order to bring about change.

The education and health-care sectors have been particularly affected by decentralization efforts in Sweden. This may be due to structural similarities and the fact that these two areas alone generally account for the biggest chunk of government spending outside of defence. Both fields involve large, highly visible service delivery systems that are seen as important social institutions (school and hospitals). Professionals (teachers, doctors, nurses and administrators) are essen-tial participants in both decision-making and implementation. These professional groups are represented by interest organizations directly involved in policy-making and prepared to engage in collective action (strikes) if their demands are not accommodated, and these have become more frequent in recent years.

The potential impact of decentralization depends in part on the existing degree of centralization prior to reform. In Sweden the highly centralized system of governance evolved over several decades. Although the Ministry of Education remains small, the central agency responsible for implementing political decision, the SÖ, grew considerably during the period of expansion and reform of the 1950s and 1960s. As demands for central co-ordination, planning, control and evaluation grew, the agency expanded its personnel and competencies. It provided experts, research, guidance and communication channels to the local school authorities. In the pursuit of egalitarian policy national standards, curricular goals, and even lesson plans were adopted by the SÖ which also oversaw their implementation in local communities through regional and local units. The central bureaucracy provided the funds and initiative for ongoing renewal and innovation at the local level (Heidenheimer, 1974; Husén and Boalt, 1967; Husén and Kogan, 1984; Marklund, 1980–83). Whether intended or not, by institutionalizing the principle of 'rolling reform' the SÖ acquired the initiative in educational reform, thereby reducing the role of political decision-making in educational innovation.

Since the early 1980s, however, efforts have been under way to scale back the central bureaucracy across policy sectors. Education has been a key target and the SÖ was successively scaled down and at last replaced by a new organization – the National Agency for Education – which is both much smaller as an organization, and has a much more narrowly defined task. Evaluation and assessment of municipal and school educational praxis is its main duty. Whether the extraordinary capacity for co-ordination, planning, and research that was internationally regarded as a model and standard for other nations to emulate will be recouped or re-created at the local level remains to be seen. At the very least, the communication and co-ordination functions have been made more complicated by the elimination of the SÖ.

In the United States the net direction of initiatives during the 1980s can be difficult to discern. Since 1980 there has been a clear trend toward decreasing the Federal Government's responsibility in the field of education. The exception to this trend is the drive toward adoption of national standards and performance testing. At the same time, state governments have tightened control over local school districts in what appears to be a more centralized policy system at the state level (Boyd, 1987; Boyd and Kerchner, 1987). Despite the Federal Government's reduced financial commitment to education during the Reagan–Bush years, a steady barrage of exhortations from Secretaries of Education Bennett and Bell was aimed at state and local authorities (Boyd, 1988; Jung and Kirst, 1986). So while the Federal Government withdrew from programmatic involvement and funding responsibilities, its leadership nevertheless continued to try to influence policy at other levels of government. National commissions have played a part in this cajoling from Washington, DC. Thus, decentralization has not led to a quieter role for federal authorities in the ideological battle over the future of the nation's schools.

What are some of the other possible consequences of decentralization and might they not produce some real results in terms of improved educational performance? On the positive side of the balance sheet, local authorities may use their new-found freedom to experiment with more efficient and effective approaches and new administrative structures. They may be able to respond more quickly to changing local needs. Funds and personnel previously dedicated to fulfilling requirements set by higher authorities especially with respect to monitoring and reporting may be freed up for purposes more directly related to teaching and learning. By concentrating greater decision-making authority at the local level, the system may provide parents, students and teachers with greater influence.

Given the reorganization of career ladders at the national level in Sweden, administrative personnel with considerable skills and experience are likely to be available to municipal and county officials now responsible for innovation. Small-scale reforms have worked elsewhere (Denmark) in part because response time and costs are reduced. Teachers can try out new approaches with less bureaucracy. Results are easier to track and remain linked with the setting in which they were generated. Teachers' jobs are enriched through a more active role in defining their work environment and methods. If the neo-liberals are correct, decentralization will unleash dynamic competitive forces which will hasten reform. School administrators will be compelled to find what works and implement it in order to meet the demands of their client groups. Decentralization may make it easier to experiment with voucher plans in both the United States and Sweden.

But the jury is still undecided on whether decentralization improves educational performance. Donahue (1990) cautioned against market-based incentive structures where performance is difficult to measure and where less tangible values than those that are generally amenable to cost-benefit analysis obtain. Education is just such a field. Under close scrutiny from the population they serve, local administrators and politicians are anxious to find quantifiable measures of performance. Testing and evaluation have become popular tools and a target of considerable investment and research by national as well as local authorities in education in both the United States and Sweden.

Decentralization may make it possible for some school districts to retain progressive programmes that are equity oriented. Bringing policies closer to home may rally neighbourhood support for the schools, drawing the community together in support of education and spending. Where public funds are in short supply, community action groups can and have been mobilized to provide volunteers and contributions of supplies and equipment.

But as Kozol's (1991) examination of school practice in the United States argued, the problems of the American school system are not going to be solved by more decentralization. As long as funding for education remains highly decentralized and fiscal stress plagues all levels of government, the much-needed resources to improve the educationally impoverished communities in the United States will not be forthcoming. Structural reforms like decentralization carry no guarantees that they will produce better educational performance, either at the level of individual students, school districts, or aggregate performance criteria including national testing. Both centralization and decentralization have their advantages and disadvantages. But as the comparison of US and Swedish initiatives shows, the degree of centralization alone cannot be the causal agent in either creating the problems or finding the solutions.

Decentralization may hinder the efficient and effective use of costly elements of educational infrastructure such as research and technology investments. Furthermore, as variation increases, competition among schools may also increase and, without a central administrative agency to facilitate communication across administrative units, the incentives may be to withhold rather than share findings related to new initiatives and approaches. Is it reasonable to expect that schools of inferior quality will be replaced by better ones? And what happens to the students who are displaced by the failure of their local school or its inability to secure funding from local resources?

Decentralization will undoubtedly have an impact on how policy is formulated and perhaps not in the direction neo-liberal reformers intend. Decentralization in Danish health care has altered the nature of decision-making at the local level in favour of professional interest organizations that work closely with bureaucrats. The producers of policy act together with a coalition of beneficiaries, personnel groups and professional representatives so closely that they learn to accommodate each other's interests. Experts and service providers work together to expand services and resist budget cuts (Heidenheimer and Johansen, 1985). Decentralization may actually create strong grass-roots organizations that are capable of resisting further attempts at cutting public services. Decentralization has also led to greater politicization of local government. School closings are controversial wherever and whenever they occur. As 'user groups' and service providers are called upon to play a more active role in decision-making, they can also be expected to put more pressure on politicians.

Current decentralization efforts provide an unusually rich setting to observe the effects of changes in administrative structure on the content, consequences and process associated with public policy. They are an experiment in the making that, if adequately studied, may offer us new insights into the nature of authority and control in contemporary democratic societies (Campbell, 1969). But if past reforms are any indication, it may be a decade or longer before we can adequately assess the results. By that time, we may confront new challenges which we will expect the educational system to address. In the meantime, expectations have been raised and perhaps disappointed yet again by the promise of reform that does little to change the heart of the matter: what and how children learn. A Carnegie Foundation study indicates that teachers are already pessimistic about the possibility of real reform (Carnegie Foundation for the Advancement of Teaching, 1990). Although decentralization may be popular at the moment, changing the administrative structure may prove to be too little too late for the demands we face at the present moment. But the flexibility and ideological commitment to decentralization that has been evident in such different contexts as Sweden and the United States are likely to keep it on the political agenda for some time to come.

REFERENCES

Bardach, E. (1977) *The Implementation Game: What Happens after a Bill Becomes Law*. Cambridge: MIT Press.

Bendor, J. and Moe, T.M. (1985) 'An adaptive model of bureaucratic politics', *American Political Science Review*, **79**, 755–74.

Bendor, J., Taylor, S. and Van Gaalen, R. (1985) 'Bureaucratic expertise versus legislative authority: A model of deception and monitoring in budgeting', *American Political Science Review*, **79**, 1041–60.

Bird, R.M. (1971) 'Wagner's law of expanding state activity', *Public Finance*, **26**, 1–26.

Boyd, W.L. (1987) 'Public education's last hurrah? Schizophrenia, amnesia, and ignorance in school politics', *Educational Evaluation and Policy Analysis*, **9**, 85–100.

Boyd, W.L. (1988) 'How to reform schools without half trying: Secrets of the Reagan administration', *Educational Administration Quarterly*, **24** (3), 295–309.

Boyd, W.L. and Kerchner, C.T. (1987) 'Introduction and overview: Education and the politics of excellence and choice', *Politics of Education Association Yearbook*, 1–11.

Buchanan, J.M. (1967) *Public Finance in the Democratic Process*. Chapel Hill: University of North Carolina Press.

Campbell, D.T. (1969) 'Reforms as experiments', *American Psychologist*, **24**, 409–29.

Carnegie Foundation for the Advancement of Teaching (1990) *The Condition of Teaching, 1990*. Princeton: Princeton University Press.

Chubb, J.E. and Moe, T.M. (1986) 'No school is an island: Politics, markets, and school performance', *Brookings Review*, **4**, 21–8.

Chubb, J.E. and Moe, T.M. (1990) *Politics, Markets, and School Performance*. Washington, DC: Brookings.

Clark, D. and Astuto, T. (1986) 'The significance and permanence of changes in federal education policy', *Educational Researcher*, October, 4–13.

Cohen, D.K. (1990) 'Governance and instruction: The promise of decentralization and choice', in W.H. Clune and J.F. Witte (eds), *Choice and Control in American Education*. New York: Falmer Press.

Corwin, R.G. and Dianda, M.R. (1993) 'What can we really expect from large-scale voucher programs?', *Phi Delta Kappan*, **75** (1), September, 68–72, 74.

Czarnizwska-Joerges, B. (1988) *Reformer och ideologier. Lokal nämnder på väg*. Lund: Doxa.

Demsetz, H. (1993) 'The private production of public goods, once again', *Critical Review*, **7** (4), 559–66.

Donahue, J.D. (1990) *The Privatization Decision: Public Ends, Private Means*. New York: Basic Books.

Eliason, L.C. (1988) *The Politics of Expertise: Legitimating Educational Reform in Sweden and the Federal Republic of Germany*. PhD thesis, Stanford University.

Eliason, L.C. (1990) 'Between rationality and politics: Swedish educational policy 1940–1962', *Policy Explorations*, **5** (1), 8–19.

Eliason, L.C. and Weiler, H.N. (1989) 'The politics of educational reform in Western Europe: Do policy systems learn from past experience?' Paper presented to the Western Political Science Association annual meetings, Salt Lake City, UT.

Elmore, R.F. (1993) 'School decentralization: Who gains? Who loses?' in J. Hannaway and M. Carnoy (eds) *Decentralization and School Improvement: Can We Fulfill the Promise?* San Francisco: Jossey-Bass, 33–54.

Friedman, M. and Friedman, R. (1980) *Free to Choose: A Personal Statement.* New York: Avon.

Gustafsson, G. (1980a) 'Modes and effects of local government mergers in Scandinavia', *West European Politics*, **3**, 339–57.

Gustafsson, G. (1980b) *Local Government Reform in Sweden.* Lund: CWK Gleerup.

Heckscher, G. (1984) *The Welfare State and Beyond.* Minneapolis: University of Minnesota Press.

Heidenheimer, A.J. (1974) 'The politics of educational reform: explaining different outcomes of school comprehensivization attempts in Sweden and West Germany', *Comparative Education Review*, **18**, 388–410.

Heidenheimer, A.J. and Nørby Johansen, L. (1985) 'Organized medicine and Scandinavian professional unionism: Hospital policies and exit options in Denmark and Sweden', *Journal of Health Politics, Policy and Law*, **10**, 100–20.

Hemerén, H. (1988) 'Intention och verklighet', in L.G. Stenelo (ed.), *Makten över den decentraliserade skolan.* Lund: Studentlitteratur.

Hirschmann, A.O. (1970) *Exit, Voice, and Loyalty: Responses to Decline in Firms, Organizations, and States.* Cambridge, MA: Harvard University Press.

Husén, T. and Boalt, G. (1967) *Educational Research and Educational Change.* Stockholm: Almqvist & Wiksell.

Husén, T. and Kogan, M. (eds) (1984) *Educational Research and Policy: How Do They Relate?* New York: Pergamon Press.

Jung, R. and Kirst, M.W. (1986) 'Beyond mutual adaptation, into the bully pulpit: Recent research on the federal role in education', *Educational Administration Quarterly*, **22** (1), 80–109.

Kingdon, J.W. (1984) *Agendas, Alternatives, and Public Policies.* New York: HarperCollins.

Kozol, J. (1991) *Savage Inequalities: Children in America's Schools.* New York: Crown.

Kristensen, O.P. (1987) *Væksten i den offentlige sektor. Institutioner og politik.* Copenhagen: Jurist-og økonomforbundets Forlag.

Lindbeck, A. (1993) 'Overshooting, reform and retreat of the welfare state'. Seventh Tinbergen Lecture, delivered on 1 October, de Nederlandsche Bank, Amsterdam.

Lindbeck, A., Molander, P., Persson, T., Peterson, O., Sandmo, A., Swedeborg, B. and Thygesen, N. (1993) 'Options for economic and political reform in Sweden'. Seminar Paper No. 540. Stockholm: Institute for International Economic Studies.

March, J.G. and Olsen, J.P. (1989) *Rediscovering Institutions: The Organizational Basis of Politics*. New York: Free Press.

Marklund, S. (1980–83) *Från reform till reform. SkolSverige 1950–1975*. Stockholm: Liber Utbildnings Förlaget, 1–4.

Marmor, T.R. (1993) 'Understanding the welfare state: Crisis, critics, and countercritics', *Critical Review*, **7** (4), 461–78.

Miller, D. (1993) 'Public goods without the state', *Critical Review*, **7** (4), 505–24.

National Commission on Excellence in Education (1983) *A Nation at Risk: The Imperative for Educational Reform*. Washington, DC: US Government Printing Office.

Niksanen, W.A., Jr (1971) *Bureaucracy and Representative Government*. New York: Aldine-Atherton.

von Otter, C. (1986) *Kan man rationalisera folkhemmet?* Stockholm: LOs offentliga samtal.

Parker, M.D. (1989) 'Vouchers for day care of children: Evaluating a program model', *Child Welfare*, **68** (6), November–December, 633–42.

Peters, B.G. (1985) 'Sweden: The explosion of public employment', in R. Rose (ed.) *Public Employment in Western Nations*. Cambridge: Cambridge University Press, 203–27.

Prychitko, D.L. (1993) 'Formalism in Austrian-school welfare economics: Another pretense of knowledge?', *Critical Review*, **7** (4), 567–92.

Rist, M.C. (1991) 'Milwaukee: Mixed results after a year of school choice'. *American School Board Journal*, **178** (7), July, 21.

Schmidtz, D. (1993) 'Market failure', *Critical Review*, **7** (4), 525–34.

Smith, B.C. (1985) *Decentralization: The Territorial Dimension of the State*. Boston: George Allen and Unwin.

Socialdemokraterna (1989a) *Förslag till nyt partiprogram*. Stockholm: Socialdemokraterna.

Socialdemokraterna (1989b) *90-talsprogrammet–en debattbok om arbetarrörelsens viktigaste frågor under 90-talet*. Stockholm: Tidens Förlaget.

Strömberg, L. and Westerståhl, J. (eds) (1983) *De nya kommunerna*. Stockholm: Liber.

Tyack, D. (1993) 'School governance in the United States: Historical puzzles and anomalies', in J. Hannaway and M. Carnoy (eds), *Decentralization and School Improvement: Can We Fulfill the Promise?* San Francisco: Jossey-Bass, 1–32.

Varian, H.R. (1993) 'Markets for public goods?', *Critical Review*, **7** (4), 539–58.

Weiler, H.N. (1983a) 'Legalization, expertise, and participation: Strategies of compensatory legitimation in educational policy', *Comparative Education Review*, **27**, 259–77.

Weiler, H.N. (1983b) 'West Germany: Educational policy as compensatory legitimation', in M. Thomas (ed.) *Politics and Education: Cases from Eleven Nations*. Oxford: Pergamon Press, 33–54.

Weiler, H.N. (1989) 'Education and power: The politics of educational decentralization in comparative perspective', *Educational Policy*, **3** (1), 31–43.

Weiler, H.N. (1990) 'Comparative perspectives on educational decentralization: An exercise in contradiction?', *Educational Evaluation and Policy Analysis*, **12** (4), 433–48.

Weiler, H.N. (1993) 'Control versus legitimation: The politics of ambivalence', in J. Hannaway and M. Carnoy (eds), *Decentralization and School Improvements: Can We Fulfill the Promise?* San Francisco: Jossey-Bass, 55–83.

Weimer, D.L. and Vining, A.R. (1989) *Policy Analysis: Concepts and Practice*. New York: Prentice Hall.

White House (1991) *America 2000: The President's Education Strategy*.

Chapter 5

The Evolution of Education Reform in Great Britain and the United States: Implementation Convergence of Two Macro-policy Approaches

James G. Cibulka

INTRODUCTION

In the United States reform of the nation's public schools is a continuous pre-occupation.[1] At almost every point in the history of the public schools major reforms of organization or pedagogy have been advocated and seriously debated. The current period of reform of elementary and secondary schools in the United States may well represent the most extensive and sustained demands the institution has experienced since the early part of the century, when institutional arrangements were largely established. These reform efforts have been under way for approximately a decade, using as a starting point the publication of *A Nation at Risk* (United States, National Commission on Excellence in Education, 1983).

In Great Britain the most recent reform period dates to the passage of the Educational Reform Act 1988, although broad-scale discussion of reform actually began in 1976 when the Labour Prime Minister, James Callaghan, gave his now well-known Ruskin College speech. Efforts to revamp the entire educational system appeared in a series of Education Acts beginning in 1979, culminating in the most radical reform Act of all in 1988, as well as more recent revisions to the 1988 Act.

In both countries then, the most recent period of reform has been the most ambitious, so significant indeed, that it is useful to ask what this period of implementation has taught us and what the implications are for the future of reform in each nation.

The underlying assumptions guiding these recent education reforms in both countries have been fundamentally similar. International global competition is the key concern, from which it has been inferred that the educational systems of both nations are ill-equipped to address these new economic challenges. In both nations some critics go so far as to blame the schools for alleged economic problems such as poor productivity. Of course, not everyone has accepted these diagnoses either in Great Britain or the United States. Still, the language and logic employed by reformers were nearly identical in both nations.

Despite this common starting point, the policy debates and policy responses began quite differently in the two countries. For example, reform in Great Britain was from the start intensely partisan, reflecting the premises of Thatcherism, and the corresponding Labour reaction to her conservative, free-market priorities. By contrast, in the United States the early years of education reform were relatively bipartisan and consensual. The nation's governors, both Democrats and Republicans, sponsored reform legislation in many states. These differences between the education reform process in the two countries are hardly accidental, of course. The two political systems operate quite differently.

What many on this side of the Atlantic have observed about recent American developments towards national standards and testing is that we may be moving in the direction which Great Britain's reforms took from the start. What is less commonly observed here is that British reforms have been in the process of modification since 1988 when the law was passed. Whether convergence is occurring is not clear, but the initial reforms are undergoing considerable modification in both countries and are likely to continue to do so.

This chapter addresses why this evolutionary process is occurring, and begins with a brief discussion of the theoretical framework underlying the analysis.

REFORM OF INSTITUTIONS: TWO PERSPECTIVES

Reform of an entire societal institution is far more complex than altering separate elements of the institution. This is such an obvious assertion that it hardly seems to bear much elaboration. Yet most of the literature on reform has ignored the question of the scope of change envisioned by reformers. Until the 1970s the change literature in the United States was dominated by the diffusion of innovation perspective widely associated with Everett Rogers. As Berman and McLaughlin (1975) commented, this literature did not focus on organizational variables. The next stage in the development of the literature on change in educational programmes was an implementation perspective associated with Berman and McLaughlin. Here again, however, the unit of analysis was a school system, or subunits within it, rather than the broader socio-political system within which the school system was embedded. This political perspective was being advanced among political scientists (e.g. Pressman and Wildavsky, 1973) but found little receptivity among education scholars.

More recently, McDonnell and Elmore (1987) distinguish among change strategies and argue that system-transforming changes pose a special set of opportunities and constraints for a higher government authority attempting to change the behaviour of lower units of government. It is this macro-level perspective, in addition to attention to the particular policy instruments in question, which represents a departure from the earlier implementation perspective. In fact, the restructuring emphasis in the reform movement signals a shift from an incrementalist model of reform to a systemic focus. Not surprisingly, this phase focuses on governance reforms as well as shifts in the authority structure towards more collaborative styles of management (e.g. site-based management) and teacher professionalization.

Despite this shift in focus in the educational change literature pertaining to the United States, relatively little attention has been paid to the politics of macro-level reform. One must turn to classic studies of the politics of federal aid (e.g. Bailey and Mosher, 1968; Munger and Fenno, 1962) for examples, and these studies portray the politics of adoption prior to implementation. In other words, Pressman and Wildavsky's politics of implementation focus on macro-level social reforms remains rare. The work on implementation in education (e.g. Berman and McLaughlin, 1975; Elmore, 1979–80; Huberman and Miles, 1984) remains more indebted to the policy design literature than the politics tradition.[2]

In recent years some American political scientists have shifted toward a focus on how institutional features shape policy outcomes (e.g. Moe, 1990; Searing, 1991; Shepsle, 1989). Thus far, little of this work has been applied to education. However, in an influential book, Chubb and Moe (1990) take this institutional perspective in attacking assumptions about school reform in the United States, predicting a bleak outcome.[3]

The literature on implementation of reform in Great Britain, by contrast, is less limited by rationalist assumptions. The explicitly partisan and ideological character of national education policy, and educational policies and practices more generally, has a long tradition there. One need only cite some recent examples of scholarship on the British Education Reform Act 1988 working from this political tradition (Ball, 1993; Edwards and Whitty, 1994; Walford and Miller, 1991; Whitty, 1991) as well as many others. British scholarship has been less dominated by empiricism and political pluralism than its American neighbours.

In this chapter I attempt to show how the case of Great Britain and the United States illustrate two alternative political processes by which public policies are established; policy-planning and pluralist-bargaining. However, given the fact that the reform of an entire institution is a complex undertaking, it could be expected that the implementation of the policy would encounter significant implementation challenges. In particular, five are addressed in this paper: faulty design assumptions, unforeseeable events, institutional impediments, operational complexities and partisan manoeuvring. These are depicted in Table 5.1.

Table 5.1 *Policy adaptation: Implementation factors reshaping initial system-transforming policies*

Original policy	Implementation factors	Adapted policy
	Faulty design assumptions	
	Unforeseeable events	
	Institutional impediments	
	Operational complexities	
	Partisan manoeuvring	

Briefly stated, *policy-planning processes* focus on the development of a rational policy by like-minded individuals. Given one or more goals, the problem becomes one of finding an optimum choice among discrete alternatives (Nagel, 1980), or at least an acceptable alternative. Policy planning can occur in an authoritarian state, dominated by a monarch, military rulers or other power élites. In a democratic state, it can reflect consensual decision-making by elected élites, usually members of the same political party, who often act in concert with career bureaucrats and sympathetic interest groups (sometimes referred to as the 'iron triangle' in the United States context). Typically, one political party has sufficient executive and legislative power to dominate the government. Whatever the specific institutional context, a policy, planning perspective strives for goal optimization through unitary policy-making (Peterson, 1976).[4]

There is no unifying theory which describes what the elements of a policy design are and what facts and values should dominate the considerations of policy-makers as they design a policy. However, in the case of an education policy, one might logically give attention to the authority structure of schools and school systems, the nature of teaching as work, how persons within the educational enterprise are motivated, their knowledge base and the skills they possess, the goals of schooling, characteristics of pupils (their abilities, level of readiness, motivation, external support, etc.) as well as a host of other questions at both a strategic and practical level. Policy development does not have to be perfectly rational for this approach to policy development to operate. Assumptions about rational policy-making and management have undergone a dithering assault in recent decades, and there is no need here to revisit that familiar ground. Suffice to say that a revisionist perspective on policy-planning argues that even if there are not clear goals to guide the information and implementation of policy, much less a sound knowledge base, it is still possible for planning to occur. Elmore (1979–80), for instance, coined the useful metaphor of 'backward-mapping' to capture a more realistic scenario for the implementation phase of policy. Regardless of the optimism one brings to this perspective about the capacity of policy-makers working from these assumptions, the problem is to arrange the parts of the system in such a manner as to maximize the likelihood that a desired outcome will occur.

Not all policy-planning is intended to be 'system-transforming', but when this is true, it poses a special challenge for policy-makers. Transformations which are broad in scope must address changes at the institutional level of governance as well as those at the level of management and technical operations.[5] From a policy-planning perspective the essential requirement is to work as intelligently as possible among these constraints to transform, or at least reform, the system. A *pluralist bargaining perspective* views policy-making as well as its implementation as a product of compromise among ideologies, values and interests. The problem of how to achieve a desired outcome, working from the perspective of policy-makers, is not a central feature of political analysis, and is relevant only to the extent that it helps explain how political outcomes emerge. Assumptions about rational planning which dominated the study of public administration for many decades, are eschewed in favour of a behavioural focus on how policy outcomes actually occur. Political analyses, working within a behavioural rather than normative tradition, for instance, focus instead on how power determines the agenda-setting process, the way interests are mobilized, how access to decision-makers and bargaining is influenced by power, and how power arrangements shape the policy settlement. Political bargaining analyses of implementation use the same lens to address what happens to a policy after it becomes official. Much of the early implementation research began from a rational policy-planning model. It was presumed that public policies carry goals which are explicit and that the task of implementation is to operationalize these goals toward a successful outcome. That view of implementation has received much criticism in recent years as being unrealistic since it blames implementers for policy failures (Palumbo and Calista, 1990).

Pluralist bargaining assumes that policy-making, and reform of institutions in particular, is largely incremental and that differences among the policy-makers can be ironed out by 'partisan mutual adjustment'. While pluralist-bargaining may be initiated at the national level and therefore may involve national élites, frequently it reflects acquiescence to a variety of élites (including local ones) and constituent pressures. As new problems arise, policy is further refined to maintain the shared interests of the policy-makers. Institutional reform, in other words, is less a master plan than a series of small steps with a cumulative impact. This bargaining perspective on public policy views implementation processes as a stage wherein the ambiguities and compromises which are inherent in adopted public policies must be worked out.

In short, a policy-planning model emphasizes a macro-level systemic perspective and centralized intervention, while a pluralist-bargaining model, even when it operates centrally, addresses particular aspects of a policy problem without pretence to comprehensiveness, with a focus on incremental goals reflecting compromise among diverse interests. While the policy-planning model views the implementation phase as requiring the protection and achievement of the original policy goals, the pluralist-bargaining model views implementation as just another stage of policy setting wherein goals and means of achieving them are clarified.

However, similar realities at the implementation stage, discussed above and depicted in Table 5.1, move the two approaches to policy setting towards a convergence. In the analysis which follows I shall illustrate how these models of policy-making have characterized education reform in the two nations, and the consequent implementation problems which have tended to push policy towards the opposite model from which it began. The chapter begins with reform in the United States.

AMERICAN EDUCATION REFORM: AN EVOLUTION FROM BARGAINING TO PLANNING

American education reform began with modest goals, not the aim of either a nationwide overhaul or a fundamental transformation of the educational system. Even before the publication of *A Nation at Risk*, countless reform efforts were under way at state and local levels, spurred on by scores of reports. There was no unitary thrust to be found among such disparate initiatives, although they tended to reflect the premise that the quality of public schooling had fallen sharply. American pupils were perceived to lack basic skills. The most academically able were not being challenged. Discipline had fallen. Schools were unsafe. A relatively small number of these reports argued for special needs to be addressed – for the handicapped, for underachievers, for limited-English proficient pupils and others. Some reports also addressed the problems of teachers.

Despite this lack of a clear focus at the start, the dominant strain was not to further equity, but to advance quality. To be sure, equity and quality were not perceived to be contradictory in the minds of some critics and were even parallel. Yet at best the theme was to hold equity constant while restoring quality.

This perhaps reflected the strong thrust of criticism coming from the business community, which financed many of the reports criticizing American schools. Even here, however, the business interests which campaigned for reform did so by appealing to public opinion, which for most of the decade had registered serious and growing concern about the deteriorating quality of schools. Only some of these efforts were focused on international competition. Many business interests, particularly those represented by the Chamber of Commerce in many cities, focused more on short-term, narrow objectives – to improve the entry-level job skills (technical or social) of the high-school graduating pool.

It was *A Nation at Risk* which gave the reform movement a new focus on international economic competition, a theme which for several years would overshadow competing approaches to reform. It is difficult to overestimate the degree to which one report reshaped public perceptions that there was a crisis in American public education. Thereafter, for several years the debate about the necessity and desirability of reform was framed within the assumptions of this report. Moreover, it had a galvanizing effect on further reform efforts in many states and local communities.

While the focus on international competition has not subsided to this day, the particular strategies for how to reform the system have. First, by the late 1980s evidence was mounting that by most standardized achievement measures, American schoolchildren were not performing any better than previously. True, individual states could point to progress against national norms, but the norms themselves came to be criticized as inflated. National measures like the Scholastic Achievement Test (SAT), American College Test (ACT) and National Assessment of Educational Progress (NAEP) continued to record stagnant performance.

At the same time, there was growing interest in how to improve the conditions for attracting and retaining good teachers. From the start, as mentioned above, this has been an element in reform discussions and was even mentioned in *A Nation at Risk*. However, the leadership of Albert Shanker, head of the American Federation of Teachers (AFT), helped convince the American public, and perhaps more important, policy-makers, that teachers were in favour of reform provided it was directed at more than cosmetic changes in schools. With powerful foundation backing, particularly from the Carnegie Foundation, efforts were initiated to experiment with professionalization of teaching and promotion of National Teaching Standards. Thus, it came to be accepted wisdom that the first wave of reform was failing to register the anticipated progress because it had sought only to raise standards through application of mandates rather than by restructuring schools as places to teach and learn. For the first time some attention began to focus on students themselves and the conditions which promote 'higher-order learning', as the catch-phrase came to be accepted. This emphasis on systematic rather than incremental changes was advanced by the nation's governors in its report *Time for Results* (NGA, 1986). Among the structural changes they proposed were greater opportunities for parental choice in selecting schools.

Further, the powerful Committee on Economic Development, which represents the thinking of the CEOs in the nation's largest corporations, issued *Children in Need* (CED, 1986). They recognized that because of a growing labour shortage, children of the poor could not be allowed to continue failing at current rates. While many had questioned whether the reform movement would hurt the poor and educationally disadvantaged by essentially ignoring them, new arguments were being mounted by the business community itself that the reform movement had to be directed at these children. Equality of educational opportunity thus re-entered the debate about educational reform. Whereas urban school systems had been virtually ignored in the early years of reform (the Council of Great City Schools' report *Results in the Making*, 1987, was all but ignored), by the latter part of the decade the needs of the educationally disadvantaged were at least being discussed. Business leaders sought to recapture influence over urban school systems which in many cities they had all but abandoned, although little was done to improve the financial condition of schools for the urban poor.

In the early years of reform the Federal Government had played only a marginal role (Boyd, 1987). The Reagan administration only accidentally came upon the platform of reform in its second term of office. In Reagan's first term of office he used 'the bully pulpit' to emphasize the need for reducing federal involvement in education and aid to private schools. After the publication of *A Nation at Risk* it was clear that the public wanted reform of public schools, and the administration switched its strategy in this direction. This new reform zeal was epitomized by Reagan's choice of William Bennett as Secretary of Education in his second term. Bennett came from outside the educational establishment and saw his role as going over the heads of entrenched interest groups and instead appealing directly to the American people. He was an articulate, if abrasive, spokesman for Reagan's 'New Federalism' in domestic policy: a retreat from socially redistributive programmes, allegedly high taxation and overregulation. The 'New Federalism' sought to return power to the states and localities. In practice, however, many mandates were retained but responsibility for funding them was shifted from Washington to the state capitals (Gold and Erickson, 1989).

President Bush initially did little to change the Reagan approach to education reform. His decision to call a summit of the nation's governors in autumn 1989, however, represented an important, if initially unintentional, demarcation with the policies of his predecessor. While the summit was dismissed as a public relations exercise by the former Education Secretary, William Bennett, one outcome of the conference was an agreement to draft national educational goals. These, in turn, were followed by the creation of a National Education Goals Panel under the sponsorship of the National Governors' Association, which was charged with developing national standards for measuring progress on achievement of the goals. From the White House perspective, the Goals Panel did not have the stamp of the President's leadership, since initially it was chaired by a respected Democratic governor from Colorado, Roy Romer.

In April 1991 Bush announced his 'America 2000' plan for reforming American schools. It called for four separate tracks to advance reform: national standards and testing to increase accountability; research and development efforts to create new models of American schools (including school choice); adult literacy for those out of school and those in the workplace; and community initiatives. The plan was an effort to provide a comprehensive approach to reform, orchestrated, if not entirely conducted, by the Federal Government. Business was guaranteed a strong role in the research and development component of the plan.

Rather than funnel funding proposals through the federal bureaucracy at the US Department of Education, the plan created a private, non-profit 'New Schools Development Corporation' (NASDC), which pledged to raise $300 million in private donations.

It would be impossible, of course, to shape a national education policy without Congressional approval of its major components. Here the problem of divided government at the national level – a Democrat-controlled Congress and a Republican President – quickly proved to be a major impediment in moving the plan forward. The Senate, for example, rejected a Bush administration proposal, largely along party lines, to spend $30 million (originally $200 million, later pared in hopes of a compromise) on a choice programme which included religious schools. Bush's bill was replaced by the Democrats' own education reform bill. The 'new American schools' proposal ran into opposition and became tied up in Congressional wrangling. The proposal for national standards and a national system of assessments was also in a state of confusion. Congress did create a 32-member panel, the National Council on Education Standards and Testing, to advise it on how to proceed. When the panel's report was released in early 1992, and recommended proceeding, it was met with mixed reactions by educators, members of Congress and the Congress's own non-partisan Office of Technology Assessment. Among the arguments which emerged was whether standards should be developed only for students, and not also for schools, whether national assessment would harm some pupils and educational quality overall, and what stakes would be attached to a system of national assessments. Since a momentum had been growing across the country against standardized paper-and-pencil tests, questions also arose over whether a national examination system could incorporate performance-based techniques and still maintain traditional standards of test validity and reliability. Debate also flared over whether a national assessment system should test every child, rather than a sample of students such as NAEP traditionally has. Some favoured revising NAEP to an annual test consistent with evolving national content standards (to be developed by a new National Education Standards and Assessments Panel and a reconstituted (politically balanced) National Education Goals Panel). Indeed, the development of national standards themselves was likely to be controversial in some subject areas; in social studies, for instance, multicultural education has become contentious, whereas in other areas such as mathematics a consensus was possible.

The partisan manoeuvring on these issues did not subside after the presidential election in November 1992. After Bush's defeat it took the new President, Bill Clinton, until 1994 to get his education proposals through Congress. The Clinton administration backed its own version of 'America 2000' (now 'Goals 2000: Educate America Act') with many of the same features which had been advocated by Bush, and predictably many of the same arguments over national standards and testing ensued in Congress. The Clinton administration, politically centrist in focus, also endorsed school-to-work initiatives, although more aggressively than Bush had, and the new President was willing to allocate more resources to education despite sharp fiscal constraints in the federal budget. For the time being educational choice and merit schools (the idea of providing high-achieving schools with financial rewards) fell out of fashion. Despite these differences of degree between the two administrations, however, the continuity of focus between them signalled that American education policy, at the federal level at least, had now embraced a policy-planning focus whose overarching ideology is one of 'systemic change'. Whether this unitary model can be adapted to a federal intergovernmental system where authority resides with states and where local school districts retain enormous influence is one of the central political questions facing American educational reformers.

In striving to interpret this evolution in American education reform we can turn to the distinction made at the outset between two alternative interpretive processes which guide the formation of public policy. American education reform is a sterling example of pluralist-bargaining rather than policy-planning. Reformers have appealed to the common interests which all Americans have in improving their schools, and in time characterized the perceived decline in public schools as an external threat. Some analyses of education reform in the United States characterize the process as being unduly influenced by business interests and large foundations which represent those interests (Shea et al., 1990). There is certainly some truth in this characterization. However, the late 1970s and early 1980s were characterized by a remarkable outpouring of reports critical of American schools, sponsored by a wide range of interest groups and reflecting broad public sentiment that schools needed reforming. Thus, the publication of A Nation at Risk merely galvanized what was already under way from the bottom up. Reforms were endorsed in most of the 50 states, led by governors of both political parties with the active encouragement of the National Governors' Association. Diverse coalitions supported these reforms.

In short, until recently education reform in the United States fitted a largely pluralist-bargaining model. Reform evolved incrementally rather than as a rational blueprint of a small group of like-minded policy-makers seeking to achieve a desired outcome. As this reform movement evolved, compromise moved the bargaining process forward so that if no policy-maker achieved all of her or his goals, at least most people received some of what they wanted.

During the Reagan and Bush presidencies these reforms and the compromises which they represented came under strident attack. Thus, a new form of bargaining emerged which focused on ideology more than compromise. Major flashpoints of controversy during this period were aid to private schools, teaching of values and criticism of educational spending. This partisan flavour began with the controversial style of former Secretary of Education, William Bennett, who campaigned against the educational establishment much like his boss President Ronald Reagan. Even defenders of American schools, prime among them teachers' unions, have been forced to concede that there is little objective evidence that the nation's schools are improving dramatically.

The implementation problems which have attended educational reform in the United States illustrate the limitations of a political process for reform which has relied so heavily on pluralist bargaining. Some examples follow.

Faulty Design Assumptions

Perhaps the major problem has been that Americans backed into institutional reform rather than facing it head on, as their British counterparts did. In retrospect, the idea that dramatic change in the performance of America's schools could come from marginal changes in the system was naïve at best.

Another faulty assumption was the reliance early in the reform movement on the use of mandates to achieve change in school performance. The recognition some years later that education reform was more complicated, and required structural reform was a matter of learning from mistakes. There is a deep strain of naïvety in American political culture which assumes that complicated problems can be fixed by passing a law. While there is enough evidence about the intractability of the education establishment to fill many library shelves, the lesson was not learned by political leaders eager to demonstrate immediate progress to a restive public. Indeed, the recognition that raising student achievement would require a radical transformation of the way schools operate was an insight which could not have been expected from elected politicians with no professional knowledge of teaching and learning. It was a conclusion that the experts looking at the evidence only gradually began to draw. Accordingly, by the late 1980s the reform movement had begun to examine alternatives to passing mandates, and the language of 'restructuring' had won currency as a preferred policy approach.

Unforeseeable Events

As was mentioned above, the development of a labour shortage in the 1980s caused business reformers to become more inclusive in their focus, not so inclined to ignore the educationally disadvantaged. From one view, the policy design as it emerged in the early 1980s was too short-sighted and should have anticipated this eventuality. Still, it seems inevitable that institutional change must occur over a prolonged period because of its complexity, and during this period of implementation new problems will arise which require policy-makers to rethink the assumptions with which they began.

Certainly, one of the key shifts within the reform movement was the decision by President Bush to call together the nation's governors for an historic 'education summit'. At the same time, this development was viewed by some as a one-shot public relations device by a President eager to fulfil his campaign promise to be the 'Education President' even though he was loath to pass much new legislation. Despite its public relations benefits, however, the summit soon led to demands for more reform activism at the national level. In response, Bush developed his 'America 2000' strategy, which eventually evolved into the reform blueprint of the Clinton administration. At the time no one could have predicted how significant the summit would prove to be for the future of the reform movement, for it marked the beginning of national goals and standards, which redirected education reform in a more policy-planning direction.

Institutional Impediments

Some implementation problems stem from the structure of a nation's political system. In the United States the splintering of authority among levels of government is a heritage of the federalists' fear of a strong monarchy. It is a system hard to govern, but viewed by Americans then and now as preferable to its alternatives. One English person observed to me that she pays more attention to developments on the European continent than those in the United States because in the latter there is 'so much to follow, to figure out what all your 50 states are doing'. The problem she so correctly pinpointed is not diminished, unfortunately, by the proximity of view on this side of the Atlantic. With 50 trains running on their own routes according to their own schedules, there is bound to be confusion, duplication, reinventing the wheel and the like. There is also jealous guarding of turf as each level of government strives to protect its autonomy from intrusion by the next higher level. On the positive side, decentralization fosters experimentation and learning from others' successes and mistakes.

One of the institutional impediments receiving considerable reform attention is the lack of co-ordination among children's services. This disarray reflects the American approach to social welfare programmes, which are lodged in private and public agencies, with autonomous missions and protective turfs, and are part of a complex intergovernmental maze. This lack of co-ordination received remarkably little attention until Kirst (1991) studied it in California and spurred a national movement to address this problem. The movement has led to a much broader conception of the school's role than in the early reform efforts.

Operational Complexities

Some of the many problems of reforming an institution can be found in the example of national standards and assessment. Few would deny that the technical issues which are embedded in this path to reform are monumental. Some are strategic choices, such as whether to use national assessment as a device for classroom appraisal and improved teaching, which would require all students to participate, or whether to use some system such as NAEP largely for accountability purposes. Whether and how to incorporate performance-based approaches also presents strategic choices. Other policy-planning problems involve largely tactical considerations which intrude nevertheless on strategic choices, such as how to relate the new standards to existing state (and local) assessment systems. The approach which has emerged, for the time being at least, is to allow each state to develop its own system and to have it validated against national goals and standards, in lieu of one national examination system (or perhaps alongside it). If policy-making is viewed as maximizing one or more goals, the technical problems of designing a solution which is capable of achieving these goals will require extensive planning. Yet this kind of planning is exactly what the American approach to educational reform has been short on.

Partisan Manoeuvring

Problems of partisanship are another dimension of the political aspects of policy. As the reform movement has turned increasingly towards the national level, these problems of partisanship have become more visible and pervasive. The recent stand-offs between presidents and Congress over the direction federal involvement in education reform would take is a sharp contrast with the bipartisan tone President Bush struck when meeting with the nation's governors for the Education Summit in 1989. These problems of partisanship are likely to continue to be resolved in the same way they always have been, through bargaining which creates compromises sufficient to command a legislative majority as well as the President's support. Despite some evidence that the stalemate was broken in 1994, when President Clinton finally won support for his 'Goals 2000: Educate America' legislation, the conflictual nature of policy-making in Washington continues – after the 1994 elections this policy came under sharp attack by Republicans.

This partisan manoeuvring is a symptomatic manifestation of a much deeper problem of political values which lurks behind the problems of education reform in the United States. Americans have created a national politics of divided government, for reasons extending far beyond education policy, but which education policy exemplifies. Americans have grown profoundly distrustful of public officials, including school boards, administrators and teachers. The faith that professional educators were worthy of the public's confidence, and that they ought to be permitted to operate autonomously, was beginning to erode as long ago as the 1950s, when Cold War fears predominated, and a decade later worsened under the demands of the civil rights and student rights movements. A growing political conservatism in the nation combined with distrust of government spurred by Watergate. Anti-tax fever mounted, as did resentment of 'big government' and 'overregulation'. American schools increasingly became battlegrounds for resolving social and cultural conflicts which other social institutions were unable or unwilling to assume. At root the lack of consensus on societal values has affected the perception that schools are to be reformed but without agreement as to how this should happen. At the moment the Federal Government is in no position to set the education reform movement back on course because Washington's conflict-ridden and discredited institutions reflect the unresolved divisions of American society.

As education reform has unfolded in the United States, its implementation processes have more nearly resembled a bargaining model rather than a policy-planning model. To the extent that reform has proved more complicated than anticipated, has moved through different stages and has jumped from one reform strategy to another, these developments are part of an implementation process which reflects the incrementalism of American policy-making. The problems of reform are less implementation failures than policy-planning ones, problems which have moved the fulcrum of American educational policy reform in the direction of more rational planning. As the next section shows, in Great Britain the educational policy pendulum has been swinging in the opposite direction.

GREAT BRITAIN: FROM PLANNING TO BARGAINING

Quite unlike the United States, education reform in Great Britain began at the national level (Halpin, 1994). The Thatcher Government's assumption of power had been a stunning rebuke of the Labour Party's management of the economy. Thatcher went beyond the claim that the Labour Party was incompetent, however. She inserted a distinctly ideological dimension into the critique of her predecessors by assailing the socialist drift she perceived, and committed her government to the privatization of many public services, among other things.

The 1988 Education Reform Act which passed through parliament reflected the heavily partisan assumptions which the Prime Minister and her Government brought to nearly every aspect of domestic policy reform. It was, by comparison with the mishmash characterizing so many state-level education reform bills in the United States, a remarkably coherent piece of legislation.[6]

Many of the provisions were intended to increase parental choice and make schools more responsive to market forces (Whitty and Menter, 1991). Open enrolment was proposed to help popular schools recruit more pupils and to force poor schools to close; Local Education Authorities (LEAs) would no longer be able to set enrolment caps artificially low in order to constrain parental choice.

Parental choice received further impetus from the new policy, which created grant-maintained schools. If so authorized from a school's local governing body, parents at a school could by majority vote apply to the (then) Department of Education and Science (DES) to 'opt out' of their LEA. Funding support (including the indirect costs previously borne by the LEA) would then come directly from the national government, bypassing the LEA. Margaret Thatcher reputedly expected that most schools in the country would, in fact, exercise this new freedom.

The legislation also authorized the creation of a second type of school not under the authority of LEAs. Up to 20 new city technology colleges (CTCs) were to serve youth aged 11 to 18 years living in urban disadvantaged areas, with a curriculum emphasizing science and technology, as well as having a vocational focus to help meet the nation's critical shortage of qualified scientists, technicians and engineers. The colleges were to be operated as private schools, run by educational trusts with heavy contributions from industry and commerce.

Greater authority for parents also was sought in the provision for local management of schools. Schools had been required to have local governing bodies for a long time, and the 1986 Education Act had expanded the powers of governors, as well as parental input and tried to attract individuals with private-sector expertise to school governing bodies. However, the 1988 Act went much further. Each LEA was required to propose a financial delegation plan for local management of schools (LMS) to the DES. The national government was authorized to develop a formula for distributing a required portion of the budget directly to local schools, thus forcing LEAs to cut their services or sell them directly to local schools.

The Education Reform Act contained other reforms intended to increase accountability of schools to external standards. A national curriculum was prescribed for core subjects. To accompany it a system of national assessment was planned, to be linked to performance standards known as 'Attainment Targets' in the various subjects. The National Curriculum and the new assessment system were to apply to schools operated by LEAs as well as the new grant-maintained schools.

While some (e.g. Demaine, 1988) saw the latter centralizing provisions as antithetical to the decentralizing focus of market reforms, most of those in the Tory Party, with the exception of some neo-liberal critics such as Sexton (1988), saw these two directions as being quite logically compatible. The Hillgate Group (1987), for instance, viewed the National Curriculum as a way of reasserting 'a solid foundation in British and European history' rather than global multiculturalism and the curse of relevance in the curriculum.

These provisions were passed with remarkable alacrity by Parliament, a fact that some found objectionable (Simon, 1988). The main provisions of the Bill had been published in a series of consultation papers by the DES, but which allowed only a two-month period for responses prior to the drafting of the Bill. Further, critics charged, the Bill was steamrollered through Parliament without adequate opportunity to debate its provisions. Apparently this was a deliberate strategy of the Government. One of the principal architects of the Bill, Kenneth Baker, later defended the Tory Government's actions, saying that the Bill would have never been passed had extensive consultation occurred.

On the other side of the coin, this meant that the Thatcher Government's plans for radically overhauling the nation's schools became law with few compromises. It was, in other words, possible to speak of a policy design with a clear and relatively comprehensive focus, at least as it appeared to the drafters of the Bill. To borrow from the terminology we have been using in this chapter, policy-planning triumphed over political bargaining. No one would deny that the design of the policy was decidedly partisan. It was rather that the adoption of the 1988 Education Reform Act represented, by American standards at least, a victory for planning over the brand of compromise and stalemate which sometimes characterizes politics when institutional reform is the goal.

Yet as the reform movement moved from adoption to implementation, policy-makers in the Thatcher Government, and later in the Government of Prime Minister John Major, were faced with a variety of political problems. The ideologically tidy assumptions of the bill's designers did not always fit institutional complexities, while at the same time differences of emphasis within the law's provisions created unanticipated complications. These complexities of implementation, in turn, required that the government re-examine some of its initial assumptions, alter its course, or in some cases put a positive spin on why change was not occurring as expected. In 1993 a new Education Act was passed by Parliament. While the 1988 reforms were not dismantled, many provisions of the original legislation were modified to address these implementation problems. Indeed, by 1994 the Government found itself confronted with public opinion polls indicating scepticism about the Government's ability to accomplish the ambitious improvements in the nation's education system which the Tories had promised.

In the sections which follow, examples will be offered of these political factors which intruded during the implementation of the 1988 Reform Act. Because of space limitations, only selected examples of these limitations will be offered, as they were originally laid out in Table 5.1. Also, it is important to point out that the particular examples cited below may illustrate several political factors operating at the same time, even though for simplicity of illustration only one political liability may be mentioned.

Faulty Assumptions

One area where the Government badly misgauged support from its supporters was with regard to the new city technology colleges (CTCs) it proposed. Some of the country's largest corporations distanced themselves from the idea, preferring to funnel donations into already established schools and fearing a possible trend toward assuming the costs of secondary education (Walford, 1991; Walford and Miller, 1991). Some business leaders even rejected the vocational focus of CTCs as merely another example of the attempt to create a 'relevant' curriculum, a trend which the Hillgate Group had derided. The Government's aim of having CTCs serve inner-city populations was frustrated by lack of co-operation from Labour-controlled boroughs, who refused to help them designate appropriate sites for the new schools. Moreover, the DES had badly underestimated the start-up costs of the CTCs, prompting one commentator to describe this as an example of 'instant policy planning' (Nash, 1988). This was in sharp contrast to the careful canvassing of Conservative Party members which had taken place when the Assisted Places Scheme was planned, spadework which had led to none of the setbacks encountered with development of CTCs. (Whitty et al., 1993). So much difficulty was encountered that, in 1991, Prime Minister John Major announced that his government would support a new type of CTC; local authorities, grant-maintained schools and voluntarily-aided schools could operate or sponsor CTCs. (*Times Educational Supplement* [hereafter *TES*], 1991c). Further, critics charged that the Government was trying to bribe LEAs with extra aid if they agreed to sponsor a new CTC, an assertion which on the face of it seemed to have some validity despite vigorous denials by the Secretary of Education.

Thus, the failure to win early assent to their radical idea of CTCs came back to haunt the Tories later. It appeared that no more than 15 new schools would ever be built, not the 20 originally announced. To help those numbers, the Government stretched its original concept of creating new CTCs by approving 11 GM (grant-maintained) schools as 'technology colleges'. Furthermore, government policy on the school-to-work transition began to move in other directions. In 1991 a pilot programme was developed which provided 'learning credits', i.e. vouchers, for school-leavers. The Government then considered expanding the concept so that it would apply to all 16-year-olds who stay in school and would permit students to select a programme of their choice, academic or vocational. While it has not been resolved how much such a comprehensive education and training system would rely on free-market principles or strategic planning, the Government promised wide consultation and a so-called 'Green Paper' and pilot scheme by 1996. Such proposed reforms could be expected to generate as much controversy as the CTCs, given the threat they pose to the traditional A level exam. Indeed, a split developed within the Government between proponents in the Department of Employment and Department of Trade and Industry on one side, and sceptics on the other.

The same observation about faulty initial assumptions could be made about many aspects of the 1988 Reform Act. As will be explained below, the Thatcher Government greatly underestimated the complexity and costs of implementing a national curriculum and national assessment. Similarly, it erred in assuming that a national policy of reform could virtually ignore teachers – their compensation, supply, expertise to implement the Reform Act, as well as their commitment.

Unforeseeable Events

When the 1988 Act was passed, public support for the Thatcher Government was high. The subsequent problems Thatcher had in managing the economy, among her other liabilities, made her policies less acceptable to the general public. The Thatcher Government's attempt to restructure financing of local government services through the 'poll tax', as it was unflatteringly dubbed, proved a serious embarrassment and indirectly placed a drag on education reform, at least for a time until Thatcher backed away from this unpopular scheme and subsequently left office. The Government intended to put public pressure for reducing rates (taxes) on local government authorities, particularly those in Labour-controlled boroughs by restricting aid from the central government and forcing local authorities to go to the citizenry for additional revenues. Due to gross misestimation of anticipated costs by the Government, as well as lack of co-operation by local authorities (many of whom raised the amount of the poll tax to compensate for anticipated loss of revenue rather than cut budgets), the Government confronted some of the worst demonstrations and public criticism showered on a British government in many decades. Despite the demise of the poll tax, 'charge-capping' of local authorities by the national government (which had preceded the poll tax) continues, with the effect that education budgets to the LEAs were reduced. (This may be consistent with the Government's aim of reducing spending on bureaucracy, but it has led to constant criticism that the Government is grossly underfunding education.)

The departure of Thatcher more or less required her successor John Major to distance himself from her policies, as he has done, in order to rebuild public confidence. However, the Major Government has done little better in restoring public confidence about its ability to manage the economy (despite its ability to survive a national election), and these larger political liabilities have weakened the Government's ability to pursue its education reforms with the same resolve and even high-handedness which was the case in 1988 when the reforms were established.

Operational Complexities

No aspect of the education reforms illustrates better the complexities of designing a 'foolproof' reform than the provision for opting out, which was intended to spur market responsiveness and efficiencies. Yet the provision immediately encountered a withering number of challenges for the Government. As a result, the Government's experience with schools opting out has been something less than a ground swell, given the prediction once made by Margaret Thatcher that most schools in the country would choose this route (Garner, 1987). By 1994 only 1.4 per cent of all primary schools had opted out, while 14.4 per cent of secondary schools had and nearly one-quarter (23 per cent) of all secondary schools had begun the process of opting out (Power et al., 1994). The Government still hoped that all secondary schools would opt out by 1997. Overall, less than 1,000 of the nation's 2,400 government schools have opted out.

Initially, the Secretary was beleaguered by governing bodies wishing to opt out of LEAs to avoid being closed by them because of falling enrolments. This had to be resisted, in part because the Government's policy of open enrolment was designed to achieve the opposite, leading to the closing of small 'inefficient' schools. As Whitty (1991) pointed out, the Government's anticipation that the first LEAs to pull out would be in Labour-controlled boroughs proved inaccurate. Indeed, many low-spending boroughs under Tory control have opted out. Still, after 1992 the number of schools opting out dropped sharply. School heads have complained about the numerous disincentives of 'going grant-maintained', such as obtaining insurance, enduring hostile inspectors from the Local Education Authority, the placement of excluded pupils in their schools by the LEA and so on.

Perhaps to create a ground swell, the Government offered generous allowances (critics charge this is a bribe) for opting out, and extended authorization to all primary schools, not merely to large ones. Further, to encourage secondary schools to opt out, in 1992 the Government announced its intention to establish a common funding formula for all secondary schools which ostensibly would increase funding in one-third of the LEAs, but only if the schools would agree to opt out. Also, in 1994 the Government created a Funding Agency for Schools to help fund capital investment for new school initiatives. Indeed, government officials spoke of seeking private promotion for new schools, a move clearly intended to bolster its flagging GM initiative.

Not surprisingly the Government was criticized because these various incentives to opt out have proven to be expensive, and this runs at cross purposes with the Government's fiscal conservatism. In response to criticism in the House of Commons, as well as pressure from its own Department of the Treasury, the Government announced in 1994 that it would cut funding to grant-maintained schools by up to 10 per cent and phase out special grants over a four-year period. Such concessions could only weaken any further interest in opting out.

Further, the Government is ambivalent about just how much cultural diversity it wishes to encourage through opting out. Some members of the New Right coalition abhor the possibility that Muslim schools and others promulgated by groups whose values may be antithetical to Christian or British values would receive encouragement by the state, either through opting out, through state aid for independent religious schools, or some other means. At the same time, the Hillgate Group has strongly encouraged new, autonomous schools of all types desired by parents. One attempt in the House of Lords to permit such schools was not supported by the Government. Here we see at play the ideological tension within the Conservative Party from those who believe liberal ideas, including market forces, should take precedence over traditional conservative adherence to cultural tradition. Indeed, this same tension has been evident in discussions of the National Curriculum, with some of the strongest supporters being those wishing to use the National Curriculum to root out the influence of the 'liberal educational establishment' in favour of traditional values, while free-market enthusiasts see the curriculum and assessment system as a dangerous usurpation of government power best regulated through market exchanges.[7]

Still another unforeseen problem with opting out is that it has mobilized angry parents protesting that the Government has left them without any secondary school for their child because of a shortage of available spaces. At the same time, parents whose children have offers from several schools weigh them and hold on to what may prove to be surplus places (TES, 1992a).

From the beginning, the Government has had to counter charges that opting out was a secret device to re-create a more class-stratified educational system, which has gradually been dismantled since the 1944 Education Act. When this charge of élitism originally was levelled, the Government could offer many assurances that this was not so. For instance, no school opting out of an LEA to grant-maintained status was permitted to change its admission policies or character within five years of opting out, a restriction the Government dropped in 1991. While it lasted, the policy prevented parents whose children were in comprehensive schools from changing their school to an élitist grammar school. Similar fears about élitism have been borne out concerning the funding formulas devised by the LEAs and approved by the DES, for allocating budgets to individual schools. The Government decided to implement financial management of schools by budgeting average staffing costs and eliminating 'positive discrimination' for low-income areas. Beginning in the 1960s the national government, as well as LEAs, had provided additional money to inner-city schools, which has been known as positive discrimination. The new formulas, however, make this difficult because they prohibit such efforts and shift toward age-weighted funding, alongside cuts in national (Section 11) grants for racially disadvantaged groups. As a result of the new financial delegation plans in some LEAs, money has been shifted from inner-city schools to suburban and rural ones (Whitty, 1991).[8] All this flies in the face of, or at least casts some doubt on, government claims that its reforms are aimed at making the system better serve failing, average and below average pupils (*TES*, 1991a). If this is the Government's aim, its policies are afflicted by contradictory effects and, just as likely, by competing impulses.

In short, the provisions for opting out were entangled in a web of operational complexities linking this provision to other aspects of the reform. In seeking to administer this novel policy, the Government found itself embroiled in controversy at nearly every turn. Its problems in navigating these treacherous seas have led to many setbacks. As a result, opting out, while not dead as a policy goal, has been robbed of much of its original threat to the educational establishment. Policy-planners had little ability to anticipate these operational complexities at the time the law was passed. Recently, they have looked to new ways of encouraging opting out, such as, among other things mentioned here, eliminating the requirement for a majority vote by parents at each school.

Institutional Impediments

The features of the 1988 reforms relating to a national curriculum and national assessment provide a sterling example of how institutional impediments can confound system-transforming policy goals. The National Curriculum and assessment also illustrate operational complexities and partisan manoeuvring, but here we shall concentrate on how the particular institutional characteristics of schools proved to be an obstacle.

When the Government first announced its intention to implement a national curriculum, one of the criticisms was that the ten mandated subjects would take up too much time. The statutory language of the 1988 Act had limited the percentage of time which must be devoted to these subjects, which critics said was an unrealistic target. The Government later retreated from these ambitious plans. When Kenneth Clarke became Secretary of Education, he announced that he intended to dismantle former Secretary of Education Kenneth Baker's goal of a universal curriculum and examinations for 14- to 16-year-olds because of the inflexibility of a curriculum with ten mandated subjects.

The National Curriculum has engendered considerable controversy apart from the assessment implications. Some subjects such as history have been highly contentious because of debates over the proposed content of the curriculum. Many teachers do not like the way material is presented in certain subjects, claiming that the curriculum does not take account of the range of activities a child is engaged in or the needs of students who start with little or no English. Indeed, teaching standard English became a point of controversy.

This argument concerning the prescriptive, time-consuming character of the National Curriculum gained credence when the Government undertook its plans for national assessment. The initial direction for the assessment system was set forth by a group convened by the Secretary of Education, known as the Task Group on Assessment and Teaching (TGAT, 1987; 1988). The School Examinations and Assessment Council (SEAC) subsequently assumed significant authority for the development of assessments, subject to specific but delimited oversight by the Minister for Education. Thus, the implementation of the Reform Act's mandate had to be channelled through a complex decision-making apparatus. Under these circumstances, the government has not always got what it wanted from SEAC.

The first year that tests were piloted brought much criticism from teachers and others as to their unwieldy character. The Government encountered so much opposition that it had difficulty creating pilots with sufficient numbers to provide scientific validity for its tests. By 1991 the Government announced that tests on the National Curriculum for primary grades would not be the ambitious scheme originally planned. The much feared 'Standard Assessment Tasks' would only be loose guidelines, making it unclear how these would permit national monitoring of comparative reading standards. Clarke announced that he wanted the amount of testing of 7-, 11-, and 14-year-olds in mathematics and science to be reduced. Criticism of the way the new tests were being developed had become so wide-spread that even the Prime Minister was prompted to publicly distance his government from them. The National Curriculum cannot be allowed to dominate the classroom, he asserted, and standardized tests should be shorter (*TES*, 1991c).

Moreover, the fact that by 1991 the Conservative Party had been in power for some 11 years placed it in an awkward position when pointing to performance shortcomings which the new assessment system highlighted. When Kenneth Clarke pointed to two reports (one commissioned by SEAC and the other by HMI, using the new assessment data) which showed that the nation's reading achievement was not good enough, a Labour Party education spokesman blamed the Government for the national scandal (*TES*, 1991b)! This problem beleaguers any regime which sets out to redefine the *status quo* but later finds that it comes to be seen as an instrument of the *status quo*, which may account for the negative public opinion polls on the Government's accomplishments which were alluded to earlier.

The National Union of Teachers and the other two major unions claimed that the national tests, which were to be phased in over a number of years for various age groups, created an excessive workload and in 1992 and 1993 waged successful boycotts with much parental support. The Government's School Curriculum and Assessment Authority was forced to halve the tests by reducing the so-called 'Attainment Targets' and redefining them to emphasize only the essential knowledge, understanding, or skills said to characterize each level of attainment. This slimming process also reduced the content of the national curriculum. The Government went so far as to consult advisory groups of teachers on some of these matters, and then proceeded to ignore much of their advice when, to no one's surprise, it conflicted with the Government's own well-known views.

An enduring source of controversy surrounding assessment is the Government's decision to publish test results without any adjustments for 'student intake', i.e. pupil characteristics. Educators have debated hotly whether accountability reporting should report raw scores or attempt to adjust for 'value added' by the school. However arcane such debates were to Tory policy-makers at the time, failure to resolve such questions early on has confounded the Government's accountability efforts ever since. Accordingly, the Government dropped 'league tables' for children aged 7 and 14 years. However, it also announced that it still plans to publish school-by-school league tables for 11-year-olds, despite fears by teachers and school heads that parents will misuse such information. The Government provoked considerable controversy by announcing its intentions to publish school comparisons on certain performance indicators such as pupil absence and the number of hours in the school day. Of course, these measures were roundly attacked as biased and flawed.

In sum, the National Curriculum and national assessment have become a tangled thicket. Neither is dead, but the original scope of the National Curriculum has been scaled back and its uses for national assessment of school performance have been sharply narrowed. Many of these problems could not be foreseen when the policies were drawn up in blueprint form, because the Tories were loath to consult with their adversaries as to the institutional complexities which may have lain ahead. The result was a protracted period of controversy and partisan mutual adjustment.

Partisan Manoeuvring

Given the strongly ideological character of British politics, when compared to the United States, and given the confrontational style of Margaret Thatcher's Government, partisanship underlies much of what has been discussed here. Margaret Thatcher blamed the Labour Party for Great Britain's educational deficiencies, since it had controlled the Government. Nine years later, when the Tory Government sought to blame the educational Establishment for low reading scores, they found themselves painted with the Establishment brush by the Labour Party.

One of the notable voids in the Reform Act, considering its otherwise comprehensive approach to reform, is the matter of teacher salaries, training, and development. A tradition of political partisanship appears to be at the root of this omission. Prior to the passage of the Act, the Thatcher Government had a long acrimonious relationship with the National Union of Teachers (NUT). Not accidentally, the reforms largely ignored the problem of low teacher salaries and the accompanying teacher shortages in some LEAs. The latter tended to be dismissed by the Government as problems created by ultra-Left politicians in Labour boroughs. While teachers are clearly unhappy with some of the provisions of the Reform Act, such as a policy which declares teachers 'redundant' in cases of budget shortages, the Conservative Governments of the 1980s made it very difficult for teachers to strike. Consequently, industrial action in response to budget cuts has been minimal (Whitty and Menter, 1991). Apparently to mollify the NUT, the Government softened its criticism of teachers at least for the 1992 elections and offered them a 7.5 per cent pay increase above the rise in cost of living, reasoning that they deserved it because of their hard work. Yet such olive branches did not go far enough to heal old wounds. As explained above, the NUT undertook industrial action to oppose the implementation of the national assessments. Tensions were aggravated in 1994 when the national government announced that it would not find a negotiated salary increase and left this responsibility to the hard-pressed LEAs, which reinforced perceptions that LMS and school-based budgeting are merely devices to deprive schools of adequate funding and to deny teachers fair treatment.

Indeed, the Government has no real policy for addressing the needs of teachers. One of the Tory's own supporters, the head of British Aerospace, who headed the School Teachers Review Body, criticized the Government for having no long-range policy for improving the supply of teachers (*TES*, 1992b). While the Government remains committed to performance pay, it has had little success in encouraging LEAs to experiment, due to its own fiscal policies, in addition to determined resistance from teachers. If the Government shifts more attention toward teacher appraisal, as has been discussed, this would only exacerbate its problem in recruiting and retraining teachers.

All of these implementation problems have led to education reform policies which over a period of time have come to look less radical, and arguably have achieved less dramatic results, than the pronouncements which emerged in 1988 after the Reform Act was passed by Parliament. When radical planning bumps up against political reality during implementation, institutional reform necessarily moves in a more moderate direction.

These examples of the implementation problems of the British Educational Reform Act 1988 do not demonstrate that the reforms are failing. Indeed, some aspects of the reform, such as local management of schools (LMS) have been judged to be relatively successful (*TES*, 1994). Yet they do show that putting in place a macro-level reform whose aim is the virtual reconstruction of an institution requires more than the politics of policy-planning. In some respects the attempts at comprehensiveness have worked against the Government, because some provisions conflict with one another. For instance, in 1994 the Secretary of State for Education, John Patten, claimed that the success of LMS was holding back efforts to push all schools in the nation to GM status. In sum, since the passage of the law a variety of implementation challenges have emerged, many of which could not be foreseen by Margaret Thatcher and her advisers, and which necessitated the passage of a new reform law in 1993. At the same time, some might have been avoided had a different style of politics prevailed, one less inclined toward a pre-emptive strike and more toward customary consultation among diverse interests and a willingness to compromise. The risk of a bargaining approach, however, may have been too high if it had eliminated the possibility that the Government might be able to act all.

CONCLUSION

Great Britain and the United States illustrate two alternative paths to institutional reform. Whereas the two nations have started from very different places, the policies have tended to converge.

One explanation for this convergence theory is that various nations face increasingly common problems, such as low student achievement, teacher training needs, inadequate vocational and school-to-work transition programmes, and inadequate money to fund reforms. Indeed, this common view was expressed by high-ranking education leaders from various countries at a conference (Celis, 1994). Stated more academically, there are structural properties underlying national developments which push policy in converging directions, and these properties are linked to the globalization of national economies. (For one version of this view, applied to urban contexts, see Grace, 1994.)

This structural perspective is not necessarily wrong. However, another explanation has been offered here. The political process in both these democratic political systems has pushed their policies in a common direction. The opportunities and constraints surrounding redesign of a complex institution such as schooling are similar, reflected in the five kinds of implementation problems which must be confronted. These implementation problems cannot be bypassed by a strategy of 'policy-planning' which the British case typifies any more than they can be catapulted out of existence by the political bargaining model of consensual compromise and partisan mutual adjustment which is so characteristic of policy-making in the United States. For instance, as policy unfolds and bumps up against assumptions which prove to have been faulty, learning from their experiences forces policy-makers to move policy in a new direction; hence, a national curriculum and assessment are being viewed by many in this country as a way of accomplishing restructuring, just as these same reform nostrums are beginning to lose a bit of their fragrant bloom in Great Britain. Institutional impediments and operational complexities, combined with unforeseeable events, reinforce the tendency for policy-makers to redesign their policies. Despite considerable differences in the political cultures and institutional frameworks of Great Britain and the United States, the politics of implementation have proved to be the politics of convergence.

Partisan manoeuvring can facilitate the process of adjusting policy, but it can also lead to stalemate. In the United States, what began as a broad consensus around the need for reform later evolved into strident disagreements about how reform should proceed, and it is not clear that this gridlock has been overcome. Partisanship in Great Britain, on the other hand, is built more explicitly into a strong political party system and the operation of government. In quite a different manner from the United States, partisan disagreements have greatly complicated implementation of education reforms.

Is institutional reform of a nation's schools an impossible undertaking? The present two cases do not take us to that extreme conclusion – yet! Moreover, the historical record flies in the face of such a conclusion, since schools have evolved dramatically over the centuries and are the products of many 'reforms', some of dubious merit and others more clearly progressive. What these two cases do show is that institutional reform, because it strives not simply for adjustment of structures and norms, but instead for surgical reconstruction, is a far more difficult undertaking than policy-makers in both nations imagined only a short number of years ago.

NOTES

1 I am indebted to William Boyd and David Halpin for their helpful suggestions on an earlier draft of this paper. In addition, John Fitz offered invaluable information and advice. To the extent that I have failed to absorb their counsel, the responsibility is mine, not theirs.

2 There is a small literature on implementation of reform which includes some political considerations, such as Odden and Marsh, 1988. These, however, are exceptions to the norm.

3 Some of their data speak to institutional features of schooling such as the managerial focus of many public school principals, in contrast to the instructional focus of many private school principals, while other aspects of their institutional argument (e.g. the supposed grip of unions on educational policy) are beyond their data and therefore conjectural.

4 Policy-planning does not require that there be unanimity of perspective among the policy-makers. For example, bureaucrats may insist on provisions which will enable them to implement the policy most effectively from their perspective. Elected officials may be inclined to focus on provisions which have symbolic merit or which promise quick results which they can boast about during their next re-election campaign. These differences generally are accommodated through covert discussion and even bargaining. Hence, in the context of modern democratic government where power is divided among different branches and where the regime reflects a balancing act among different groups within the political party, policy-planning must accommodate partisan mutual adjustment as it is shaped. To the extent that one branch of the party holds pre-eminent power at a point in time, the policy is likely to be less attenuated by these internal compromises. None the less, because of the complexity of policy-making in the modern democratic state, given these institutional features of divided government and political party rule, it is unlikely that the policy-planning will reflect entirely unitary processes. Rather, such a model has utility as an example of what Max Weber fondly called an 'ideal type' which is rarely if ever found in pure form in the real world.

5 Here I use Talcott Parsons' distinction between the levels of authority structure in any organization – institutional, managerial and technical – which are characterized by gaps and tensions (see Parsons, 1960).

6 This is not to ignore the fact that the reform bill was the product of internal bargaining in the Thatcher Government. Various provisions were favoured by one or other wing of the party and by particular individuals. Opting out, for example, was popular with Thatcherites, but far less so to the career civil servants at DES who cast a sceptical eye on any reform which might lead to institutional instability and thereby threaten their power and legitimacy. Thus, DES insisted to the Prime Minister's Cabinet that restrictions must be placed on opting out, at the same time that these bureaucrats enthusiastically expanded LMS, a reform which they saw as compatible with and even a means of strengthening their power. DES, for instance, wrote in penalties for Local Education Authorities which refused to co-operate with LMS. In short, the development of a 'rational' comprehensive reform plan was influenced and to a degree constrained by the divisions within the party and the divided powers in the government (see note 5 above). For examples of these political compromises at the adoption stage see Ball (1991).

7 Some free-market Tories such as Stuart Sexton also are strong protectors of cultural tradition.

8 At the same time, as a result of a controversial decision to budget schools on the basis of average staffing costs rather than actual ones, some inner-city schools were confronted with surplus budgets. Further, the Government claimed that there would be a 'safety net' to reduce the immediate effect of large budgetary losses to a school stemming from the new formulas. London was not required to begin financial delegation until 1992. Thus, the final distributive outcome of the policy remained unclear.

REFERENCES

Bailey, S.K. and Mosher, E.K. (1968) *E.S.E.A.: The Office of Education Administers a Law*. New York: Syracuse University Press.

Ball, S. (1991) *Politics and Policy Making in Education: Explorations in Political Sociology*. London: Routledge.

Ball, S. (1993) 'Education, markets, choice, and social class: The market as class strategy in the UK and the USA', *British Journal of Sociology of Education*, **14** (1), 3–19.

Berman, P. and McLaughlin, M. (1975) *Federal Programs Supporting Educational Change*, Vol. IV. Santa Monica, CA: Rand.

Boyd, W.L. (1987) 'Public education's last hurrah: Schizophrenia, amnesia, and ignorance of school politics', *Educational Evaluation and Policy Analysis*, **9** (2), 85–100.

Celis 3rd, W. (1994) 'Nations envied for schools share Americans' worries', *The New York Times*, 13 July.

Chubb, J.E. and Moe, T.M. (1990) *Politics, Markets and America's Schools*. Washington, DC: Brookings.

Committee on Economic Development (1986) *Children in Need*. New York: CED.

Council of Great City Schools (1987) *Results in the Making*. Washington, DC: CGCS.

Demaine, J. (1988) 'Teachers' work, curriculum, and the New Right', *British Journal of Sociology of Education*, **9** (3), 247–64.

Edwards, T. and Whitty, G. (1994) 'Inequality and inefficiency in schooling', in A. Glyn and D. Miliband (eds) *Paying for Inequality: The Economic Costs of Social Injustice*. London: Institute for Public Policy Research.

Elmore, R. (1979–80) 'Backward mapping: Implementation research and policy decisions', *Political Science Quarterly*, **94** (4), 601–16.

Garner, R. (1987) 'Mrs. Thatcher enthuses over opting out proposals', *Times Educational Supplement*. 18 September.

Gold, S.D. and Erickson, B.M. (1989) 'State aid to local governments in the 1980s', *State and Local Government Review*. Winter, 11–22.

Grace, G. (1994) 'Urban education and the culture of contentment: The politics, culture, and economics of inner-city schooling', in N.P. Stromquist (ed.), *Education in Urban Areas: Cross-National Dimensions*. Westport, CT: Praeger.

Halpin, D. (1994) 'Lessons in school reform from Great Britain? The politics of educational policy appropriation and transfer'. Paper delivered at the annual meeting of the American Educational Research Association, New Orleans.

Hillgate Group (1987) *The Reform of British Education: From Principles to Practice*. London: Claridge Press.

Hofstadter, R. (1955) *The Age of Reform: From Bryan to F.D.R.* New York: Alfred A. Knopf.

Huberman, M. and Miles, M. (1984) *Innovation Up Close*. New York: Plenum.

Kirst, M.W. (1991) 'Improving children's services: Overcoming barriers, creating new opportunities', *Phi Delta Kappan*, April, 615–18.

McDonnell, L. and Elmore, R. (1987) 'Getting the job done: Alternative policy instruments', *Educational Evaluation and Policy Analysis*, **9** (2), 132–52.

Moe, T. (1990) 'Political institutions: The neglected side of the story', *Journal of Law, Economics, and Organization*, **6**, 298 ff.

Munger, F.J. and Fenno, Jr, R.F. (1962) *National Politics and Federal Aid to Education*. New York: Syracuse University Press.

Nagel, S. (1980) *Improving Policy Analysis*. Beverly Hills, CA: Sage.

Nash, I. (1988) 'CTCs forced to change tack', *Times Educational Supplement*, 17 June.

NGA (National Governors' Association) (1986) *Time for Results*. Washington, DC: NGA.

Odden, A. and Marsh, D. (1988) 'State education reform implementation: A framework for analysis'. Paper presented at the annual meeting of the American Educational Research Association.

Palumbo, D.J. and Calista, D.J. (1990) *Implementation and the Policy Process: Opening Up the Black Box*. Westport, CT: Greenwood.

Parsons, T. (1960) *Structure and Process in Modern Societies*. New York: Free Press.

Peterson, P.E. (1976) *School Politics: Chicago Style*. Chicago: University of Chicago Press.

Power, S., Halpin, D. and Fitz, J. (1994) 'The grant-maintained schools policy: The English experience of educational self-governance'. Paper presented at the annual meeting of the American Educational Research Association, New Orleans, Louisiana.

Pressman, J. and Wildavsky, A. (1973) *Implementation*. Berkeley, CA: University of California Press.

Searing, D.D. (1991) 'Roles, rules, and rationality in the new institutionalism', *American Political Science Review*, **85** (4), 1239–60.

Sexton, S. (1988) 'No nationalization curriculum', *The Times*, 8 May.

Shea, C.M., Kahane, E. and Sola, P. (1990) *The New Servants of Power: A Critique of the 1980s School Reform Movement*. New York: Praeger.

Shepsle, K.A. (1989) 'Studying institutions: Some lessons from the rational choice approach', *Journal of Theoretical Politics*, **1**, 131–47.

Simon, B. (1988) *Bending the Rules. The Baker 'Reform' of Education*. London: Lawrence & Wishart.

TGAT (Task Group on Assessment and Teaching) (1987) *A Report*. London: Department of Education and Science.

TGAT (1988) *Three Supplementary Reports*. London: Department of Education and Science.

Times Educational Supplement (1991d) 'Delicate balancing acts', 6 December.

Times Educational Supplement (1992a) 'Greater choice or none at all', 31 January.

Times Educational Supplement (1991a) 'Reading achievement not good enough', 11 January.

Times Educational Supplement (1991c) 'Major revives CTCs project', 5 July.

Times Educational Supplement (1992b) 'No more than they deserved', 4 February.

Times Educational Supplement (1991b) 'Retreat sounded on 14–16 syllabus', 11 January.

Times Educational Supplement (1994) 'Report finds LMS fails to deliver', 20 May.

United States, National Commission on Excellence in Education (1983) *A Nation at Risk: The Imperative for Educational Reform: A Report to the Nation and the Secretary of Education, United States Department of Education*. Washington, DC: The Commission.

Walford, G. (1991) 'City technology colleges: A private magnetism?', in *Private Schooling: Tradition, Change, and Diversity*. London: Paul Chapman Publishing, 158–76.

Walford, G. and Miller, H. (1991) *City Technology College*. Philadelphia: Open University Press.

Whitty, G. (1991) 'Making sense of urban education after Thatcher'. Lecture given at University of Liverpool, 1 May 1991.

Whitty, G., Edwards, T. and Gewirtz, S. (1993) *Specialization and Choice in Urban Education: The City Technology Experiment*. London: Routledge.

Whitty, G. and Menter, I. (1991) 'The progress of restructuring', in D. Coulby and L. Bush (eds) *The 1988 Education Reform Act: Conflict and Contradiction*. London: Cassell.

Chapter 6

School Effects from Decentralization

David Reynolds

INTRODUCTION

It is a truism to state that the increased devolution of educational powers to schools is now an international phenomenon, since virtually every industrialized society is now attempting various kinds of devolution schemes. Like many of the other educational innovations of the last two or three decades, school-based decision-making and management promises a great deal to virtually all educational interest groups, although of course there will be different anticipated gains for each interest group. For governments, school-based decision-making may consign to a local level inevitable conflicts of values which have been so evident at national level in most industrialized societies (see Hargreaves and Reynolds, 1989), thus defusing various tensions. For parents, the arrival of apparently substantial powers at their local schools may encourage further investment of their efforts into a concern with the education of their children. For teachers, the arrival of enhanced powers may lead to increased professional self-esteem, which they may well wish to be reflected in enhancement of the material rewards of teaching to reflect the added workloads that are likely to be generated by the policy changes.

The literature on the 'why' of locally based school management and curriculum planning is, therefore, extensive (for example, Beare and Boyd, 1993; Chapman and Dunstan, 1990). What we need to do here, though, is to look beyond the *explanation* and the *description* of what is being done to the governance of schools and think more critically about whether key educational processes may be changed by school-based management and planning, and whether, crucially, the student outcomes from their school educational experiences are changed positively. To do this, we need to survey the research literatures that are available in three different areas:

- the school effectiveness research base;
- the school improvement research and practice base;
- the educational policy research and practice base.

SCHOOL EFFECTIVENESS RESEARCH

There is now a substantial body of research on the effects of different ways of organizing schools based on their students' academic and social progress over time and there are a number of recent summaries and codifications of the knowledge base available (e.g. Mortimore, 1991; Reynolds and Cuttance, 1992; Scheerens, 1992). What does the research tell us about the possible effectiveness of the introduction of local curriculum planning in terms of its effects on students' outcomes?

It is important to note, of course, that most of the school effectiveness literature predates the arrival of school-based planning/management, which in most industrialized societies only arrived on the educational scene from the late 1980s/early 1990s, and which restricts the amount of the literature that is relevant to us here. Also, it is clear that the variable 'the presence of local curriculum planning' simply does not feature in any studies. What does feature more frequently is a 'teacher involvement' variable which measures the effects of the increased involvement of teachers in schools in determining their organizational priorities, school functioning and school processes. One of the earlier reviews of the literature, by Purkey and Smith (1985), noted the importance of school-site management and democratic decision-making, whereby the staff of a school are given a considerable amount of responsibility and authority in determining the exact means by which they address the problem of increasing academic performance. This included, in their review, giving staff more authority over curricular and instructional decisions and the allocation of building resources. However, it is important to note that this widely quoted review is the authors' summation of factors which they believe likely to create effective schools, not a review of research findings. Their own review of school effectiveness research findings generated six factors, none of which related directly to school-based decision-making: effective curriculum and teaching, clear goals and expectations, the monitoring of performance, ongoing staff development, parental involvement and school district support.

Nevertheless, the 'staff involvement' variable does appear important in generating effectiveness in a number of studies. Rutter *et al.* (1979) noted that school outcomes were more favourable when there was a combination of firm leadership with a decision-making process in which all teachers felt that their views were represented. Work in the UK (Reynolds, 1982; Reynolds *et al.*, 1987) linked teacher participation in decision-making, headteacher delegation of power and the generation of high levels of 'added value' to students' academic and social development. The well known *School Matters* study of Mortimore *et al.* (1988) also noted that the involvement of teachers was associated with enhanced school effectiveness over a wide range of academic and social outcomes, such as academic achievement in mathematics and reading, self-esteem, student attendance rate and student attitudes to school and teachers. Specifically, in effective and successful schools, the teachers were heavily involved in curriculum planning and also played a major role in developing their own curriculum guidelines, in determining which class they were to teach and in determining financial allocations. More 'experiential' evidence to support the effectiveness-producing value of teacher involvement comes from the British Schools Inspectorate whose summary of effective schools' characteristics concludes that in such schools: 'effective communication and confident relationships enabled teachers to contribute to the formulation and implementation of school policies. Effective schools had clear goals ... the production of these goals and objectives had been the result of discussion by all staff' (Department of Education and Science, 1988).

It is important at this stage to enter a number of caveats, however. First, not all existing studies show a positive relationship between teacher involvement and schools' levels of effectiveness. The reanalysis by Scheerens *et al.* (1989) of the data collected within the IEA Second Mathematics and Science Study shows no clear relationship between an involvement variable (number of meetings held by the Mathematics Department) and student mathematics achievement, nor between an autonomy variable (the teachers' use of their own personally or school-generated tests) and the achievement of students. There are also Dutch studies which show a *negative* correlation between the frequency of staff meetings and school effectiveness (Stoel and Knuver, 1986, cited in Scheerens, 1992).

Secondly, some reviews of the literature such as that by Scheerens (1992) do not even mention 'staff involvement' or 'school autonomy' as crucial effectiveness variables, and those reviews which do argue for the importance of what Americans call 'faculty input into decision making' usually note that:

> it is not clear that stress on faculty input always or usually has been a
> critical consideration in generating unusual effectiveness, nor is it
> clear whether the input has been most valuable when defined
> narrowly in terms of solicitation of suggestions or broadly in terms of
> full partnership in decision making.
> (Levine and Lezotte, 1990, p. 49)

The authors of the latter review conclude quite sensibly that efforts which involve devolution of power to schools, 'are unlikely to suceed unless serious attention is paid to other correlates of effectiveness' (Levine and Lezotte, 1990). Thirdly, we should be aware of the danger of extrapolating to other contexts factors which have been shown to be effective within other countries and cultures, in view of the increased evidence that some school effectiveness factors may be 'context specific' (Reynolds and Cuttance, 1992).

All in all, though, the effectiveness research on balance would be supportive of the effectiveness of increased school control, assuming that teacher involvement is in turn enhanced.

SCHOOL IMPROVEMENT RESEARCH AND PRACTICE

The second body of knowledge which has potential usefulness for us is that generated from within the school improvement 'paradigm' or way of thinking of the 1980s and 1990s. While there is some evidence that people within this group have partially espoused philosophies of empowerment, teacher ownership, collegiality and the devolution of power to the school level as a reaction to the failure of the 'top-down' curriculum and organizational change of the 1970s (Reynolds, 1988; Reynolds *et al.*, 1993), there is no doubt that the people within this tradition have found considerable evidence to support their position. Fullan (1991) has argued consistently that certain process factors are essential to generate effective schools, and that the mere presence of some of the effective schools' factors, or 'correlates' as the Americans call them, that we have noted above would not be enough to generate effectiveness. These process factors included two staff involvement variables, namely, 'intense interaction and communication which refers to simultaneous support and pressure at both horizontal and vertical levels within the school' and 'collaborative planning and implementation which needs to occur both within the school and externally'. The large-scale International School Improvement Project (ISIP) that was funded and co-ordinated by the OECD in the mid- to late 1980s reflected and further developed these views through its schema of the relatively autonomous school, which by a process of collaboration between its members within the school and support from outside the school could, in the view of the project, become an educational setting in which the capacity to manage the educational change process is developed (see Hopkins, 1987).

Other reviews of the literature within the 'improvement' tradition have generated similar findings. Leithwood *et al.* (1990) found that effective principals and school leaders use participatory decision-making selectively but frequently, depending upon the leader's assessment of context. They were seen as working towards the development of widespread agreement concerning goals and organizational standards. The most recent work on 'transformational' principals who were experimenting with radically different, laterally oriented school governance structures is also relevant here, as are the beliefs of the American restructuring movement (Murphy, 1993) which celebrates teacher ownership and through that an enhanced pupil ownership of the educational process which it believes will improve student achievements in traditional and 'new' knowledge areas.

More recently it seems that authorities such as Fullan (1991) and others have come to believe that successful school improvement needs more than merely 'ownership' of the school by its teachers to generate high-quality processes, since 'pressure' from principals or external forces is now argued to be necessary. 'Steering' of the relatively empowered school and its individual teachers is now given considerable emphasis (Hopkins and Ainscow, 1994).

What are we to conclude from this improvement literature about the potential effects of introducing local school development planning? Most of the improvement authors would be inclined to predict that this would generate an enhanced quality of school educational processes. However, research in this tradition very rarely measures whether students are learning more in their schools following the guidance of the 'improvement principles' than in those which are not, and indeed there is some absence of rigour about the knowledge this paradigm has collected. (We rarely have reliability estimated, rarely have the sampling frames, rarely have the alternative explanations entertained by the authors and, in some cases, rarely have any empirical data produced by the often ideologically based school improvement person!) None the less, the improvement literature like that on effectiveness above would be supportive of the utility of school-based planning.

EDUCATIONAL POLICY RESEARCH AND PRACTICE

This literature too is full of enthusiasm for the positive results for devolution of power to schools. Australians like Chapman and Dunstan (1990) and Caldwell and Spinks (1988) argue that devolution and 'self-management' are productive of a wide range of positive effects, from enhanced professionalism to higher quality school processes, greater school efficiency and of course enhanced outcomes. In addition to this literature, there is a considerable volume of supportive material from other countries such as Canada (Brown, 1991) and, of course, the United Kingdom (Bush *et al.*, 1993).

This literature is generally within the tradition of policy analysis, where the arguments utilized tend to be based upon extrapolation from semi-theoretical material more than upon the empirical material which forms the basis of the school effectiveness literature and, to a lesser extent, the school improvement literature also. The one exception to this is the recent, highly influential work of the Americans Chubb and Moe (1990) which argued that the problems of academic performance within American schools are the direct result of the structure of school governance and that building level autonomy which removes principals and their teachers from the hands of government and school boards is the solution, leaving them free to create higher-quality schools. However, the authors' empirical support for their position is, in this case, very weak. Their data on school organizational factors only explains about 5 per cent of the variation in student outcome scores (the R^2 is under .25), and crucially the direction of the causality between 'school autonomy' and 'student high achievement' is open to different interpretations. The authors claim that the type of control of the school affects school organization which then positively influences achievements, but it is perfectly possible that the school-achievement levels influence in turn the school organization and the degree of autonomy of the schools. It is likely that a school that is doing well in terms of achievement levels will not evoke much involvement from the local educational state; by contrast, a poorly performing school is highly likely to find its autonomy restricted by outside interventions. Whether school autonomy is the cause or, perhaps just as likely, the result of school effectiveness is difficult to discern from this study, and the strongly argued case within the educational policy literature, too, is best regarded as not completely proven, although suggestive.

THE EFFECTS OF ENHANCED SCHOOL SELF-MANAGEMENT – SOME SPECULATIONS

We have so far looked at the evidence from three areas – school effectiveness, school improvement and educational policy analysis – and found that on balance we may expect some positive effects resulting from the devolution of power to schools upon their students' achievement outcomes. We have used studies which look at teacher involvement within schools, mostly, rather than those which utilize the 'local planning' variable, but in general the school effectiveness literature, the more qualitative and case-study based improvement literature, and the policy literature tend to support the case for high teacher involvement being productive of higher student achievement. Although none of the studies spell out the intervening links or the causal variables in the chain that links governance and outcomes, it is likely that devolution of planning functions to schools, if it is linked with teacher involvement in the planning, would generate the following:

1 More commitment among teachers to the tasks of the school through greater involvement in its planning and organization.

2 More collegiality among teachers, who might be expected to relate to each other as professional supports because they have been 'brought together'.

3 More enhanced professional self-esteem, an enhanced internal
locus of control and a more 'active' professional orientation as a
response to being judged worthy of power-holding.

It is important, though, to add some caveats to these inevitable speculations.
First, the studies which show beneficial effects of teacher involvement only do so
when the teacher involvement variable is also linked with principal leadership to
'steer' the activity. Self-management *on its own* is unlikely to have positive educational effects. Second, it is unlikely that any one variable on its own – such as higher
degrees of school self-management – will make a considerable difference to student
achievement, particularly since all school organizational factors together do not
explain more than 10–12 per cent of total student variation, as shown by the most
recent cutting-edge studies reviewed by Reynolds and Cuttance (1992). Third, the
power of the 'self-management' variable to affect outcomes positively is likely to lie
in the capacity of this organizational change in the 'governance' area of the school to
have effects upon the areas of school organization that directly influence learning,
such as teachers' classroom behaviours, teachers' professional collaboration and
the like. If the change in the 'governance' variable of curriculum decision-making is
not followed by changes in other variables, and there is no guarantee that it will be,
the positive potential change in student achievement may not appear.

It is also important to note that there may be, additionally, possible adverse
effects, or at the least effects that require policy attention, during the process of
schools picking up their local planning functions:

1 Transfer of powers to schools may increase the variation in the
quality of school organizational processes between schools, since
the schools will vary in their capacity to plan, work collaboratively,
or even at the most basic level to think about educational matters
constructively.
   There may need to be an enhanced evaluative function, and an
interventionist quality control function for certain school cases, that
is retained and developed by central authorities, to cope with the
effects upon students of the potentially increased school variation.

2 Certain schools may find that the transfer of functions may unleash
greater volumes of within-staff conflicts. In the current absence of
significant powers at school level, many schools may not possess
much educational discourse within them at all, and the arrival of
the need for that discourse as schools discharge their planning
functions may find individuals lacking the personal and intellectual
skills necessary for productive educational discussions.
Programmes of professional educational development may be a
necessary adjunct to enhanced school-planning functions.

3 The role of the school principal is likely to become a more crucial
and powerful one after the change in policy. The principal will
have to manage a further audience, his or her teachers, and will
have to handle the planning process. There must be a concern as
to whether all principals have the requisite skills to fulfil their new

role adequately, and in particular as to whether they have the skills to manage conflict within their staff groups.

4 Positive effects upon student achievement of an enhanced school role in planning are likely to come from the wider changes in school organization, ethos, etc. that are generated by the governance change. This wider school-level change may not be permitted within certain schools because it may threaten the principal. There is a need for specific attention to ensure principals permit the useful 'lateral ripples' that change in governance arrangements may generate.

5 As long as central authorities held on to all, or most, of the determination of educational policies, centrally determined goals such as equity, excellence, equal opportunities and the like could be mandated directly into school curricula. Permitting schools to develop their own policies to a greater extent runs the risk of a greater variety of educational goals being reflected in the school, goals which may in certain instances conflict with, or be antithetical to, national goals.

6 It is possible that the power transferred to schools will be taken up differently within schools, with certain groups opting out of the process of planning, particularly perhaps older teachers, female teachers and those in very junior positions. The selective nature of those who may be fully involved in planning may result in an equally selective determination of school content, goals, etc.

7 Transferring responsibility to schools for planning has time implications. The additional time associated with meetings, committee work and the generation of planning documents can contribute to increased tiredness and stress, which can in turn affect staff attendance and teaching performance.

8 A multifaceted system of education, with responsibilities allocated to a greater number of levels, is likely to be a much more complex system also. There may be difficulty in the relations between schools and local regions and the educational 'centre', and in the precise boundaries, responsibilities, etc. that attach to the three different levels.

9 With a planning function, there will be enhanced organizational complexity within schools also, with the probable existence of consultative groups, committees and working parties generating an enhanced need for increased clarity in organizational design, lines of communication and in the functional responsibilities with respect to staff, senior staff and principals.

SOME RESEARCH POSSIBILITIES

This is inevitably a tentative and exploratory discussion of the possible effects of an enhanced school role in planning. What is important is that the changes in educational policy that are being generated in the schools of any country are fully evaluated, so that the literatures within school effectiveness, school improvement and educational policy, and the professional practice of education itself, can be added to and enhanced in quality. Possible research avenues could include the following:

1 Comparing schools who make considerable changes to their curricula with those who make fewer changes to see the effect upon school processes and students' outcomes over time, utilizing a 'contrast' design which compares the two school types against each other.

2 Studying the extent to which all schools change in their organizational procedures as a result of the changes on a 'before and after' basis.

3 Comparing the experience of schools in different types of contexts, which may be different social class of catchment areas, urban/rural, effective/less effective, newly established/old established, etc. It is likely that rich case studies would be most profitable here.

4 Since it is highly likely that the educational districts or regions will differ in their support activities for schools as the changes towards school planning are implemented, it is important that any potential effects of this upon school processes and students' outcomes are evaluated.

5 Studying the extent to which mean student achievements vary during the implementation period and the institutionalization period of the policy changes. Although change over time is difficult to pin down to educational policy changes rather than to more general social and economic change, a comparison of a country's changes in students' academic and social outcomes with those of other societies of similar socio-economic and cultural composition, but which are not implementing the same policy changes, might be constructive.

6 Educational policy changes may have different effects on the students exposed to them within schools, by social class, ability, achievement, gender, ethnicity, etc., particularly if schools utilize their enhanced planning powers to generate quantitatively and qualitatively different curriculum form and content in different organizational regimes.

7 Studying those organizational factors within schools and/or their districts that are associated with variation in the planning process and their possibly different curricula. (These might include principal factors, staff factors, school organizational or ethos factors, etc.)

8 Studying the extent to which additional planning functions have wider effects upon levels of staff ownership, collegiality, etc.

It is recommended that a varied sample of schools of differing prior levels of effectiveness and of differing social and economic contexts is chosen and the changes in the educational policy input, the schools' organizational responses and the students' levels of academic and social outcomes are studied, in order to find what is the optimum mix of macro-level policies, district initiatives, and specific school organizational planning and management factors that is associated with exemplary work and/or positive effects upon student achievement outcomes.

References

Beare, H and Boyd, W.L. (1993) *Restructuring Schools*. Lewes: Falmer Press.

Brown, D.J. (1991) *Decentralization and School Based Management*. Lewes: Falmer Press.

Bush, T., Coleman, M. and Glover, D. (1993) *Managing Autonomous Schools*. London: Paul Chapman.

Caldwell, B and Spinks, J (1988) *The Self Managing School*. Lewes: Falmer Press.

Chapman, J. and Dunstan, J.F. (1990) *Democracy and Bureaucracy*. Lewes: Falmer Press.

Chubb, J.E. and Moe, T.M. (1990) *Politics, Markets and America's Schools*. Washington, DC: The Brookings Institute.

Department of Education and Science (1988) *Secondary Schools: An Appraisal by HMI*. London: DES.

Fullan, M. (1991) *The New Meaning of Educational Change*. London: Cassell.

Hargreaves, A. and Reynolds D. (eds) (1989) *Education Policies: Controversies and Critiques*. Lewes: Falmer Press.

Hopkins, D. (ed.) (1987) *Improving the Quality of Schooling*. Lewes: Falmer Press.

Hopkins, D. and Ainscow, M. (1994) *School Improvement in An Era of Change*. London: Cassell.

Leithwood, K.P., Begley, J. and Bradley Cousin, J. (1990) 'The nature, causes and consequences of principals' practices: An agenda for future research', *Journal of Educational Administration*, **28** (4), 5–31.

Levine, D. and Lezotte, L. (1990) *Universally Effective Schools: A Review and Analysis of Research and Practice*. Madison: NCESRD Publications.

Mortimore, P. (1991) 'School effectiveness research: Which way at the crossroads?' in *School Effectiveness and School Improvement*, **2** (3), 213–29.

Mortimore, P., Sammons, P., Ecob, R. and Stoll L. (1988) *School Matters: The Junior Years*. Salisbury: Open Books.

Murphy, J. (1993) *Restructuring Schools*. London: Cassell.

Purkey, S. and Smith, M. (1983) 'Effective schools: A review', in *Elementary School Journal*, **83**, 427–52.

Purkey, S.C. and Smith, M.S. (1985) 'School reform: The district policy implications of the effective schools literature', *Elementary School Journal*, **85**, 353–89.

Reynolds, D. (1982) 'The search for effective schools', *School Organization*, **2** (3), 215–37.

Reynolds, D. (1988) 'British school improvement research: The contribution of qualitative studies', *International Journal of Qualitative Studies in Education*, **1** (2), 143–54.

Reynolds, D. and Cuttance, P. (1992) *School Effectiveness: Research, Policy and Practice*. London: Cassell.

Reynolds, D., Hopkins, D. and Stoll, L. (1993) 'Linking school effectiveness knowledge and school improvement practice: Towards a synergy', *School Effectiveness and School Improvement*, **4** (1), 37–58.

Reynolds, D., Sullivan, M. and Murgatroyd, S. J. (1987) *The Comprehensive Experiment*. Lewes: Falmer Press.

Rutter, M., Maughan, B., Mortimore, P. and Ouston, J. (1979) *Fifteen Thousand Hours: Secondary Schools and Their Effect on Children*. London: Open Books.

Scheerens, J. (1992) *Effective Schooling*. London: Cassell.

Scheerens, J., Vermeulen, C.J. and Pelgrum, W. J. (1989) 'Generalizability of instructional and school effectiveness indicators across nations', *International Journal of Educational Research*, **13** (7), 789–99.

Chapter 7

Decentralization by or for School Improvement[1]

Ulf P. Lundgren and Kerstin Mattsson

Improvement means a change in a process from one mode to another, but it connotes also a change towards a mode of higher quality. Quality in its turn – concerning human artefacts like schools – is, of course, a question of value judgement. From the history of education we can learn that what has been labelled school improvement is often the articulation of specific social and political interests. The history is full of changes or discourses about changes in which a proposed change in itself, by definition, is an improvement. In reality, educational changes that can be described as moving to higher quality are not that easy to find.

The improvement of education is, however, a relative matter. Two questions can be formulated. Can improvement of education be anything more than an adjustment of schools or institutions of education to changed conditions in society? Can schools improve within their own cultures and thereby perhaps even supersede or 'futurize' the society?

Given these two questions, we can discuss school improvement from two viewpoints. One is to see improvement as related to the society (the external context). The other is to see improvement as related to a specific educational institution (internal context). What is an improvement – a change to a better quality – is in the first case related to criteria determined outside the school. In the second case it is related to criteria valid inside the school. Of course, this is an analytic distinction. Changed external conditions alter the frames for the internal work and thereby have an impact on the educational process. But, while aware of the simplicity in the distinction, it delivers a starting point. It may also help us to analyse and understand the nature of different reform programmes.

Decentralization is a change of power and control over processes from the centre to the periphery. Such a change, if aimed at improvement of education, ought to change the quality of education. In order, then, to analyse the relationship between decentralization and improvement we have to see how the idea and the reality have emerged.

DECENTRALIZATION

After the Second World War educational systems the world over expanded to an extent that has no precedent in history (Coombs, 1968). Educational systems in the Western world have only partly been able to cope with this expansion. Traditions and various types of system factors have delayed the adaptation of the educational systems to the new demands and challenges.

During the 1950s and 1960s several economists were able to establish correlations between investments in education and economic growth (Blaug, 1976). In the field of economics of education two main theories were formulated. The first was the theory of human capital, which was formulated during the 1950s and 1960s, and became one of the foundations of educational expansion (Schultz, 1961). The other theory can be labelled the filter- or sorting-theory. According to this, the aim of education was not first and foremost to refine human resources but to sort subjects. At the risk of oversimplifying, this theory can be expressed in the following way. Education aims at sorting the students according to their ability. An educational system is, then, a 'filter' for sorting and an information system for those who receive the products (Arrow, 1974). The first of these two theories was used as an important tool in educational planning and in arguments for large investments in the educational sector, in Sweden as well as elsewhere. The belief in the power of education was strong – education was assumed to promote wealth for citizens as well as for the nation at large. The general assumption, however, proved to be context-bound, rather than generally valid. The 1970s and the 1980s showed new patterns and problems.

Today we are facing a situation in which the outcome of public education – its productivity – again is clearly related to the economy, but in a world of new economic challenges and competitions. These changed economic conditions have renewed theories on the economics of education. But now these ideas are not linked to human capital and sorting functions, but to the concept of markets.

During the expansion period political administration of reforms was relatively straightforward. Decision-makers ascribed the system's well-articulated goals, defined according to priority, and provided resources that, it was assumed, would guarantee their attainment. The various sectors appeared as possible instruments for reaching political goals. If the administration failed, the blame was often ascribed to shortcomings in the original plan. These problems, it was felt, could be solved at the next stage. Moreover, by systematic use of research, an accumulation of knowledge was assumed to prevent future failures. It was possible to plan in a rational way or, to use the words of Wildavsky, 'the method called the "rational paradigm" (order objectives, compare alternatives, choose the highest ranking)' was generally accepted (1979, p. 8).

This rational paradigm called for centrally administered reforms, and it seemed possible not only to make plans but also to fulfil them. It can be, as Wildavsky argues, that this rational paradigm 'is mistaken as describing either how decisions are or ought to be made' (*ibid.*). But, perhaps more importantly, it fitted well into educational systems with a long-centralized tradition and strengthened the role of central managers to provide oversight and advice about measures to be taken.

During the expansion and as a consequence of the rational paradigm, in many countries central policy-making became important. The centre made the plans, even controlled the development work and was, by being central, capable of negotiating and meeting various and often contradictory demands. The Swedish comprehensive school reform in the 1960s gives us perhaps the best illustration of this (Lindensjö and Lundgren, 1986; Lundgren, 1979; 1985).

In the 1970s we saw a change in educational policy. Evaluations as well as pure statistics pointed out that the earlier and basic expectations of many of the post-war reforms had not been fulfilled. Centrally administered and controlled reforms had not been implemented as they were supposed to be. In Sweden, as in many countries, earlier formulated arguments for decentralization were renewed and in the first instance realized by local school improvement projects, school evaluation and a change in the role of school leaders from being executors of given rules and directives to being policy-makers and managers in a process of school development. The reform period in Swedish upper-secondary education during the early 1980s illustrates the change from a belief in centrally governed reforms to demands for more decentralized strategies.

Changes from centralization to decentralization or vice versa, however, are seldom total. In many countries the changes are going in both directions at the same time. Again, Sweden provides us with a good example. Bills were passed in the parliament, according to which a rather extensive decentralization would be implemented. Reform programmes have been implemented during the last 15 years, which can easily be described as decentralized. At the same time, however, the central school administration is currently developing a set of central tests that in reality will mean a rather heavy – in relation to the past – central steering of the content of education (see Franke-Wikberg, 1989). And while improving the academic content of upper-secondary education reflects a newborn belief in decentralized strategies, the reforming of the vocational upper-secondary education at the end of the 1980s and the beginning of the 1990s has been almost as centralized as the Swedish school reforms of the 1960s (Heyman et al., 1979; SOU, 1989, p. 16; SOU, 1990, p. 16).

The case of Sweden is, of course, in some aspects unique. However, it seems to illustrate a rather general tendency. The interpretation of demands on national education from an international economy renews models for labour-force planning and calls again for central initiatives; at the same time these changes have to be carried out without additional resources. Thus, in order to develop the efficiency of education, reforms have to be implemented at the management level concerning the governing of schools. Reforms towards decentralization seem to respond to demands for efficiency. Productivity of education is linked to central decisions and efficiency of education is linked to a decentralized decision structure (Lundgren, 1982).

The reforms aiming at decentralization are not exclusive to education. They reflect a reconstruction of the public sector and, 'It is certainly not an exaggeration when Nelson Polsby calls the issue of centralization and decentralization "one of the great, resonant themes of contemporary politics" (Sharpe, 1979, p. 1)' (Weiler, 1988, p. 1).

There are, however, irrespective of changes in the direction of moving policy-making towards or from the centre, some changes in the relationship between the state and public education and in the relationship between civil society and public education that are basic in any discussion on how central control is exercised. Thus, it is necessary to briefly discuss these changed relationships between centre and periphery.

In order to establish a point of reference we must assume, with Wildavsky (1979), that problems are permanent and solutions bound to time and context. Hence, the 'great, resonant themes of contemporary politics' – centralization and decentralization – are to be understood as a renewal of instruments for governing and the handling of permanent problems. Following such a line of argument it seems inevitable that the identification of what is the problem has to be renewed or refreshed. What has to be reformed has consequently to be identified as being in a state of crisis (Goble, 1986) and, furthermore, the crisis must be identified as having been caused by what has to be the solution; that is, the crisis is not due to lack of economic resources but rather to misuse of human resources. If the causes are identified as being human and possible to control, then the solutions seem possible to implement by new or renewed instruments like decentralization, in-service training, school improvement, professionalization, etc., not by adding new resources. The organization has to be boosted.

What is pointed out by many political scientists (Wildavsky, 1979) is that the governing subject – the political leadership – has problems in taking the initiative for an active reform policy. We can see examples of a fragmentation of educational administration, which creates problems with overall planning and the ability to resolve complex groups of interrelated problems. We can also see tendencies towards more policy-making being carried out by the administration itself.

The movements towards decentralization can be interpreted as one way of solving the contemporary problems (Granheim *et al.*, 1990; Lindensjö and Lundgren, 1986). By reforming the educational system through decentralization some of these problems can be dealt with. Some of them will, however, disappear with the submerging of decisions. Decentralization is not a solution in itself. If the aim is a reconstruction of power and control, decentralization has to be followed by measures that demand action. School improvement, as it has taken form in for instance Swedish reform programmes, can be understood as such a measure; an attempt to develop new strategies for action.

Here we face the main problem in comparing developments within the various OECD countries. It seems as if we can identify two patterns: one in which the demands on school improvement are internal, growing out of the schools themselves and thereby forming demands for a restructuring of power and control, that is decentralization; the other in which the implementation of decentralization is articulated in the external demands for programmes for school improvement. These two patterns, of course, reflect various educational traditions and how, within these traditions, power and control over education are exercised.

At the same time, the motives for decentralization do not directly point out the problems of governing. Indirectly, however, the problems of governing are there. Weiler (1988, p. 2) points to one or more of three models or arguments for decentralization behind various decentralization movements. His classification of models gives a good analytical starting point:

1 The 'redistribution' model, which is predicated on the sharing of power.

2 The 'efficiency' model, which is geared to enhancing the cost-effectiveness calculus of the educational system through a more efficient deployment and management of available resources.

3 The 'cultures of learning' model, which emphasizes the decentralization of educational content.

Going back to the earlier notes on two patterns for the relationship between decentralization and school improvement, we can see that when a decentralization reform generates demands for school improvement, the first and second models are envisaged. When school improvement programmes demand decentralization, the second and third models are envisaged. The efficiency model seems to be common to both patterns.

However, any decentralization of the educational system, irrespective of motives, puts into focus the balance between political and professional control over education. The governing or steering of an educational system can be described in two dimensions: the location of power (where) and the agents (who has the power). These two dimensions can be illustrated in a graphic scheme, which also points out four main models of steering and governing of education:

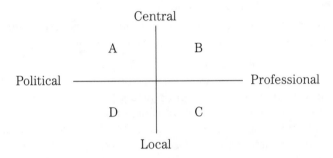

A movement towards decentralization focuses questions on the professional ability and the professional responsibility of teachers. In countries where there has been a rather strong professional power we can see a change to political power. In other countries we can see a struggle for more professional power. These changes, in their turn, seem to be directed not only towards teacher training – initial and in-service training – and its content, but also towards evaluation and how political power can be exercised and on what ground decisions can be taken.

The concept of decentralization is, as was said in the first introductory remark, rather difficult to define in a precise way. In 1988 Weiler pointed out that:

> In the national and international glossaries of educational policy,
> 'decentralization' has been a principal for some time now, right next
> to such other favourites as 'participation', 'autonomy', and 'reform'.
> . . . This is so in spite of considerable difficulties in agreeing on what
> exactly 'Decentralization' means in practice, and in spite of a less
> than overwhelming record of success in those attempts at
> decentralization that actually have been undertaken.
>
> (Weiler, 1988, p. 1)

How decentralization in reality is taking 'gestalt' reflects administrative, budgetary and legal traditions. Decentralization can on one level be rhetorical, but on another level a concrete process involving a rather drastic change of the entire educational system.

An educational system is governed mainly by three sets of instruments or governing systems (Lundgren, 1979):

- the legal steering system;
- the economic steering system;
- the ideological steering system (goal and content).

The evaluation system could be viewed as a fourth steering system. The more the first three steering systems are loosened up and become diffuse and thus give space for various interpretations, the more evaluation will govern by giving interpretations in an operationalized way.

If we accept the patterns of thought lined up here, that is:

- there is a renewal of models for the economics of education in which productivity is defined in relation to international economic competitiveness, and efficiency has to be created within a declining frame of expenditure;
- there are problems in political governing demanding a renewal of political resources and a restructuring of the arena of formulation;

then there will be a development in which the governing of education has to find a balance between central and local power and control. The educational reforms we are facing will then, irrespective of starting points, be possible to describe as both decentralizing and centralizing. In such a reform movement it will be necessary to develop two measures. On one hand the demands for productivity will be strengthening the central control of education by an emphasis on evaluation. On the other hand the demand for efficiency will strengthen the local control over how resources are used. School improvement programmes will be essential for developing models and strategies for local power and control. At the same time there is an inbuilt contradiction between central control and local control that will be visible in how evaluation will take shape at central and local levels, and thereby on how knowledge will be organized and 'spoken'.

The dilemma we are facing then is that the intention to increase decentralization – in a system where central governing becomes complicated – demands co-ordination and a renewal of information resources, and this will be interpreted as a demand that can be satisfied by evaluation. At the same time an evaluation system can replace the earlier central systems for governing. What on one side turns out to be a change in steering systems directed towards a distribution of policy-making from the centre to the periphery will, on the other side, be a strengthening of a central steering system.

In order to chain these two streams of changes to each other, it is important that a change in governing will be met by a change in how schools are led. The leadership of schools will, as a consequence, come into focus. It is the school leaders who have to interpret the new central signals and transform them into local decision-making and a professional structure.

In order to make ongoing changes visible they are often blown up in public discourse by being described as 'dramatic'. Even at the risk of misusing the word, the changes in the public discourse about education during the last decade must be described as being rather dramatic.

The teaching profession has been facing severe criticism and new challenges (see Lundgren, 1985). Some of these challenges have been responded to rather rapidly by using traditional measures like changed teacher training, pre-service and in-service. Other responses are slower, but perhaps more profound. It can even be argued that public distrust of education has been created in order to find a problem for already existing solutions. In any case, if the statement is accepted that this change in the public discourse about education reflects more profound changes in the conditions for education, existing models for the governing of education have to be renewed. If so, the focus on school leaders, their work and education in so many ongoing educational reforms has a possible context of explanation.

The concern for the quality and standards of education is, to use economic terms, a concern for productivity. Seeing the concern for productivity in relation to an international economy, it seems important to centralize standards for education by curricula and/or evaluation. At the same time the space for increasing resources to the educational sector is restricted. This creates new demands on school management. The economy of education is related to productivity. The economy of schools is related to efficiency.

Within this perspective, changes in demands on school leaders and their work cannot be related to decentralization alone. Decentralization is part of the boosting of the economy of schools. But a movement towards decentralization puts specific demands on school management and on the work of school leaders.

SCHOOL IMPROVEMENT AND SCHOOL MANAGEMENT

Every school unit consists of a heterogeneous group of teachers. Teachers enter a specific school at various times and with various backgrounds (in teacher education, in-service education, ambition, expectations, etc.). Whether teachers are professionals can, of course, be discussed but they have a rather lengthy education and an ethos. At the same time this professionalism has, for divers teacher categories, various and sometimes different backgrounds.

Educational systems have become more and more heterogeneous with an increasing division of labour. The post-war expansion had among its consequences a development of specialities. It also brought into schools new groups of specialists such as psychologists and guidance personnel.

Individual schools are often embedded with a rather heterogeneous professional staff, in which the various categories do not necessarily perceive their work from a common educational background and with a common ethos. School management means – as a consequence of this differentiation – to bring together independent subjects with different interests, attitudes and knowledge in a work process that is to form a united organization from a differentiated staff of employees.

At the same time the functions of education have been broadened and the length of schooling prolonged. Schools have been forced to take over more and more of the upbringing of children and youth, which in its turn creates value conflicts. Furthermore, as discussed previously, the demands on education have, over time, become related to outcomes of economic relevance. The reality of schooling is filled with complex social and individual problems, yet the pressure for reform is increasingly restricted to specific outcomes. It is in this context that the division of labour within schools is of decisive importance for possible strategies of school management. Teachers perceive and identify problems in relation

145

to their specific education and specific tasks. A student problem can be identified by one teacher as a learning problem, by another as a social problem.

How strategies for management of schools are formed is, of course, related to goals given and selected. Successful management is the art of foreseeing problems and the ability to deal with acute problems. For those in the schools, that is teachers, successful management is often related to how acute problems are handled (Lundgren, 1982). For those outside the schools success is shown in the ability to foresee problems, allocate resources and manage information. Briefly, we can state that successful leadership is the ability to improve schools both in relation to the external and the internal – and changing – context. In the process of change there are stabilizing elements. The profession of teaching, built on various ideas and various types of education, various identities and various traditions, is one such factor. Ideas about schools from parents and politicians is another.

In this plurality of stabilizing factors the management of schools is one component. Within the task of management is embedded the integration of what is differentiated, the finding of a common course in respect to many and often different opinions and ideas. The successful handling of such management amounts to school improvement. In a process towards decentralization school management is accentuated.

Management of public education is intended to transform political governance into concrete strategies for leadership that form a common course for a school. But to shape this common course the management must build on interests within the internal context of the school.

The difference between school management and management of other organizations is that the goals are rather abstract and there are no clear criteria for success, in other words, the feedback system for governing and leading is rather blunt. In enterprise, the market gives signals according to which production responds and to some extent evaluations can be seen as fulfilling the functions of a market. But besides the measurement problems in any evaluation, educational evaluation is internal. Educational correspondence with, for example, economic demands is a matter that is likely to be responded to all too late to have consequences for actually governing education and teaching.

External demands are, for these reasons, more difficult to respond to for school leaders than are internal demands. Given this level of complexity the division of labour within schools becomes problematic. In order to respond to external demands the central issue in school management is to integrate what is differentiated and to shape from various and often different interests a common course; to handle leadership as policy-making and policy control.

But policy-making concerning school management is a new concept in many countries, not least in Sweden. Decentralization in countries with a long tradition of central governing of education demands that school leaders do something contrary to tradition. Schools have been a part of the state apparatus and teachers as well as school leaders have primarily been civil servants; school leaders have been expected to administer schools according to given laws and rules, and vigilantly see that the rules are followed. Educational policy-making was a part of politics and was formed in specific arenas. The influence on policy-making was channelled over the political and sometimes the co-operative structure. In a decentralized system the borderlines between political governing and professional leadership have, however, become blurred and diffuse. Accountability and responsibility are now linked to processes and outcomes and not so much to laws and rules. To formulate policy will in itself be an anxiety-evoking task. This means that school leaders have to depend on the support of their staff and are thereby more vulnerable. At the same time, a change of role of school leaders that makes them more autonomous can also make them even more sensitive to central signals.

Going back to the statement that ongoing educational changes can be described as moving towards both decentralization and centralization, school leaders seem to have been given the task of integrating these two movements – an integration that results in school improvement.

NOTE

1 In this chapter Lundgren and Mattsson apply a line of analysis outlined in Lundgren (1990). It was then built up to scrutinize the evaluation concept, but this time the focus is widened to include school improvement and management.

References

Arrow, (1974) 'Higher education as a filter', in K. J. Lumsden (ed.) *Efficiency in Universities*. Elsevier.

Coombs, P.H. (1968) *The World Educational Crisis*. London: Oxford University Press.

Blaug, M. (1976) 'The empirical status of human capital theory: A slightly jaundiced survey', *Journal of Economic Literature*, **14**, 827–55.

Franke-Wikberg, S. (ed.) (1989) *Skolan och utvärderingen. Fem professorer tar ordet*. (The school and the evaluation. Five professors' statements.) HLS Förlag: Stockholm.

Goble, N. M. (1986) 'New challenges for teachers and teacher education'. Opening address to WCOTP, Council of Europe Seminar in Strasbourg, 28–30 April.

Granheim, M., Kogan, M. and Lundgren U. (eds) (1990) *Evaluation as Policy-making. Introducing Evaluation into a National Decentralized Educational System*. London: Jessica Kingsley.

Heyman, I., Mattsson, K. and Pettersson, S. (1979) *Reformarbete i gymnasieskolan*. (School improvement in upper-secondary education.) Stockholm: HLS Förlag.

Lindensjö, B. and Lundgren, U. P. (1986) *Politisk styrning och utbildningsreformer*. (Political governing and educational reforms.) Stockholm: Liber.

Lundgren, U. P. (1979) *Model Analysis of Pedagogical Processes*. Lund: Liber.

Lundgren, U. P. (1982) 'Between schooling and education'. Invited address to the annual meeting of the American Education Research Association, New York, March. Washington: Educational Research Information Center. Ed. 218 193.

Lundgren, U. P. (1985) *Att organisera skolan*. (To organize the school.) Stockhom: Liber.

Lundgren, U. (1990) 'Educational policymaking, decentralization and evaluation', in Granheim *et al*.

Schultz, T. W. (1961) 'Investment in human capital', *American Economic Review*, **51**, 1–17.

Sharpe, L. J. (ed.) (1979) *Decentralist Trends in Western Democracies*. London: Sage.

SOU 1990:16 (1979) 'Utvärdering av försöksverksamhet med 3-årig yrkesinriktad utbildning i gymnasieskolan. Första året'. (Evaluation of vocational education within upper-secondary school. The first year.) Stockholm: Allmänna förlaget.

SOU 1990:16 (1990) 'Utvärdering av försöksverksamhet med 3-årig yrkesinriktad utbildning i gymnasieskolan. Andra året'. (Evaluation of vocational education within upper-secondary school. The second year.) Stockhom: Allmänna förlaget.

Weiler, H. (1988) 'Education and Power: The Politics of Educational Decentralization in Comparative Perspective'. Stanford: unpublished manuscript.

Wildavsky, A. (1979) *Speaking Truth to Power. The Art and Craft of Policy Analysis*. Boston: Little, Brown and Company.

Chapter 8

Redefining the Concept of Educational Equality through Decentralization

Gunnel Gustafsson and Anders Lidström

INTRODUCTION

After the Second World War a coherent system of primary and secondary education was created in Sweden, based upon the idea of egalitarianism and established through continuous reforms. This project coincided with the Social Democrats' gradual implementation of their main agenda, the welfare state. One of the goals was to reform elementary schooling and provide the same education for everybody independent of social class, sex, place of residence, etc. Primary and secondary education was seen as a crucial agency for social change. Working-class children were to get the same education as middle- and upper-class children, and this was supposed to lead to a social restructuring of society.

As pointed out by Lindensjö and Lundgren (1986) a new wave of reforms emerged during the mid-1970s and a series of steps have been taken since then toward decentralization of the decision-making system and the introduction of a higher degree of flexibility in public education. However, the tradition of collective responsibility for compulsory education up to high-school level has proved to be very strong. Primary schooling is still, in the main, publicly organized and financed. In 1993 less than 1 per cent of all children attended private (independent) schools. The purpose of this chapter is to put the policy decisions taken from the mid-1970s in a political, administrative and ideological context, and thereby increase the understanding of what has been changing and why. The questions we ask are: What is the problem that decentralization is supposed to solve, and what are the major developments during this period?

First, we present the official version of what happened as it is described in documents and statements made by the actors involved. An explanation frequently used by official decision-makers is that decentralization of formal rights to make decisions is improving the equality of education through better adjustment to local circumstances. Secondly, we argue that such efforts have to be seen in the light of the rise and fall of the Swedish centralist welfare state. Thirdly, we ask if it is possible to interpret the present developments as an emerging new type of egalitarianism. Our thesis is that the egalitarian educational ideology which meant equal opportunities for the same education is gradually being changed into stress on education of the same value. These changes are accompanied by changed central local government relationships and a general strengthening of local powers. Thus, formal rights and duties to make decisions and take responsibility for primary and secondary education (as well as for many other policies) is transferred from state to local governments as well as downwards within the state bureaucracy.

At the end of the chapter we return to the question of the relationship between policies concerning the content of education and those dealing with division of power and responsibility (for elementary schooling) between levels of government. Our conclusion is that the question of degree of decentralization is closely related to the emergence of a new urban middle class. Reconsideration of elementary education with regard to access, curricula, teaching, etc. is often described by decision-makers as rational, almost unavoidable, adjustments of inter-governmental relationships. This is a long-term management strategy deeply rooted in the Swedish pragmatic culture of consensus and co-operation between strong local and national powers.

IDEOLOGY AS REALITY – RATIONAL ACTOR EXPLANATIONS

Since the beginning of the 1970s the official policy has, as mentioned, been to transfer power and responsibility from national to local governments as well as downwards within local and national government agencies (administrative decentralization). The Royal Commission Report 'Make decisions nearer citizens' (SOU, 1978, p. 52) served as the basis for a far-reaching and continuous increase in administrative as well as political decentralization within almost all policy fields, not least education (Gustafsson, 1987).

The official story to be told by the politicians charged with responsibility for the developments within the school sector is the following. At the end of the 1960s, great concern was expressed about the quality of primary and secondary education. For example, it was argued that discipline problems were severe and that an increasing number of students had difficulties at school. The government appointed the so-called SIA-commission, with the task of investigating the internal working of the school.

The commission presented its proposals in 1974 (SOU, 1974, p. 53). A series of measures were suggested in order to improve the situation. Of principal importance were the proposals aiming at decentralizing responsibilities, which ran contrary to the previous tradition. According to the commission, improvements of the internal work required a greater scope for adjustment to local conditions. Therefore, the suggestion was that decision-making powers should be moved from central to local level. For example, it was proposed that the use of central government grants should be less restricted by detailed rules. It was also stressed that other interested groups, such as parents, students, and local branches of trade unions, should have more influence over local decisions. During the later 1970s, other commissions dealing with problems in the school sector, such as the SSK-commission (SOU, 1978, p. 65), suggested measures along the same lines. The underlying idea was that greater responsiveness to societal conditions and problems in education would make students more motivated and willing to learn.

Most of the proposals of the SIA-commission were adopted by the Government and in principle accepted by Parliament in its 1975–76 session. From then onwards, a number of decisions were taken, aimed at gradually transferring power and responsibility from national to local level. In 1978, a new system of central government grants for compulsory schooling was introduced. The previous system of numerous earmarked grants was replaced by a limited number of block grants. Local authorities were able, to a greater extent, to set their own priorities for the use of resources. In 1980, the Government decided on a new curriculum covering the years of compulsory schooling, that is, Grades 1–9 (Lgr 80, 1980) adjusted to the new principles of decentralization. It contained fewer details than previous curricula and, instead, emphasized the goals of the school system.

Reform initiatives for the upper secondary school (Grades 10–12) have also been taken during this phase of the reform movement. Here, the reform path in itself has followed decentralist principles. Instead of presenting a complete reform, local authorities were invited to take initiatives in experimenting with new ways of organizing education at this level. A major restructuring of the last three (non-compulsory) years of high school was suggested at the beginning of 1990, and this was, after some compromises, accepted by parliamentary majority. As a result, local authorities are now free to decide whether to have upper secondary schools of their own and what programmes to offer. Alternatively, they can decide to fully or partly buy this service from a neighbouring municipality. Also, apart from a nationally set minimum time for each subject, timetable dispositions are now decided locally to a significant extent.

The position of the local authorities was further strengthened in the late 1980s, as a new Minister of Education with extensive local government experience transferred full responsibility for the employment of teachers to the municipalities, despite strong opposition from one of the teacher unions and the bourgeois parties. A new system of central government grants was introduced, replacing the previous earmarked allocation of resources with a lump sum for schooling in each local authority. Further, decisions on how to use these resources were fully handed over to the local level, although they were expected to comply with the pragmatic consensus tradition and restrict their policies to the frames of nationally set goals, curricula and regulations.

In order to adjust the administrative organization to the decentralist changes, the role of the National and Regional Boards of Education was revised. The strong position of the National Board (Heidenheimer, 1977), due to its extensive powers to issue and interpret regulations and curricula, was reduced at the end of the 1980s when it was given a more supervisory and advisory role with respect to the local authorities and the schools. Correspondingly, the tasks of the Regional Boards of Education were altered and greater emphasis was put on supporting local school development.

The administrative reforms continued. In 1990 it was decided to abolish the entire level of Regional Boards of Education and to reduce the size and functions of the National Board of Education (see Proposition, 1988/89, p. 154). One year later, decisions were taken also to abolish the National Board of Education. It was replaced by a much smaller National Agency for Education which included a limited regional organization. The previous administrative superstructure was regarded as unnecessary in the decentralized school system now taking shape.

Instead, the new state administrations were to focus mainly on evaluating the implementation of national goals and controlling the performance of schools and local authorities (see Proposition, 1990/91, p. 18).

As a result of the Social Democratic defeat in the 1991 general election, four bourgeois parties formed a coalition government. School reforms were one of the new government's major priorities and a goal was set to develop the best school system in Europe. Decentralization was going to continue, but with a difference in focus. The 'new' policies were in some important respects a continuation along the Social Democratic reform path. In 1992 it was decided to bring together all sector specific central government grants into one large lump sum for each local authority (see Proposition, 1991/92, p. 150). Thus, local authorities were given larger discretion on how to use their grants, but at the same time the school sector became more involved in local financial decisions and, thus, had to compete with other local government services for money.

Even during the Social Democratic reign, parents were given the right to choose schools for their children. The schools were also encouraged to develop their own specific profiles. However, the bourgeois government has stimulated the establishment of independent schools, thereby extending student and parental choice (see Proposition, 1991/92, p. 95; Proposition, 1992/93, p. 230). Independent schools include not only private schools but also those run by, for example, religious organizations and those based on a different pedagogy, such as Montessori or Waldorf. Wide freedom to start new schools, generous central government grants and permission to raise resources from parental contributions have facilitated a slight increase in the number of independent schools (so far including up to approximately 2 per cent of the pupils). Independent schools, however, figure more significantly in urban and suburban areas. The Social Democrats regained power after the 1994 elections. However, no major changes have occurred in terms of education policies, apart from a reduction in the financial support to independent schools.

THE RISE AND FALL OF A CENTRALIST WELFARE STATE

School attendance from the age of 7 was made obligatory for every Swedish child in 1842. Simultaneously, the then already existing local tradition of collective responsibility for primary education was formally granted to parishes. It now became the duty of these small local units, in the main responsible for the religious matters of the state church, to run schools and employ teachers. This remained the case up until the period between the two world wars, when the responsibility for elementary education was gradually transferred to municipalities; it is in this local political setting that the coherent and comprehensive national programmes regarding primary and secondary education were specified and implemented after the Second World War.

The governmental system within which the egalitarian educational policy was formulated and carried out has commonly been perceived and described as highly centralized and uniform (cf Heidenheimer et al., 1983). Such a characterization is, in our view, an oversimplification. The structure of government was more complex and the processes of decision-making far more complicated than noted by foreign observers. The establishment of the welfare state took place within a culture of consensus based upon ideas and actions reflecting strong 'rational' and pragmatic considerations. The central–local government relationships were characterized by a combination of strong central and local powers with basically the same interests, rather than two centres of powers in conflict with each other. Primary education has, thus, long been an important component in the strong tradition of local self-government. Through their rights to taxation, parishes and municipalities have been in a position to provide the means necessary for an adjustment of local needs, not least in the field of education. Thus, there is and always has been a balance rather than a dichotomy between central and local powers. Local authorities in Sweden have wanted basically the same system of education as national government.

This consensus regarding elementary schooling is a reflection of the homogeneity of Swedish society. The level of service provision has, however, varied considerably between local authorities, especially in earlier days. For example, during certain periods, the big cities tended to provide a longer comprehensive education than rural authorities (Marklund, 1980, p. 8). The historically strong position of local governments increased when the welfare state was developed.

During a 40-year period (1936–76) the Social Democratic party gained so many seats at each election that they could stay in power continually. From the beginning of the 1930s until around 1970, when the traditional electoral basis – the industrial working class – started to decrease, the Social Democrats were the principal political force in Sweden (Einhorn and Logue, 1989). The welfare state was built and gradually extended during the 40 years of Social Democratic governance. The long-term goal was to create an efficient and egalitarian society and the school system was considered to be an important and well integrated part of it. Strong national government authority was held to be important for two reasons. First, the ideology of 'equal distribution of welfare' among different social groups, as well as between more and less developed parts of the country, presupposed a national policy. Secondly, nationally formulated rules were perceived as necessary guidelines for the successful implementation of national programmes by local governments, and consequently for 'efficiency'.

The egalitarian policy style, based on a combination of a strong centre and strong local government, is thus part of a Social Democratic ideology. This is, of course, not to say that the rise of the uniform Swedish educational system is entirely a Social Democratic 'construction'. During the period when the welfare state emerged a number of favourable conditions were at hand. First, there was a unique period of economic growth. As Sweden was not involved in the Second World War its means of production stayed intact. Secondly, the political system was reformed and democratic principles were settled and, in addition, there were important institutional, cultural and demographic preconditions for the gradual establishment of an advanced social prototype. Finally, people in general identified with 'their own' political party and in the main the same political parties were active at national, regional and local level. Both the political parties and the labour market organizations formed strong integrative forces.

In the late 1940s there was an intense political debate over the speed and degree of the social measures to be undertaken as well as over the tax system.

The Social Democrats managed to introduce progressive income taxation to constitute the financial basis for their egalitarian policies. This was opposed by non-socialists, whose basic philosophy was that high income earners should be allowed to keep a relatively high proportion of what they earn, to avoid them bearing a disproportionate share of costs for social welfare in a broad sense. Some elements of the new social order were, however, never questioned by non-Socialists. Economic growth and full employment were seen as important economic policy goals by all political parties.

The declining support for the Social Democratic party during the 1970s reflects a decline in the proportion of workers within the electorate (Berglund and Lindström, 1978). Since the beginning of the 1970s the emphasis has not been on industrial production but on service and Sweden's industrial society has gradually changed into a service or post-industrial society. A major characteristic in this transition is the emergence of a large, well-educated middle class, particularly in big cities and towns. This group not only make more individualized demands on public policies but are also capable of articulating their individual preferences in order to influence political decision-making (Petersson et al, 1989). The situation is characterized by political instability, and the relative importance of the progressive income tax system has decreased. Emphasis is now more on proportional taxes and taxes on goods and services. Social Democratic leaders now believe that progressive income taxes, above a certain level, constitute obstacles to people's willingness to work. State transfers to local governments have diminished measured as a percentage of local government income, whereas municipal taxes, which are proportional income taxes, have tended to increase until the mid-1980s. In 1935 the proportion of the income paid in tax was approximately 9 per cent (Årsbok för Sveriges kommuner, 1935). For 1955 and 1993 the comparable figures were 12 per cent and 31 per cent respectively (Årsbok för Sveriges kommuner, 1955; 1993).

A NEW TYPE OF EGALITARIANISM?

Foreign observers have admired the Swedish welfare model for its successful combination of capitalism and socialism; the so-called middle way to pragmatic solutions of problems which are not necessarily easy to solve in many other countries (Childs, 1936; 1980). Today it has become obvious, however, that this type of society is not immune to problems. Both ideological and economic reasons contribute to the difficulties which egalitarian policies have confronted since the mid-1970s. In his book *The Welfare State and Beyond* Professor Gunnar Heckscher concluded that, 'Scandinavians are increasingly unwilling to sacrifice too much of their individual liberties for the establishment of the millennium. In this they are not very different from other Western peoples' (Heckscher, 1984, p. 253).

As described above, the balance between centre and local area has clearly changed during the last two decades. This means less legal and economic restrictions for variation in service delivery, and thus stronger incentives for discretion. In reality there is consequently considerable local variation within the present school system (Gustafsson and Lidström, 1989; Lidström, 1991; Löfquist, 1988). Relevant policy documents are, however, in the main still stressing equal opportunities for the same education for everybody, and the cultural commitment to consensus on this element of the welfare ideology is of crucial importance in the public debate.

The gap has, however, widened between actual service variation and the official norm of equal service delivery. At the same time the formal efforts to decentralize power and responsibility from the state to local governments as well as downwards within the bureaucracy have led to uncertainty, complexity and often-changing divisions of labour between actors and agencies. Decentralization of power and responsibility from state to local governments may be regarded as an attempt to make the political system more appetizing. The crucial question is, however, whether local governments will accept their responsibility for solving potential future conflicts concerning, for example, school finance or deviations from the old norm of equal education for everybody. Local authorities, too, may export their problems, and thus 'give them back' to families or individuals. Local decentralization through the development of neighbourhood councils is one way for local government to cope with their inner tensions and conflicts (Kolam, 1987). Also, practically all local authorities have delegated power and responsibilities to principals and schools.

If decentralization efforts, be they transfers from national governments downwards or from local governments downwards, result in official maintenance of consensus but with tensions and conflicts underneath which cannot be discussed openly, then democratic mechanisms are threatened at their roots. The result may be further diffusion of power and this in turn can lead to damage to the mechanisms for accountability.

In Sweden collective action is often undertaken in order to prevent something which might cause future problems. This anticipatory attitude is a main ingredient in the radical/consultative policy style. As described, there are emerging visible contradictions between policy norms and the actual provision of equal education. In the present economic situation, with a huge state budget deficit and severe problems for local authorities to finance their activities, it seems unrealistic to spend large financial resources on the provision of the same education for everybody. Therefore a more 'rational' long-term 'agenda of management strategy' might be to redefine the policy norms. The first indications of slight policy changes of this type were included in policy documents such as the 1988 Bill on the development and governing of schools, in which the Minister of Education states:

> Behind the comparatively extensive regulation of the school system
> lies, among other things, a wish to guarantee an equal standard of
> education all over the nation. According to my view, it is important to
> reach a balance between this need, on the one hand, and on the
> other hand the previously mentioned endeavour for simplification and
> decentralization.
>
> (Proposition, 1988/89:4, p. 6, our translation)

The Swedish tradition of gradual reforms which allows for pragmatic consensus building is illustrated in the following suggestion made by a Social Democratic Minister of Education: 'There should be scope for the individual school to profile itself when it comes to content and ways of working. In order to try different alternatives for proliferation, experiments should be carried out with modifications of the time schedules in the curricula' (*ibid.*, p. 53, our translation).

Brown (1991) argues that one of the key beliefs on which decentralization is based is that 'variability is good'. As egalitarianism lies in the very heart of the old Swedish welfare ideology, redefinitions of this key concept may turn out to be a 'rational' strategy for the future. Our interpretation is that a new type of egalitarianism is emerging. The stress is on 'equally valued' service rather than on 'equal provision'. The reform of upper-secondary schooling has provided the municipalities with greater scope for developing and offering their own distinctive courses and programmes. The present emphasis on freedom of choice in conjunction with the emergence of independent schools is likely to increase differences further. These are steps away from the standardized system which to such a large extent has characterized Swedish education, hence making the old equality norm less relevant. Educational content is clearly going to vary between municipalities in the future.

Previously, the main aim was to facilitate for the less privileged to enter the most prestigious theoretical programmes. Today the emphasis is on curricula and teaching that responds to the diverse tasks and problems of the present society, and on giving theoretical and vocational programmes equal status. It is considered important that students of all high-school programmes have a chance to choose topics which make them eligible for higher education at universities and similar institutions.

The length of practical training programmes has increased so they, just like the theoretical training programmes, last for three years. This makes it easier to update industrial work and argue that vocational education is of the same value as theoretical education. Vocational programmes at upper-secondary level did not result in a dead end for further education previously. Students training to be metal workers or staff nurses still obtained the formal requirements for starting university studies, just by completing their last years of upper-secondary training. The additional year provides more practice in subjects like languages and mathematics, and thus make these students more able to cope with the demands of higher education.

The gradual redefinition of the concept of equality has been facilitated by the reduction of central government control over schooling. For example, a previous abolishment of a national government grant for the financing of chief education officers is likely to have changed these key persons' identification with the system. From previously regarding themselves as representing national policies on local level, they now tend to identify themselves with local interests. Also, the abolishment of the Regional Boards of Education can be interpreted along the same lines. Local authorities and schools will be able to develop much more individual solutions to problems, not necessarily in line with nationally formulated goals.

PRAGMATIC RESPONSES TO THE NEW URBAN MIDDLE CLASS

During the last few years further signs of increasing differences within the Swedish school system have been noted. In particular, major differences seem to emerge between citizens in urban and rural areas. In large municipalities, where there is a numerous and well-educated middle class, voucher systems, support for independent schools and other measures that can increase parental choice are put on the agendas of elected local councils. Smaller local authorities tend to guard the old criteria of egalitarianism, that is, equal provision of primary education (Lidström and Hudson, 1995). The attempts already described to 'legalize' a new type of educational equality thus come as a response to demands by a new middle class and reinforce the already existing ideological cleavages between urban and rural regions.

A tendency towards recentralization has recently appeared as a response to the rural challenges of the ongoing changes towards decentralization and increased flexibility within primary and secondary education. One example is the changing functions of the National Agency of Education. It is now regarded necessary for the agency not only to be concerned with evaluation and support, but also to actually investigate whether rules are complied with and how national policies are implemented locally. These changes reflect attempts to strike a new balance between national and local powers favouring central unitary goals somewhat more, and thereby putting renewed stress on the old commitment to equal delivery of the same education. As we see it, these developments reflect the strong cultural commitment to consensus, in this case between urban and rural areas. However, central–local relationships are only marginally characterized as a tightening of a national grip over primary education. The overall tendency is rapidly changing divisions of labour and responsibility downwards and upwards as well as between different types of authorities (public/political, public/administrative and semi-private). There is a diffusion of power and symbolic policy components have developed (Gustafsson, 1983). The welfare project is clearly in a new phase of development characterized by stronger dependence on the outside world. The debate concerning Sweden's future membership in the European Union reflects these new conditions which can be perceived as pragmatic responses to increased transnational activities and patterns of dependency. There is at present a weakening of incentives for policy-makers to be concerned about whether policy is implementable, and a reduction in agreement on the division of responsibilities between national, regional and local governments for primary and secondary education. This new uncertainty about educational policy content and division of responsibility for its implementation between levels of government and types of authority is not unrelated to the Swedish perception of identity with the larger European community.

Today very few people think that the system of primary and secondary education will prove crucial for social mobility. In our view, there is no way to avoid considerable differences between urban and rural districts with regard to possibilities for choice of education. However, when education is looked upon in a social welfare or quality of life perspective in a broad sense, the norm that prescribes 'equal value' rather than 'equal delivery' might still be acceptable. This future scenario is based upon the pragmatic attitude to change which is typical of Swedish culture as well as upon the historically strong commitment to local self-government (Greenwood, 1979). As we see it, the present attempts to redefine equality of education have a fair chance of success as 'policy instruments' in the establishment of a new balance between different levels of government as well as different ingredients (such as environment, education, labour, health, etc.) in the emerging welfare definitions which take Sweden's new position in the European context into account.

References

Årsbok för Sveriges kommuner 1935. P.A. Norstedt & Söner, Stockholm. (Statistical Report of the municipalities of Sweden 1935).

Årsbok för Sveriges kommuner 1955. Statistical Report, SCB, Stockholm. (Statistical Report of the municipalities of Sweden 1955).

Årsbok för Sveriges kommuner 1993. SCB, Stockholm. (Statistical Report of the municipalities of Sweden 1993).

Berglund, S. and Lindström, U. (1978) *The Scandinavian Party System(s)*. Lund: Studentlitteratur.

Brown, D.J. (1991) 'The recentralization of school districts'. Paper prepared for presentation at the annual meeting of the American Educational Research Association, Chicago.

Childs, M. (1936, 1980) *Sweden: The Middle Way on Trial*. New Haven: Yale University Press.

Einhorn, E.S. and Logue, J. (1989) *Modern Welfare States*. New York: Praeger.

Greenwood, R. (1979) 'Relations between central and local government in Sweden: The control of local government expenditure', *Public Administration* **57**, 457–70.

Gustafsson, G. (1983) 'Symbolic and pseudo policies as responses to diffusion of power', *Policy Sciences*, **15**, 269–87.

Gustafsson, G. (1987) *Decentralisering av politisk makt*. (Decentralization of political power). Stockholm: Carlssons.

Gustafsson, G. and Lidström, A. (1989) *Handlingsutrymme i skolans värld*. (Freedom of action in school life). Skolöverstyrelsen F89:2, Stockholm.

Heckscher, G. (1984) *The Welfare State and Beyond*. Minneapolis: University of Minnesota Press.

Heidenheimer, A.J. (1977) 'Achieving equality through educational expansion. Problems in the Swedish experience'. *Comparative Political Studies*, **10**, 413–32.

Heidenheimer, A.J., Heclo, H. and Adams, C.T. (1983) *Comparative Public Policy*, 2nd edn. London: Macmillan.

Kolam, K. (1987) *Lokala organ i Norden 1968–1986. Från idé till verklighet*. (Neighbourhood councils in the Nordic countries 1968–1986. From idea to reality). Forskningsrapport 1987: 7, Statsvetenskapliga institutionen, Umeå universitet.

Lgr 80 (1980) *Läroplan för grundskolan*. Allmän del. Stockhom: Liber. (National curriculum for the compulsory school).

Lidström, A. (1991) *Discretion – an Art of the Possible*. PhD thesis. Department of Political Science, Umeå University.

Lidström, A. and Hudson, C. (1995) *Skola i förändring. Decentralisering och lokal variation*. (Schooling in Transition. Decentralization and Local Variation). Stockhom: Nerenius & Santérus förlag.

Lindensjö, B. and Lundgren, U.P. (1986) *Politisk styrning och utbildningsreformer*. (Political governing and educational reforms). Stockholm: Liber.

Löfquist, S. (1988) *Resursfördelning efter behov – politik i skolan*. (Resource allocation on need criteria and politics in school). Licentiate dissertation, Statsvetenskapliga institutionen, Umeå universitet.

Marklund, S. (1980) *Skolsverige 1950–1975*, del 1, 1950 års reformbeslut. (Concerning schools in Sweden 1950–1975, part 1. Reform decision of 1950). Stockholm: Liber.

Petersson, O., Westholm, A. and Blomberg, G. (1989) *Medborgarnas makt*. (The power of the citizens). Stockholm: Carlssons.

Proposition 1988/89:154. Om en ny regional statlig förvaltning (Bill on a new regional state administration).

Proposition 1988/89:4. Om skolans utveckling och styrning (Bill on school development and governing).

Proposition 1990/91:18. Om ansvaret för skolan (Bill on the responsibility for school).

Proposition 1991/92:150. Kompletteringspropositionen (Complementary bill on the state budget).

Proposition 1991/92:95. Om valfrihet och fristående skolor (Bill on freedom of choice and independent schools).

Proposition 1992/93:230. Om valfrihet i skolan (Bill on choice in school).

SOU 1974:53 Skolans arbetsmiljö. Allmänna Förlaget, Stockholm. (Royal Commission Report on the conditions on work in school).

SOU 1978:52 Lägg besluten närmare människorna. Liber Förlag, Stockholm. (Royal Commission Report: 'Make decisions nearer citizens').

SOU 1978:65 Skolan. En ändrad arbetsfördelning. Allmänna Förlaget, Stockholm. (Royal Commission Report on changed division of labour in schools).

Chapter 9

Curriculum Implementation and Change

Christine E. Deer

Curriculum change is a complex process. It requires teachers to work out new ways of undertaking their roles as teachers and manage this change while at the same time teaching their regular classes. It is fortunate that in Australia in the mid-1990s there is a more highly qualified teaching profession than ever before. A recent nationwide survey sponsored by the Schools Council of the National Board of Employment, Education and Training, the Australian College of Education, the University of Queensland and the Division of Education, Griffith University (Logan *et al.*, 1990, p. 18), showed that 78 per cent of teachers had completed three or more years of initial certification. Of these, 32 per cent had four or more years, almost 16 per cent had only two years of teacher education, while 5 per cent had one year – a considerable improvement on those figures of a decade ago. This change to a much better-educated teaching profession is exceedingly important as, in the final analysis, it is the quality of the teacher that influences the quality of learning in the classrooms across the nation.

While there is a more highly educated teaching force, there is a growing trend to a more centralized framework of curriculum decision-making by the commonwealth, state and territory governments. This trend is in part a reaction to the patterns that existed in the 1970s and early 1980s when there was an increase in school-based curriculum decision-making in most Australian states, allowing teachers to take account of the needs of students in the particular communities in which their schools were located. However, it is also a reaction to the difficult economic situation in which Australia now exists and the move to gain more value from all Australian enterprises. The vocational values of schooling are being deemed more important by many than the value of a broad and general education base from which later career choices can be made. It is notable that at the federal level there is a Minister for Employment, Education and Training, and recently in New South Wales (NSW) the name of the counterpart has been broadened to give the title Minister for Education, Training and Youth Affairs, with 'training' being a 1993 addition.

At the same time as the centralized framework for curriculum decision-making is being established more firmly, all state and territory governments are decentralizing the operation of their school systems. Head office bureaucracies have been greatly reduced in size, regional offices are being given greatly increased roles. In the most populous state, NSW, staffing in government schools is being decentralized (a move that would have been inconceivable a decade ago).

Within this context, issues of quality, equality and control in curriculum matters are discussed in this chapter. Inevitably, however, the issues tend to overlap when one attempts to discuss curriculum matters. What will become clear, however, is the increasing federal government intervention in education as a result of: 'a general uncertainty about the nation and its future [which] has led us to look closely to the education of the next generation as a key to solving Australia's problems' (Walker, 1993, p. 8).

ISSUES OF QUALITY

How the word 'quality' is interpreted will always be open to discussion as it is a subjective term. Over the last decade there has been much criticism of schools in Australia by the media, by politicians and by those close to schools. In 1984, in an attempt to answer this criticism in an informed way, the Commonwealth Minister for Education appointed the Quality of Education Review Committee (QERC) to examine the effectiveness of government involvement in primary and secondary education with a view to developing more efficient strategies for the use of its funds in school-level education. The committee's report, entitled *Quality of Education in Australia* (Report of the Quality of Education Review Committee, 1985), was published in 1985. In tracing the outcomes of commonwealth government expenditure during the period 1974 to 1984 the Committee stated:

> There is no simple and effective way of measuring the outcomes of particular educational policies and programs or of the schooling process. Assessing the effectiveness of schooling is constrained by such things as the absence of unanimity about what students should achieve, by the lack of effective measures of achievement across the spectrum of objectives which might be pursued and by the difficulty of separating the effects of schooling from the effects of the complex of social processes experienced by learners.
>
> (ibid., p. 25)

The publication of the QERC Report in 1985 did not result in a sudden rush of commonwealth funds to assist the states in their capacity to resource needy school systems. This report is, however, very significant in Australian education as its publication marked the shift in emphasis of government concern with addressing quality through inputs to that of outputs of educational systems. The Whitlam Labor Government, elected in 1972, had established the Disadvantaged Schools Program (DSP) and the Innovations Program as means of improving education across Australia by providing schools and teachers with the funds to improve their curriculum offerings. For the next ten years or so, it was believed that the quality of education would improve if the emphasis was on increasing inputs to education systems. After 1988 the emphasis shifted to outputs, so much so that the new syllabus documents for all Key Learning Areas produced under the auspices of the statutory Board of Studies in NSW must include a statement of desired outcomes. This Board held its first meeting in July 1990 and has responsibility for the curriculum and examinations from kindergarten to the end of senior secondary schooling.

Nevertheless, concerns over the quality of education systems in Australia continue. This concern that systems should be more accountable for the quality of education they provide has encouraged system administrators and researchers in the investigation and development of new ways of reporting education progress: 'Among these innovative approaches has been the emergence of the concept of education indicators as a means of presenting relevant and timely information to a variety of audiences' (Wyatt, 1989, p. 1).

While no education system in Australia has yet implemented a system of indicators, they have been the subject of much discussion. At a conference held in Sydney to discuss performance indicators in education Brathwaite and Low presented a paper entitled 'Determining school effectiveness through performance indicators: Have we got it right?'. They defined an effective school as: 'one which sets performance objectives acceptable to its system and to its community and improves its achievements of these over time' (Braithwate and Low, 1989, p. 117). They went on to outline the issues they considered should guide the introduction of performance indicators. They stated that performance indicators should: 'help schools and teachers improve their performance, provide guidance and management information to systems, provide consumers and the public with indicators of school effectiveness, and guide policy formulation and research' (ibid.).

I believe that it will be in Australia's interest to make much better use of performance indicators in our schools. They can be used constructively to improve the output of Australian schools. If performance indicators are to be used on a widespread basis they must be used wisely. Braithwaite and Low (1989) have provided the necessary guidance so that their implementation will be acceptable to those who work in schools.

In a number of states, mechanisms for quality assurance have been established. In NSW the Department of School Education formed the Quality Assurance Directorate in 1992. Its first reviews of how government schools were providing for community needs took place in 1993. These reviews:

> are concerned directly with student outcomes and school
> development to support their improvement. They focus on the
> effectiveness of a range of structures and processes required for the
> support of student learning, such as management and leadership,
> curriculum, training and development, student welfare,
> communication and community participation within the perspectives
> and parameters of statewide priorities and resources.
>
> (NSW Department of School Education, 1993, p. 1)

Ashenden and Milligan (1993) wrote about six independent schools participating in the National Good Schools Strategy showing how they have attempted to restructure the work and workplaces of both their students and teachers to make them more productive. It can be seen that round the nation there are important efforts to improve the quality of schooling.

At the national level the National Project on the Quality of Teaching and Learning (NPQTL) was formed in 1991 bringing together the Federal Government, government and non-government employers of teachers and the teacher unions. It had three working parties:

1 Work Organization and Related Pedagogical Issues leading to the National Schools Project focusing on how changes in work organization could lead to changes in student learning.

2 National Professional Issues concerned with developing a nationally consistent framework on recognizing teacher qualifications.

3 Professional Preparation and Career Development.

Following the release by the Federal Minister for Employment, Education and Training in January 1993 of *Teaching Counts* (Department of Employment, Education and Training, 1993) the Federal Government announced the provision of A$60 million for teacher professional development over the next three years. At the time of writing (March 1994) these funds were being distributed following submissions from stakeholders across Australia.

A further development at the federal level was the formation in June 1993 of the Australian Teaching Council (ATC) with the expressed aim of giving Australia's 250,000 teachers their own professional body to improve the quality of education. However, as Maling noted:

> Few professions have had their national body established by government rather than by members of the profession. Most other professional bodies elect their own council and determine their own constitution. In the case of the ACT a substantial number of those on the council are government nominees and outside the focus group – school teachers – whose status is to be served by the council.
>
> (Maling, 1994, p. 7)

EQUALITY

In Australia under the constitution, education is a state responsibility. To discharge this responsibility centralized bureaucracies in each of the Australian states were established to organize government schools. This centralization was seen as necessary, as in places away from the capital cities there were insufficient bases to establish and support schools. It was intended to ensure that children in even the far-flung and sparsely populated parts of each state would have access to teachers of similar quality to those available to children living in metropolitan areas. This goal deserves recognition especially when it is considered that the state of Western Australia is about one-third the size of Australia.

However, a study by Turney *et al.* (1980) in rural areas of NSW shows that there was a difference in the quality of teachers in the more favoured parts of the state compared with the more remote areas. The former were better qualified. They found a preponderance of youth and inexperience and a high rate of mobility among country teachers. These findings were confirmed by other studies in Queensland (McGaw *et al.*, 1977) and in Western Australia (Education Department of Western Australia, 1979). Admittedly these studies were completed over ten years ago but there is little reason to expect that there have been dramatic changes.

During the 1970s and early 1980s, in some systems there was a movement away from this centralized approach to curriculum decision-making as bureaucra-

Table 9.1 *Key Areas of Learning Defined in Seven Reports*

Curriculum Development	NSW Primary Schools (1989)*	N.T. (1981)	S.A. (1980)	Tasmania (1980)	Victoria (1988)	W.A. (1984)
Communication	English	Eng/Lang	Language studies	Language	Eng/Lang** LOTE	Language and communication
Social cultural civic	Human society and its env/ment inc. mod. language	Social and cultural	Human society	Social studies	Social education	Social studies
Maths	Maths	Maths	Maths	Maths	Maths	Maths
Science and technology	Science and technology	Science	Science and computer ed.	Science	Science	Science and technology
Health ed.	Pers. devt. Health and phys. ed.	Phys. ed. Health ed.	Health ed. Pers. devil.	Phys. ed. Health ed.	Pers. devt.	Physical and health ed.
Work leisure lifestyle		Life and work skills	Transition education	Life problems	Commerce	Vocational and personal awareness
Arts and crafts	Creative and practical arts	The arts	The arts	The arts	The arts	Practical and creative art
Environmental studies			Environmental studies			
Moral reasoning and action beliefs						
		Computer education			Technology studies	

References:

Report of the Committee of Inquiry into Education in Western Australia, 1984:51.
Metherell, 1989: 16–17.
Ministry of Education (Schools Division), Victoria 1988:7.

* In secondary schools 'science and technology' became two independent Key Learning Areas: 'science' and 'technology and applied studies'. Similarly, 'modern and classical languages' becomes a Key Learning Area.

** Two separate Areas of Learning

cies attempted to respond to the diverse needs of the educational community in the pluralist society of Australia. During these years schools in Victoria, for example, were given the chance to design their own curricula to Year 10. However, over time there has emerged a growing reaction to this freedom, a growing concern that the curriculum has become too diffuse and a belief that freedom of choice by students meant that many missed out what was considered essential learning.

In the last ten years there have been numerous reports concerned with the curriculum and Table 9.1 summarizes seven of these to show how much uniformity there is in regard to the subjects considered essential for school curricula. There is thus an attempt to ensure that all children have access to what is considered knowledge of most worth, at least in its broad outline. In NSW the report *Excellence and Equity: A White Paper on Curriculum Reform in New South Wales Schools* (Metherell, 1989) set out six Key Learning Areas for primary schools and eight for secondary schools.

For example, one of the Key Learning Areas for secondary schools is languages other than English. The identification of this area reflects the growing concern that Australians should have better skills in languages other than English. Until the 1970s, following the curriculum of English schools, French and German were taught as foreign languages in many secondary schools. In the 1970s and early 1980s language studies in schools declined, being perceived as too difficult, and unnecessary as English was spoken by all the people who mattered. However, as a result of post-Second World War migration, Australia has a multicultural community and about one quarter of its 17 million population have parents from a language background other than English. Changes in trade and business relations have led to the revaluing of European languages and the recognition of the importance of Asian languages, particularly Japanese and Chinese (Mandarin). As a result in NSW: 'The study of a language for one year (around 100 hours) will become mandatory for the School Certificate for the 1996 Year 7 cohort students (that is, for the 1999 School Certificate)' (Metherell, 1989, p. 73).

NSW government policy is thus directing or controlling what shall be taught in government secondary schools. It is determining the centralized framework of the curriculum which shall be for all students and passing to the regions and the schools the task of implementation.

The School Certificate is completed at the end of Year 10 in NSW schools when students are aged about 16 years. There are state-wide reference tests for both government and non-government schools students in English, mathematics and science. The remainder of the assessment is completed within the schools. There are also Basic Skills Tests given at ages 7, 11 and 14.

It is important to realize that teachers are responsible for implementing whatever subject-matter government authorities consider should be part of the school curriculum. As outlined at the beginning of this chapter, the Australian teaching profession is better educated than ever before. Nevertheless, in most systems there are schools with complex problems of disadvantage: isolation; recently increased retention rates in the senior secondary years; diverse student populations; and, until recently, a high staff turnover. (With the continuing recession during the 1980s and early 1990s the resignation rate for teachers has fallen to an all-time low.) These schools are disproportionately staffed by teachers with relatively few years' experience. With this background in staffing schools, equality of curriculum provision does not exist.

There are still great difficulties in providing appropriate resources for Aboriginal education, for teaching English as a second language, and for the education of students with special needs whether the physically and/or intellectually handicapped or the very talented. In 1972, at the federal level, when the Whitlam Labor Government came to power and dramatically increased spending for education it set up the DSP and the Innovations Program. In the former, schools with special needs received extra resources while in the latter teachers were able to apply for funds to develop their own innovations to serve the needs of the students in their classrooms. These extra funds were cut in the late 1970s when economic conditions worsened. Later the Participation and Equity Project (PEP) was devised as a means of encouraging students, particularly girls and other disadvantaged members of the population, to stay on at school to complete Year 12. The QERC Report acknowledged the concerns:

> Tensions have been created by these attempts to achieve more diversity among schools. Some parents fear that their children will be disadvantaged by divergences from standard curriculum provisions and that, in deciding what is appropriate for students of a particular school, teachers may provide offerings which limit their students' subsequent options. This concern is evident in public expression of parental dissatisfaction with the decision in a few Victorian secondary schools to cease offering the Year 12 courses generally necessary for university admission. Another concern is that curriculum diversity may make student mobility from system to system, and even from school to school within a system, generally more difficult.
> (Report of the Quality of Education Review Committee, 1985, p. 80)

Retention rates have risen. In 1982 the apparent retention rate to Year 12 (the final year of secondary schooling) was 3 per cent, in 1991 this figure had increased to 71 per cent. The Commonwealth Government is claiming success for its initiatives such as increasing the value of AUSTUDY, a scheme to financially assist needy students to stay at school. The removal of eligibility for the dole for 16- and 17-year-old school-leavers has also been a powerful force.

It can be seen that there have been a number of attempts to improve the quality of education in Australia. The QERC Report was an attempt to address the issue and yet there was no reallocation of resources to achieve its goals. Perhaps there should not be. I think equality is an impossible goal. There are always going to be differences in resources whether human or material.

CONTROL

Already there has been some discussion of attempts to show how control exists in Australian education systems. There have been attempts to make changes in the curriculum and the following definitions provide a base for this discussion. First, 'implementation of programmes' is primarily concerned with teaching and learning. It involves: 'selection and design of learning activities for students;

presentation of those activities for students; involvement of students in the most appropriate way; assessment of individual student success' (Caldwell and Spinks, 1988, p. 141).

Curriculum implementation means the putting into practice of new objectives, or new materials or new content. In making changes to the curriculum, it is obvious that 'change is a process and not an event' (Hall *et al.*, 1973, p. 1) and it is widely recognized that curriculum change is itself a complex social process as Fullan and Stiegelbauer (1991) document. It is therefore important to consider the human face of curriculum implementation and change, the personal matters that affect those who are to change. Bird in an American publication describes well a situation that is just as true of the Australian scene:

> At any time, about half of the persons needed to pursue a solution
> are getting married or divorced, tending a sick or well relative; going
> bankrupt or coming into money; just starting getting ready to leave,
> or near retirement; taking care of babies or putting children through
> college; making up or breaking up; getting sick, getting well, getting
> chronic, or dying. Living can distract prospective adopters of a
> solution and thus frustrate its proponents. Fortunately about half of
> the proponents of the solution are spared the full frustration because
> they too are getting married or divorced or so forth.
>
> (Bird, 1986, pp. 45–6)

These points highlight the individual differences of the human condition. They are the backdrop to people's daily working lives. They can make abrupt changes very much harder to accommodate especially when regular duties must still be fulfilled. In Australia today the teaching profession and the administrators within the various school systems across Australia are being asked to change to a much stronger, centrally devised framework for the curriculum. It is people with these happenings in their daily lives who are charged with the implementation of the enormous changes that are currently being made by governments across Australia in regard to school organization and curriculum.

Centralization of the curriculum decision-making means that those who make these decisions are usually far removed from the day-to-day operations of the classroom (see Deer, 1985). The proponents of centralization argue that with centralization comes more effective use of scarce resources. In contrast, decentralization of curriculum decision-making allows those who have to implement the curriculum at school level, the teachers, to make decisions on what should be in the curriculum. It is argued that motivation is increased in this means of decision-making, that is, behavioural changes are effected and there is curriculum change.

Historically in Australia, curriculum documents have been prepared at the central level in each of the states and distributed to teachers in schools for implementation. Schools in the Australian Capital Territory followed the New South Wales curriculum while those in the Northern Territory followed the South Australian curriculum. The curriculum documents have been prescriptive and a system of inspectors operated in an attempt to ensure that centrally determined policy was implemented.

During the 1970s and early 1980s, beginning in Victoria, teachers in primary and junior secondary schools were given even more responsibility for curriculum decision-making and indeed, in some instances, for determining their own curriculum within the centrally determined guidelines. Teachers met for long hours, often after school, sometimes within school hours where relief teachers could be provided, to devise their own curriculum based on an analysis of the needs of the students in their schools. In metropolitan areas where schools, particularly primary schools, are not far apart, groups of teachers in each school worked on in isolation despite the fact that not far away, another group of teachers was at work on a curriculum for the same subject using the same state-provided guidelines. As teachers still had all their other responsibilities, the development of the curriculum was a slow process. Where there were staff changes some staff felt committed to the new curriculum while others, new to the school, did not. In primary schools where there are few specialist teachers and the class teacher is responsible for teaching all the subject areas, school-based curriculum decision-making was an enormous and wearisome task for many teachers.

The QERC Report summarized the situation as follows:

> The potential avenues for collaboration have become more complex in recent years because schools have increased responsibility for curriculum decisions. This is in part a recognition of increases in the level of education of teachers and in part an expression of the view that accommodate the background and interests of their students. On the other hand not all teachers have the capacity or the desire to assume responsibility for such detailed curriculum development and there is some evidence of a reversal of the trend towards school-based curriculum development.
>
> (Report of the Quality of Education Review Committee, 1985, p. 80)

'Capacity' and 'desire' are the two key words in the last sentence. There was thus a growing recognition by central authorities that the time was ripe for a change in curriculum decision-making.

In 1989, the Australian Education Council (AEC), composed of Ministers of Education from all states and territories and from the commonwealth, issued a document entitled *Common and Agreed National Goals for Schooling in Australia* (Australian Education Council, 1989). This publication represented a move towards greater uniformity of goals across Australia, though as yet there appears to be little grass-roots support for them. It does, however, mark commonwealth intervention in curriculum decision-making. The AEC has also undertaken the task of mapping what is required in each of the school subject areas and the results of this mapping exercise were published in 1993. These maps will form an important base for all future curriculum development in Australia. In December 1993 the AEC held its final meeting and regrouped to combine three ministerial councils – the AEC, the Council of Ministers of Vocational Education, Employment and Training (MOVEET), and the Youth Ministers Council (YMC). The new Ministerial Council of Employment, Education, Training and Youth Affairs (MCEETYA) will co-ordinate strategic policy at the national level, negotiate and develop national agreements on shared objectives and interests in the area of responsibility, negotiate on the scope and formation of national reporting, share information and collaborate in the use of resources towards agreed objectives and priorities as well as co-ordinate communication with, and collaboration between, related national structures (Maling, 1994, p. 6).

It is also intended that in future much curriculum development related to the national profiles will be undertaken by the Curriculum Corporation (CC) of Australia which is based in Melbourne. Nevertheless if, as Kemmis writes: 'It is perceived as imposing curriculum solutions on systems, school communities or teachers, or if its proposals are not regarded as educationally credible and practically feasible, the Curriculum Corporation will generate resistance to its work', (1990, p. 1). However, as education is a state, not a commonwealth responsibility under the Australian constitution, not all states are likely to share in the funding of the Corporation. Nevertheless the establishment of the CC reflects a concern that in a nation of only 17 million people there should be more co-operation across state and territory boundaries in regard to establishing a framework for the curriculum.

Any type of change involves some form of anxiety and loss or 'deskilling'. To try a new approach to teaching means 'letting go' of accustomed ways of operating and trying the unfamiliar. More and more curriculum changes in Australia are coming as a result of government directives. These directives are providing new guidelines within which schools must operate. Ministers of Education in the various states and territories have the *ultimate responsibility* for the curriculum which is implemented through these centrally determined guidelines. Across Australia there are variations in how support for teachers in curriculum change is being organized, but overall the picture is similar.

To support teachers in the changes being introduced by the Victorian Government, Curriculum Frameworks have been issued by the Ministry of Education. They are designed to give teachers, 'a clear direction for the curriculum, drawing on good school practices and current educational research' (Ministry of Education (Schools Division) Victoria, 1988 p. 3).

The School Curriculum and Organisation Framework:

> is concerned with whole school issues involved in the development of curriculum and school organisation. As such it is intended primarily for those who are responsible for planning developing and implementing school policy: school councillors principals and school administrators curriculum coordinators curriculum committees class, unit or year-level coordinators of areas of study program team leaders.
>
> (*ibid.*, p. 6)

This list of people who need assistance in curriculum change highlights the many players in the 'game' of curriculum change and thus the complexity of the whole issue. Missing from it are the students, although any change in the curriculum needs to take account of the way students are advised and involved in curriculum change. Deer and Thompson (1990) discuss the needs of senior secondary students in NSW in the introduction of a new curriculum.

For each of the Areas of Learning Victorian teachers are provided with a Core Document containing a rationale, recommendations for teaching and explanations on how to implement the proposals. These frameworks are thus a recognition by the central authority in Victoria, the Ministry of Education (Schools Division), that teachers need support to make significant and effective curriculum change in an efficient way so that classroom practice changes.

In Queensland, *Education 2000* (Department of Education, Queensland, 1985) has proposed similar system-level guidelines for the preparation, approval and development of curriculum documents for Pre-school to Year 10. In the post-compulsory years a separate central management committee operates with a similar brief.

One of the most significant forms of support for teachers in curriculum change in NSW schools are the professional teacher associations. These are run by the teachers themselves and, aside from regular meetings, have annual conferences and workshops for teachers on particular curriculum issues such as those related to curriculum change. For example, the Primary English Teachers' Association (PETA), has a regular journal and has been of major support to teachers in the introduction of process writing.

These associations are linked in the Joint Council of NSW Professional Teachers' Associations, an umbrella group containing representatives of all the professional associations and recognized by central government and non-government authorities as an important organization. These associations have representatives on all curriculum or syllabus development committees.

CONCLUSION

There is no doubt that curriculum change in Australia is complex, and that teachers need support if it is to take place and they are to move from 'the comfortable cradle of convention' (Rudduck, 1984, p. 66). In the final analysis it is the teacher in the classroom who implements curriculum change and much curriculum change has been cosmetic, that is, the documents show the grand new vision but little has changed in some classrooms. However, more administrators are coming to have a longer-term view of the change process. In NSW at Head Office level for government schools ten-year Corporate Plans are being prepared, as are five-year strategic plans which will be rolled over each year. These plans are being translated to individual school plans which are used in quality assurance reviews. This type of planning is a central recognition of the fact that 'change is a process and not an event' (Hall *et al.*, 1973, p. 1).

Furthermore, MCEETYA and its antecedent body, the AEC, are calling on higher education institutions to develop closer relationships with employing authorities as a means of better initial preparation of teachers and of providing existing teachers with more opportunities for professional development in both short courses and those leading to specific awards up to and including doctorates. Given the changes that are taking place throughout education, this closer partnership has the potential to offer teachers more support in curriculum change and to enable them to gain this support while completing award-bearing courses. As the means of staffing schools change, teachers who successfully complete such courses will find career recognition for their extra studies. In the long term this change will be of enormous value to the children in Australian classrooms and thus to the nation as a whole.

Increasingly, however, there is growing recognition of the importance of workplace learning for teachers evidenced in the publication of *Workplace Learning in the Professional Development of Teachers*. Among its six recommendations are: 'Universities and education systems/schools should give more consideration to processes for the accreditation of teachers' workplace learning; and the concept of the school as an educative workplace/learning community should be made a more explicit feature of restructuring efforts and school reform throughout the nation' (National Board of Employment, Education and Training, 1993, p. ix).

As teachers are the key to change in classroom practices, the final word in this chapter goes to the former Commonwealth Minister for Employment, Education and Training. In a paper entitled *Quality of Teaching: An Issue for All* he wrote:

> Keeping the best teachers in the profession will improve the
> efficiency of learning in our schools. No employer can afford to train
> a workforce at great expense only to lose large numbers of them after
> only five or ten years. By retaining the best teachers and giving them
> clear responsibilities as educational leaders – in schools, in
> classrooms and in curriculum and teacher development – schools will
> be more efficient and more effective in meeting their responsibilities
> to the community.
>
> (Dawkins, 1990, p. 3)

References

Ashenden, D. and Milligan, S. (1993) *Signposts to Restructuring Schools: Opportunities and Directions for School Leaders*. Canberra: National Council of Independent Schools' Association.

Australian Education Council (1989) *Common and Agreed National Goals for Schooling in Australia*. Canberra: Office of the Minister for Employment, Education and Training.

Australian Teachers Union (1990) *Response to Teacher Education in Australia: A Report to the AEC by the Working Party on Teacher Education*. Carlton, Victoria: Australian Teachers Union.

Bird, T. (1986) 'Mutual adaptation and mutual accomplishment: Images of change in a field experiment', in A. Lieberman (ed.) *Rethinking School Improvement: Research, Craft, and Concept*. New York Teachers College: Columbia University.

Braithwaite, J. and Low, B. (1989) 'Determining school effectiveness through performance Indicators: Have we got it right?' *Educational Administration*, **4**, 16–19.

Caldwell, B.J. and Spinks, J.M. (1988) *The Self-Managing School*. London: Falmer Press.

Dawkins, J.S. (1990) *Quality of Teaching: An Issue for All. An Initial Statement*. Queanbeyan: Better Printing Service.

Deer, C.E. (1985) 'Curriculum development', in N.L. Baumgart (ed.) *Education:*

A Map for Introductory Courses. Sydney: Novak.

Deer, C.E. and Thompson, H. (1990) 'Curriculum implementation: Student views an issue for teacher education', *The South Pacific Journal of Teacher Education*, **18** (1), 27–39.

Department of Education, Queensland (1985) *Education 2000, Issues and Options for the Future of Education in Queensland. A Summary of the Discussion Paper*. Brisbane: Department of Education, Queensland.

Department of Employment, Education and Training (1993) *Teaching Counts*. A Ministerial statement by the Honourable K.C. Beazley, Minister for Employment, Education and Training. Australian Government Publishing Service, Canberra.

Education Department of Western Australia (1979) 'Teacher transfers', in C. Turney, K.E. Sinclair and L.G. Cairns, *Isolated Schools: Teaching, Learning and Transition to Work*. Sydney: Sydney University Press in association with Western Region Disadvantaged Country Area Program.

Fullan, M. with Stiegelbauer, S. (1991) *The New Meaning of Educational Change*. New York: Teachers College, Columbia University.

Hall, G.E., Wallace Jr, R.D. and Dossett, W.A. (1973) *A Developmental Conceptualisation of the Adoption Process Within Educational Institutions*. Austin, Texas Research and Development Center for Teacher Education: The University of Texas.

Kemmis, S. (1990) 'The curriculum corporation: Observations and implications', *Occasional Paper 1, Australian Curriculum Studies Association*. Canberra: ACSA.

Laws, K. and Turney, C. (1993) 'The Australian school system', in C. Turney, N. Hatton, K. Laws, R. Philps and R. Teo (eds) *Closing the Gaps: Neglected Knowledge Needs of Beginning Teachers*. St Ives, NSW: Sydmac Press.

Logan, L., Dempster, N., Berkeley, G., Howell, M. and Warry, M. (1990) *Teaching in Australian Schools: A 1989 Profile*. Canberra: Australian College of Education.

Maling, J. (1994) 'Australian College of Education review: 1993 in retrospect', *Unicorn*, **20** (1), 5–14.

Metherell, T. (1989) *Excellence and Equity: A White Paper on Curriculum Reform in New South Wales Schools*. Sydney: NSW Ministry of Education and Youth Affairs.

McGaw, B., Warry, R. S., Varley, P. J. and Alcorn, J. (1977) 'Prospects for school leavers', in *School Leavers: Choice and Opportunities, Poverty and Education Series*, Canberra: Australian Government Publishing Service, cited by Turney, C., Sinclar, K.E. and Carins, L.G. (1979) *Isolated Schools: Teaching Learning and Transition to Work*. Sydney: Sydney University Press in association with Western Region Disadvantaged County Area Program.

Ministry of Education (Schools Division), Victoria (1988) *The Schools Curriculum and Organisation Framework P-12*. Melbourne: Publishing Services,

Statewide Support and Production Centre, Ministry of Education (Schools Division), Victoria.

National Board of Employment, Education and Training (1994) *Workplace Learning in the Professional Development of Teachers*. Commissioned report 24. Canberra: AGPS.

NSW Department of School Education, Quality Assurance Directorate (1993) *Quality Assurance Review Report 1993*. Seven Hills, NSW: Agency Printing.

NT Department of Education (1983) *Northern Territory Schools: Directions for the Eighties*. Darwin: NT Department of Education.

Report of the Committee of Inquiry into Education in Western Australia (1984) *Education in Western Australia*. (Beazley Report). Perth: Government Printer.

Report of the Management Review: New South Wales Education Portfolio (1990) *School-Centred Education: Building a More Responsive State Schools System*. (Scott Report). Marrickville, NSW: Southwood Press.

Report of the Quality of Education Review Committee (1985) *Quality of Education in Australia*. (QERC Report). Canberra: AGPS.

Rudduck J.S. (1984) 'Introducing innovation to pupils', in D. Hopkins and M. J. Wideen (eds) *Alternative Perspectives on School Improvement*. London: Falmer Press.

Turney, C., Sinclair, K.E. and Cairns, L.G. (1979) *Isolated Schools: Teaching Learning and Transition to Work*. Sydney: Sydney University Press in association with the Western Region Disadvantaged Country Area Program.

Walker, J. (1993) 'A focus on policy' in I. Walker (ed.) *Review of Australian Research in Education Number 2 Educational Policy Development and Implementation*. Canberra: Australian Association for Research in Education.

Wyatt, T. (1989) *Indicators, Evaluation and Accountability Mechanisms in Public School Systems*. Sydney: Australian Conference of Directors-General of Education.

Chapter 10

Decentralization and Teachers: Professional Status Cannot be Granted, it Has to be Acquired

Kjell Granström

As a consequence of decentralization aspirations in Sweden, teachers in elementary schools are organized in so-called teams or working units comprising several classes. Pastoral care and special education are both responsibilities of the teaching teams. The working unit is sometimes said to constitute 'a small school' within the large school. Furthermore, teachers are expected to meet regularly to discuss common tasks such as the planning of instruction, especially thematic studies. They are also responsible for developing forms for and the content of democratic co-operation between children and adults in school. The organization of teams (implemented since 1980) is intended to increase the educational decision-making power and responsibility of teachers.

This aspect of decentralization can be seen as resulting from a combination of democratic aspirations and interest in efficiency. One of the crucial matters for management during the 1980s, outside and inside schools, has been to increase efficiency by making more use of the resources of subordinates. Education policymakers have gradually adopted this view.

The reform strategies in Sweden are based on the assumption that many of the decisions which previously have been managed by a centralized rule-directed management system now can be handled by the professional actors themselves. This important change in the Swedish school system also involves a radical simplification of the rules and regulations governing the school. The change was introduced in order to reduce the centralized and rule-directed control of the schools in exchange for a decentralized, goal-directed and professionally governed work.

The allocation of educational resources (e.g. classes, groups and special education) is one example of aspirations towards decentralization. Such measures have, previously, been distributed among different schools by the Regional State Boards of Education. However, as a consequence of decentralization measures these boards were abolished in 1991 and such decisions are nowadays a local affair. The political intentions behind these changes presuppose that working units exist composed of and by teachers with a common responsibility for surveying the educational wants and needs within the working unit and with authority to handle resources and to put their educational plans into action.

As can be inferred from this brief description of decentralization measures in Sweden, there is a trend towards reducing the loneliness and isolation of the single teacher, and entrusting and empowering the teachers and the working units with added responsibility. The teachers are expected to manage – by united efforts – such educational duties as general planning of instruction and planning of special contributions toward pupils with social and learning disabilities. However, as has been shown in a national evaluation concerning the effects of a new national curriculum and of school leader education, this decentralization is making slow progress at the local level (Ahlstrand, 1994; Ekholm *et al.*, 1987). In this chapter I intend to explain the absence of decentralization effects as a consequence of context, that is, as an artefact of the organization, notwithstanding the fact that resistance is also offered by the staff.

The political purpose of shifting central power to local levels also entails a shift from political to professional power. However, this change is by no means an uncomplicated one. The working units, mentioned above, are to be seen as an organizational token of local professional power and responsibility. Although this shift was decided more than ten years ago, the experiences of working units and teacher teams are still not quite satisfactory. A recurring observation is that teacher team meetings take the form of 'make-believe games' and not of genuine teamwork.

Here I shall not go into examples of the inability of the teacher teams to make use of the power they actually have or of their usurping authority they have not yet been granted. This mechanism has been noted and is well known. In this chapter I will concentrate on three plausible and concurrent reasons for this state of affairs.

ROOTS DEEP IN HIERARCHICAL TRADITIONS

The Swedish school system has, like other Western school systems, a bureaucratic and hierarchical tradition. Each separate school usually has its own well-established order of rank for its staff. This, historically, has its roots in the time when education was the sole responsibility of the Church. The clerical pyramid from the holy archbishop to the simple sinner also included the headmasters and teachers. All power flowed from God the Father. In a secularized society this power has been transferred to a civil service trinity (the department, the board of education and the local authority). In hierarchical organizations confidence in individuals is low, the importance of authority, rules and regulations is stressed. Individuals are regarded as being not particularly mature and the organization structure is stable and rigid.

Teachers have a hereditary faith in authority and this faith has developed over several generations. On the other hand, in such systems, managers do not have faith in their subordinates, which may be seen as a logical consequence of the humility among the staff. Certainly these behavioural patterns cannot be eliminated simply by a decision taken in Parliament.

If you talk to teachers and headteachers they will seldom admit they are unequal. They refer to the fact they can talk and laugh together. However, this is more a social veneer and has nothing to do with working conditions and the distribution of work and power. A very important condition of work is the accessibility and control of economic resources. As a matter of fact decentralization of pedagogical matters is not possible without a concurrent decentralization of operative means; this is the crucial point of decentralization. Expecting teacher teams to be responsible for education, pupils' welfare, planning lessons, etc. has nothing to do with the redistribution of power. Teachers have always been responsible for matters of this kind. On the contrary, it is possible that the introduction of teacher teams has meant less autonomy and power for the individual teacher. Considerations and decisions which were formerly the concern of a single teacher now have to be agreed at the teacher team meeting. If, while individual autonomy is decreasing, no power and means are allocated to the working units the teachers will perceive themselves as losers.

In agreement with the hierarchical tradition, the teacher teams are not entrusted with operative resources (for instance money), but in order to satisfy decentralization aspirations they are expected to be responsible for daily pedagogical matters. This is an incompatibility and a very crucial reason why the allocation of responsibility and power among working units is hard to realize. Teachers are not believed capable of handling capital. And teachers sometimes do not feel that they are capable of being responsible for economic resources. It is a reciprocal process that is characteristic of a centralized and hierarchical system. If teacher teams are not in control of operative resources available for their assumed assignments no real changes are to be expected.

The above reasoning may seem to be self-evident. However, to the people involved in a traditionally hierarchical organization this is by no means the case. Distrust of responsibility exercised by subordinates makes its appearance at all levels. Local authorities do not have complete faith in their headteachers, headteachers do not fully credit their teachers and teachers lack confidence in their pupils. Economic control is one distinct mark of that; another indication is a high number of written tests, the strict control of truancy, etc. Much of what James Anderson wrote about the conditions in the 1960s is still applicable to the situation as it is at present:

> Since the determining factor in accomplishment of the goals of the school is the contact between students and teachers in the institutional framework of the school, the main control that the organization has over the action of teachers in the accomplishment of the school's goals is the enforcement of rules concerning teacher behaviour. Thus, the administrator can measure teacher compliance with these norms rather than teacher effectiveness since, unfortunately, for many administrators the two are synonymous.
>
> (Anderson, 1967, p. 136)

It is obvious that hierarchical traditions and values entail a distrust of human beings which could easily jeopardize many decentralization attempts. A crucial point in this context is the control of means and other resources. Decentralization of duties without a coherent decentralization of means will only create suspicion among the subordinates and, if the worst comes to the worst, turn them into eager opponents of attempts at decentralization.

LACK OF PROFESSIONAL KNOWLEDGE

In addition to the means at one's disposal, competence is also an important prerequisite for realizing a decentralized distribution of work. In order to handle problems in your daily work you need knowledge and competence to analyse, examine and formulate hypotheses about these problems.

Teachers often have a sense of belonging to a professional group. However, compared to occupations traditionally considered as professional, such as physicians, lawyers and psychologists, the occupation of teaching is not distinguished by the same distinct characteristics of professionalism (see Gyarmati, 1974; Lortie, 1977). Among other characteristics, professional groups are distinguished by having a common scientific basis for their work. Teachers do not have a distinct professional language and they do not share common theoretical models or theories. Decentralization is often described as a shift of power and responsibility from central political levels to local professional units. This is assuming that a local professional level actually exists. Suppose now that the employees at the local level are deficient in special competence and are lacking a useful language for the new system. In such a case the new duties will be unsatisfactorily carried out or not performed at all.

Compared to many other organizations the school is very hard to manage and perform in. An important difference between schools and, for instance, companies is the character of production goals. In a factory the products are concrete and what is produced can be expressed in specific numbers. In the case of the school, the production goals, as manifested in curricula, are ill-defined both in specification and in extent. Furthermore, the goals are often contradictory. For instance, the pupils are expected to be trained in co-operation while at the same time they are encouraged to compete for grades.

There are a number of poorly defined areas within the school organization. The vague goals are but one example. Another ambiguity is the indistinct professionalism among the teachers. To hold a position as a teacher one does not need to have a certificate or be trained. There is no requirement for a common scientific basis. The only rules governing a teacher are to be found in the Statute Book. However, as regards autonomy, teachers are permitted to design their own teaching without public control. The above criteria (scientific basis, certification, ethical rules and autonomy) have been used to describe professionalism (Collins, 1979; Greenwood, 1957; Lortie, 1975, Parsons, 1964) and the recurrent conclusion is that teachers cannot be considered as entirely professional. Gardner (1985) concluded that much daily practice in schools is in opposition to what research has shown to be useful. This can hardly be considered as a professional attitude among teachers.

The question whether the criteria for professionalism are applicable to teachers or not is of minor importance. What is significant in this case is the vagueness of the goals in the school and the fact that teachers are not trained to construe curricula and other documents concerning goals. Teachers do not share a common scientific language useful for analysing and planning, and for evaluating decentralized and collective working conditions which include accountability for educational goals, pupils' welfare, special education, social and emotional growth, democratic schooling and children's personal development. In a hierarchical

177

system many of these duties have been regulated by directions, rules and forms. The educational goals have been fulfilled by following the instructions in the schoolbooks. Cases of pupils' welfare and special education have been referred to specialists. Personal development has been left to the pupils themselves or to their parents. Democratic schooling has been carried out by the pupil council, etc. The individual teacher has in the main been responsible for his or her own lessons.

The above pattern seems to be recurring in Western society in general. Rosenholtz (1989) found in her study on the teacher's workplace that teachers in what she calls low consensus schools seemed more concerned with their identity than a sense of shared community. McQuillan and Muncey (1994) concluded that making a school's philosophy problematic for its staff tends to disrupt the fragile assumption that shared purposes, values and beliefs underlay the everyday world of the school. Such results can be interpreted as a lack of professional readiness among teachers for organizational and policy changes such as, for instance, decentralization.

Decentralization in the school implies a shift from hierarchical control (rule-directed) to a collective task-oriented (goal-directed) performance. This is something quite new and calls for high degree of competence on the part of teachers, not as teachers but as educationists. Keddie (1984) used this concept as opposed to a traditional teacher context. Usually it is the world of the present in which teachers anticipate interaction with pupils in planning lessons, in which they act in the classroom and in which they usually recount or explain what has happened. This 'presentism' is a hindrance to elaborating theories or models for educational development. Conversely, ideology and theory are enunciated in the educationist context, which may also be called the context of the discussion of school politics. It includes the discussion of educational theory, and here talk of the curriculum often evokes statements about its alignment with or opposition to programmes constructed by, for instance, authors of schoolbooks.

In a centralized, hierarchical school system the teacher approach is adequate. One condition that must be fulfilled in a decentralized, goal-directed school is that the teachers act in a educationistic manner. The need for a comprehensive knowledge base for teachers has still not been met in the Swedish school system. This is evident from a recent study concerning mental models and teacher ethics (Granström, 1992). This study revealed that decision-making concerning students with learning and social disabilities is usually very stereotyped. The concept of the empowered teacher (Corrigan, 1989) has not yet become a reality. As the policymakers and decision authorities seem to be unaware and naïve concerning these important conditions, the administrative reform of decentralization has not been preceded by any expanded training programme. It is unrealistic to expect teachers without essential professional tools to handle complicated and delicate tasks in a school with vague and sometimes contradictory goals. Decentralization of responsibility and means has to be accompanied by enlarged competence and a useful professional language, otherwise the expected increase in the power and potency of teacher teams will turn into powerlessness and a perception of inadequacy among the teachers. However, from 1995 a new national curriculum is valid in Sweden. This document is very concise and offers the individual school a great deal of freedom. Perhaps this can be an instrument to empower teachers in Sweden.

COLLECTIVE REGRESSION

Decentralization in school, including participation in teacher teams, implies co-operation between teachers. Co-operation is by no means uncomplicated and self-evident. The lack of success in the attempts to fulfil co-operative demands is revealed by individual and collective regression in groups. This interpretation may seem a bit too broad to some readers. However, in this context, it is important to be aware of important forces against decentralization and not to neglect any of the circumstances which complicate the process. As mentioned above, one condition that must be fulfilled if decentralization attempts are to be successful is the presence of a local professional level – professional in the sense of competent, mature and responsible employees. Manager distrust of subordinates and of their sense of responsibility has already been discussed, as has the limited competence among teachers. In this section I will concentrate on concepts such as maturity and regression.

The adequate development of professional planning and problem-solving procedures in and by a teacher team pre-demands certain and specific enabling conditions. When group members take part in a common task and co-operate and strive towards a common goal, a rational and work-directed condition is present and dominating. Bion (1961) preferred to call this condition a work group. Several authors (see Granström, 1986; O'Conner, 1971) have described this condition.

The main characteristics of a work group are the following:

1 The members keep the task in sight at all times and can define and redefine the task whenever this is called for.

2 The activity is related to reality and the methods are 'scientific', at least in a general sense.

3 The members meet and act in the common interest of getting a job done and there is a spirit of co-operation in the group. However, the members need not be afraid of losing their individuality.

4 They are willing to refrain from emotional gratification, putting the task first.

5 Thoughts and ideas developed in the work group are directed towards action.

The last characteristic may be seen as very rational and is also often very effective; it is an optimal state for performing professional work. However, this condition, rarely, if ever, exists as such for any length of time in the school.

Rational activity in most teacher teams is unfortunately hampered by other psychic activities, which seem to contain a lot of emotionality. Instead of being rational individuals, members seem to share common but unconscious assumptions or fantasies. These fantasies are often associated with the headteacher, they are highly irrational and will mostly prevent the group from working. Bion considered acting in the work condition as more 'mature behaviour' while the non-work activity is regressive in nature. Bion and his interpreters distinguished four different strategies or behavioural modes jeopardizing rational work. Rice (1976) has a very concise and apposite definition of the conditions determining this special group behaviour. Three of them, recurring in most schools, are:

- *dependency*: to obtain security from one individual;
- *fight*: to attack somebody or something;
- *flight*: to run away from somebody or something.

It should be emphasized that the descriptions are 'as if' terms, which means that a group behaves as if some specific conditions prevailed while the reality is quite different. Every group (teacher team, a committee meeting or a conference), oscillates between a work condition and a non-work level in the course of a session. In arduous, troublesome and anxiety-promoting situations a regressive descent is very likely to occur. The frequency with which the three defence strategies mentioned above appear varies from one organization to another. Of interest in this case is the fact that hierarchical organizations such as the Church and schools are impaired by more dependence behaviour than are more task-directed organizations. A comparison between schools and factories (Granström, 1986) demonstrated a high frequency of dependency in schools, while the companies were characterized by a high degree of rational work, sometimes interrupted by fight activities. In the present study I will concentrate on dependence behaviour as it is expressed in school.

The practice of dependence behaviour has nothing to do with lack of intellectual ability. Every well-educated and gifted individual able to act rationally and logically can be a victim of collective regression. This will occur when, for some reason, the anxiety in the group increases. A plausible reason for anxiety increasing in a group could be vague and contradictory goals. Another factor could be ambiguity and double-bind communication on the part of the managers. For instance, the leader tells the subordinates they are important and responsible while at the same time distrusting them and refusing them economic means. Certainly, it is a frustrating situation when mature and experienced teachers are offered imaginary tasks or tasks impossible to perform. But that is exactly what happens when decentralization is forced upon an unprepared hierarchical organization.

The fundamental base for emotionality in the dependence state is an assumed underlying anxiety, a fear among the members of being absorbed or homogenized by some unknown forces (for instance, the spectre of decentralization). As the group members in this special state are frightened of analysing reality they share a mindless confusion, which is an effective mechanism of defence. The proper aim is to preserve emotional security. The headteacher is often perceived as omnipotent, and the power and influence attributed to him are such that the members abandon their autonomy while at the same time denying any responsibility for their actions. They present a picture of themselves as helpless and dependent. This dependence state works as an effective defensive play against decentralization.

In the dependence phase there is no need for competence or ideas among the members. They become confused by facts and demands. They behave as if their ability to draw conclusions, to imagine and remember, has been lost. The members share a myth of equality; differences in competence, experience and knowledge are not acknowledged, and the resulting emotions are denied. Every attempt to start working is sabotaged, and demands from the leader in this direction are immediately turned down.

When the members in a teacher team enter a dependence phase they lack confidence in themselves, preferring instead to put their faith in structure, procedures and tradition. They show anxiety about sampling and testing new situations and ideas, which in a genuinely decentralized context is something the members have to do. In contrast to a hierarchical tradition teachers must not trust in rules, structure and tradition; they need to have confidence in their own competence, creativity and co-operation. It is evident that this form of group process, frequently recurring in school organizations, constitutes a real hindrance to decentralization which is very hard to master.

Concurrent hindrances

Decentralization attempts in the school system will bring about inconveniences and obstacles on several levels. Any serious attempt to change the balance of power and authority in a system will meet with resistance and opposition. Usually this has been described as a struggle for power where the oppressed people fight for space, freedom and authority. However, this picture is not quite applicable to decentralization in the school. Certainly, decentralization is not unopposed among those in power, politicians and administrators, but in this case teachers will also be opponents of a dislocation of power. In this chapter the last aspect of decentralization has been discussed.

There are several concurrent reasons why teachers are not overjoyed at decentralization. They sometimes perceive themselves as misunderstood but seldom as oppressed. On the contrary, they conceive themselves as autonomous and they appreciate the freedom in their classrooms. Administrative, economic and other managerial matters have, with pleasure, been left to headteachers and the local authority. Many teachers cannot see any immediate and obvious advantages in a more decentralized system. Such a change would entail new duties and these are not wanted in a hierarchical system.

The hindrances to decentralization suggested in this article, that is, the hierarchical tradition in the school, the lack of professional knowledge among teachers and the inclination to collective regression, will guarantee that the established order of formal relationships, rewards and controls is maintained in spite of political ambitions.

The professional status of teachers has a crucial role in decentralization. Without knowledge and theories regarding organizational structure, power distribution, planning strategies, etc., and without a language useful for discussing aims, goals and teaching strategies, teachers will be victims of hierarchical thinking and collective regression. They will be easily caught lambs for the sacrificial altar of the Establishment. Not until the teachers have collectively acquired the requisite tools will they be able to carry the hierarchy's position. Professional language, concepts, theories and knowledge are indispensable weapons in this struggle. Competence and professional status cannot be granted, they have to be acquired.

References

Ahlstrand, E. (1994) 'Professional isolation and imposed collaboration in teachers' work', in I. Carlgren, G. Handal, G. Vaage and S. Vaage (eds) *Teachers' Minds and Actions – Research on Teachers' Thinking and Practice*. London: Falmer Press.

Anderson, J. (1967) 'The authority structure of the school: System of social exchange', *Educational Administration Quarterly*, **3**, 136.

Bion, W.R. (1961) *Experiences in Groups*. New York: Basic Books.

Collins, R. (1979) *The Credential Society. A Historical Sociology of Education and Stratification*. New York: Academic Press.

Corrigan, D. (1989) 'The context of teacher education: An American profile'. Paper presented at 10th World Congress Association for Educational Research, August, Charles University, Prague.

Ekholm, M., Fransson, A. and Lander, R. (1987) *Skolreform och lokalt gensvar*. (School reforms and local responses). Publication from the Department of Education. Gothenburg University.

Gardner, H. (1985) *The Mind's New Science. A History of the Cognitive Revolution*. New York: Basic Books.

Granström, K. (1986) *Dynamics in Meetings. On Leadership and Followership in Ordinary Meetings in Different Organizations*. Linköping: Communication Studies, Linköping University.

Granström, K. (1992) 'Professional language and teacher ethics'. Paper presented at the 1992 AERA Annual Meeting, San Francisco. California.

Greenwood, E. (1957) 'Attributes of a profession', in N. Gilbert and H. Specht (eds) *The Emergence of Social Welfare and Social Work*. Illinois: Peacock Publishers Inc.

Gyarmati, G. (1974) 'Ideologies, roles and aspirations', *International Journal of Sociological Science*, **28**, 1.

Keddie, N. (1984) 'Classroom knowledge', in A. Hargreaves and P. Woods (eds) *Classrooms and Staffrooms. The Sociology of Teachers and Teaching*. Milton Keynes: Open University Press.

Lortie, D. (1977) *Schoolteachers. A Sociological Study*. Chicago: The University of Chicago Press.

McQuillan, P. and Muncey, D.E. (1994) 'Change takes time: A look at the growth and development of coalition of essential schools', *Journal of Curriculum Studies*, **26**, 265–79.

O'Connor, G. (1971) 'The Tavistock method of group study', *Science and Psychoanalysis*, **18**, 100–15.

Parsons, T. (1964) *Professions. International Encyclopedia of Social Science*. No. 12.

Rice, A.K. (1976) 'Individual, group and intergroup processes', in E.J. Miller (ed.) *Task and Organization*. London: John Wiley & Sons.

Rosenholtz, S.J. (1989) *Teachers' Workplace. The Social Organization of Schools*. New York: Longman.

Chapter 11

Secondary Headteachers' Perspectives on Locally Managed Schools

Hywel Thomas

INTRODUCTION

Headteachers have a pivotal influence on the quality and nature of educational opportunities for children in schools in England and Wales, an influence which is probably greater following recent legislation. Despite the centralizing of curriculum control and the consequent diminution of teacher influence, we should not lightly ignore the place of headteachers as managers of the teaching and support staff and its consequence for the quality of the curriculum in practice. Moreover, because implementing the National Curriculum is a statutory duty for headteachers, it may make them more involved than hitherto in monitoring and managing their school's curriculum. Management powers at the level of the school have been enhanced by delegating to headteachers and school governors much greater control over financial and other resources than has typically been the case. This delegation has occurred, however, through regulations which create a quasi-educational voucher system where the jobs of teachers and support staff depend upon levels of pupil enrolment. The consequence is pressure to compete with other schools for pupils. How headteachers respond to these pressures will shape the extent and nature of competition between schools, circumstances which raise concerns about the quality of educational opportunities for pupils in those schools, especially, which fail in this competitive environment.

How headteachers are interpreting and responding to this changed environment is, therefore, a matter of considerable importance. The views of one group of headteachers may be of particular interest for early identification of the direction of change. The experience of managing the school's financial budget predates local management of schools (LMS) in a small number of Local Education Authorities (LEAs) in England and Wales and this section draws upon interviews conducted with six headteachers in an LEA which had operated local financial management (LFM). All six were in secondary schools with full local management responsibilities and were interviewed in the autumn and spring of 1990 and 1991. Each was familiar with managing a budget and, for them, the introduction of LMS did not also mean becoming familiar with budgets and financial information systems; they were free of the administrative clutter associated with this innovation and more able to focus upon the strategic impact of LMS compared with LFM.

In outlining the purpose of each interview, it was explained that the intention was to explore each interviewee's view of the difference between LFM and LMS and, then, how relationships with other interests in the service and the community were altering. A later question invited the heads to comment upon the effect on their role of the introduction of the National Curriculum. Each interview lasted one hour or more, all were tape-recorded and then fully transcribed.

FROM HISTORICAL TO FORMULA FUNDING

LMS has meant the introduction of public and explicit rules for funding schools with most of the money dependent upon the numbers and ages of the children. Since the earlier LFM scheme in the LEA was based substantially upon the principle of historical funding, LMS meant new funding arrangements. Mrs Duke at Southbridge School and Mr Bishop at Fourgates School suggested that the new rules gave schools more freedom. Under historical funding, Mrs Duke was aware of 'a hidden agenda of what ought to be spent on various matters. Now it is a much cleaner slate and, although there haven't been tremendous variations in what one could have done before, there is a greater capacity for there to be if the need arises'. Mr Bishop also commented on the limited use of earlier freedoms, suggesting that LMS gave 'a lot more freedom of action than we formerly had', a change he also saw as creating a greater obligation 'to plan more effectively'.

Comments on the impact of the formula at Langford School and High Crest School were affected by the budget deficits which arose from the change. Both schools had substantial reserves, ranging from £90,000 to £200,000, in one case built up partly in anticipation of the change to a formula. Neither school used up these reserves to cover the immediate deficit and both reduced their teaching complement as part of the process of adjusting to their new circumstances. At High Crest, Mr Adlington viewed a budget surplus accumulated over six years as something 'we were not going to wipe out . . . though we always had a fall-back position. If we couldn't quite achieve the staffing target, we knew we could support one or two extra teachers'. Since this target was achieved some of the surplus was spent on improving facilities, notably £20,000 for the flooring of a sports' hall and £10,000 for IT enhancement. At Langford the reserve is to be used as a buffer to cover the worse period of declining numbers. It does not cover the full deficit and teachers were made redundant in 1990, an issue to which I will return.

Redundancies at Langford are a stark reminder that LMS requires schools to work within cash-limited budgets. Since local management also delegates powers for making staff appointments and dismissals, there is no way the employing local authority can require a school to take staff surplus to requirements at another; redeployment of those staff is replaced by redundancy. The change puts a premium on revenue enhancement.

INCREASING THE BUDGET

Increasing enrolment is the most effective way of adding to the budget. An over-subscribed High Crest School increased its admissions figure by 30 children for September 1990 in order to reduce the anticipated budget deficit. It was a change in standard number 'which took the governors all of 30 seconds to agree to. The

LEA were even quicker because they did not then have the problem of re-allocating all those kids'. When a neighbouring school closed, Mr Carrington at Langford 'went straight into the area, like a ton of bricks, to get those children to come to this school'. He faced competition. 'I found I wasn't fighting for the full market and half the market had already been taken, and that fight is continuing.' His account of this struggle for enrolment included the loan of facilities to local primary schools, publicity and invitations to school events. These are examples of marketing, accounts of which arose in every interview.

Mention was made of expenditure on producing more lavish brochures. At Fourgates, Mr Bishop referred to 'a much more up-market brochure . . . a glossy' and, at Crossfield, a new brochure was produced costing £6,000: 'a super new school brochure but, then, I think if it brings in ten, it's paid for anyway'. At Langford, Mr Carrington referred to booklets and a brochure costing £2,000. He also described the use of school concerts as a means of attracting children from the local junior school and meeting the costs of hiring buses to bring the children to the concert.

Mrs Church, at Meadow School, drew attention to discussion and disagreement over spending about £5,000 on the preparation of a 'more lavish school brochure to get more pupils into the school'. The issue led to a difference of view between the staff's finance committee and that of the governors, 'and there was strong feeling from at least one governor, a parent governor, that wherever possible all funding ought to be going towards pupil education in the narrow sense. Not on the environmental expenditure for example, and so on. It should be going on books and equipment at a time when people are saying there are not enough resources for schools'. This governor was swayed by the argument that five additional pupils would pay for the expenditure. The headteacher's own comments also reveal the positive aspect of 'marketing' as a means of improving positive communication:

> Yes, I thought there should be a brochure. I thought that. I have
> ambivalent views about marketing, perhaps the luxury of having
> ambivalent views simply because I haven't yet been a head of a
> school that has been under real threat as far as finance and numbers
> go. Time will tell. I do believe wholeheartedly in promoting the
> school in the community and, knowing the funding of the school at
> that stage, I thought that ... money being allocated to producing
> something attractive that told the community, potential parents,
> visitors to the school about the range of things that the school did
> well, involving all sorts of pupils, was probably money well spent.
>
> (Church, Meadow School)

The dual purpose of marketing was reflected also in the comments of Mrs Duke at Southbridge. She argued that 'it's an LMS issue in that we have become more and more aware of the need to promote the school' but was 'not terribly keen on the word marketing as such. I think it is much more promoting the positive values of the school and identifying what is good'. At Southbridge, this included reviewing relationships with the community, including local industry and feeder schools. It has also included looking at the decoration of the building and the quality of the school environment, as well as planning a new publication for parents in addition to the official handbook. Her approach rejected marketing if it meant 'amending a product and being very cut-throat with people in the area' but she took a much more positive view of marketing if it was concerned with communicating and educating:

> I think it is all right to amend a product if it is wrong but, I think at the end of the day, you have got to be quite certain of what your values are as a school and not amend those because of people out there. At a simplistic level, I think there are some people who don't send children to Southbridge because we don't have a blazer; well frankly, I would rather they went elsewhere. It is cavalier of me but I think that, then, you have got to have the role of educating parents ... marketing what you are doing, what you believe in.
>
> (Duke, Southbridge School)

Linked to the various facets of marketing are relationships with industry and community, interests which also provide means by which schools can increase their budgets. Lettings, cash grants, support-in-kind from local employers were all mentioned as means by which schools tried to improve their basic budgets. Compared with the LEA budget and the effect of increased admissions, however, none were significant amounts. How intense competition for pupils will become will be shaped by the relationships between headteachers and mediated through the role and attitudes of other key interests, including the school staff, the governing body and the LEA.

EMERGENT RELATIONSHIPS

A View of the School Staff

Several headteachers mentioned different facets of the insecurity of their teacher colleagues as they became more aware of the nature of LMS. The awareness of the link between pupil enrolment, the size of the budget and the availability of jobs seemed well understood: 'I think that what the staff have realized much more is that their position, what they do, depends on the children coming through the gate' (Mrs Duke). This understanding of local management affected perceptions of relationships with other staff, as in Mr Bishop's comment that 'every member of staff now feels either an active or passive part of the team, and the need to promote the school in a proactive way in and outside the classroom'. This was having an effect upon the internal organization of the school and its planning processes, as well as the external promotion of the school and school events. Internal changes mentioned in several schools included greater emphasis on annual planning by departments and processes of departmental reviews; these heads had increasing expectations about the management role of the head of department with respect to their curriculum and staff leadership responsibilities but also included more discretion over a part of the budget. The previous experience of LFM meant that there was little evidence of change in arrangements for consulting with staff over school finance, although heads at two schools – Crossfield and High Crest – indicated that their staff finance committees did not function.

Comments by Mrs Church highlighted changes in staff perceptions about the role of the governors: 'I think that staff were increasingly sensitive about the powers of governors as far as appointment and dismissal ... there were some feelings of insecurity and wondering, questioning whether the governors would be sensitive to their position in the school.'

Mr Carrington, memories still fresh from the redundancy process, reflected on changes in staff perceptions of the headteacher, linking his comments to early training on LMS in 1988:

> I remember way back in the training days, when the course leader stood up and said 'The greatest effects will be the fact of separating your senior staff from all of the other staff'. I remember taking him up on the point and saying I didn't believe it, but that has certainly occurred, there's no doubt about that, there's very much a feeling of 'Us and Them'.
>
> (Carrington, Langford School)

He then illustrated his point with an account of the process by which staff had agreed to an increase in the teaching week and his use of powers over the budget to give an undertaking that, if they agreed to the change, further redundancies would not be made in the current year. Others gave accounts of using the governing body's discretion over salaries to restructure staffing and to introduce honoraria for jobs.

Emerging from these accounts is a contemporary restatement of teacher-headteacher relationships which reflect that long-standing tension characterized by Hughes (1973) between the head as 'leading professional', seeking involvement and commitment from colleagues through the peer ethos of the co-working professional, and the 'chief executive' exercising management responsibilities through a hierarchy which makes the head the super-ordinate role holder in the school. What LMS does is alter the formal balance between those two aspects of the role by enhancing those powers which reside with the chief executive. Ironically, this occurs when professional development work nationally – see, for example, the position of the Secretary of State's School Management Task Force (DES, 1990) – is giving more emphasis to the need for headteachers to secure greater professional-like involvement in shaping the policies and purposes of the school.

What involvement the LEA will have as an influence upon this changed environment will partly depend upon the nature of emerging relationships between headteachers and LEA officers and advisers.

Governors and the Governing Body

The six heads spoke rather differently of their relationships with their governors and the roles they played within the school, whether as individuals or as a corporate body.

Some accounts, as in Fourgates, Meadow and Southbridge, show governors contributing as a collectivity, through committees and working groups of one kind of another. The three heads took the view that governor involvement in policy-making was likely to increase and also saw this as having more benefits than disadvantages. This expectation was described by Mrs Duke:

I think at first they didn't quite grasp all the implications of the powers and responsibilities they had, but I think more and more they are becoming more aware of their role and, I think, more slowly seeing from that the influence that they can have on items of school policy: that's when they are prioritizing.

(Duke, Southbridge School)

At the other three schools, the headteacher accounts suggest a more passive governing body. At Crossfield, the governing body's finance committee had 'been very disappointing in turn-out' and budget reports to the full governing body little more than formal reports. Some concern was expressed about governor involvement and, after the failure of a recent initiative to increase involvement, the problem is 'on ice at the moment'. At Langford, Mr Carrington remarked that 'the financial page at the governor's meeting is usually covered over in a few minutes because they can't understand it'. Yet, both heads referred very positively to the contributions of individual governors who, they suggested, had made significant contributions to the life of the schools, not least through their advice on management decisions.

The role of the governing body at High Crest is less clear. While much of Mr Adlington's account suggests a relatively passive governing body ready to take advice, his comments about the size of the school's contingency reserve suggested a degree of caution about spending which may have had its origins with the governing body.

Reflecting upon the comments of these six heads suggests that it may be helpful to distinguish those schools where governors principally contribute as individuals from those where, in addition to the role of the governor as an individual adviser, governors act as a corporate body – through committees and otherwise – when contributing to the decision process. Of course, there may also be schools were there is no effective contribution by governors as individuals or as a body. From each of these circumstances it would be possible to learn more about the processes by which governing bodies might effectively discharge their statutory responsibilities.

Research into how governors discharge their responsibilities would also illuminate the relationship between the governing body and its headteacher. Mrs Church and Mrs Duke commented upon their pivotal role in shaping the involvement of governors in the school and their relationship with staff. Speaking of governors Mrs Duke remarked:

Mrs Duke: I think heads have got to be much more political with a small 'p' than ever they were.

HT: With governors?

Mrs Duke: Yes, and with staff, with everyone.

HT: What do you mean by that?

Mrs Duke: Well, I think that I am really thinking that one has to analyse much more the means of working, discussion and decision-making than, perhaps, used to be the case.

HT: Why do you think that it's more important?

Mrs Duke: Well, because I think, probably, the power base of involvement has widened.

Mrs Church developed her views on the changing perceptions of staff about the governing body into an analysis of its implications for the head:

> The more I think of it really, the more I think that the head's role is absolutely critical in representing the school's needs, the staff's needs, describing the staff's feelings of insecurity to the governors so that they will appreciate that . . . the head really has got to be that funnel of advice and information and feelings, and so on, between the two.
>
> (Church, Meadow School)

The head often also acts as the funnel through which perceptions of the role of the LEA are received by others in the school. What view did these headteachers have of the role of LEA officers and inspectors?

LEA Officers and Inspectors

Typically, a distinction was drawn between the views of the heads about the officers of the LEA as compared with its inspectors. Great enthusiasm was evinced by some about the role of the inspectorate. Mr Enfield's comments reflect this position:

> Certainly, the relations with the inspectors have never been as good as they are now. If you talk about value for money, that is where schools are getting value for money, I think. They are also a very intelligent lot and David Walcott (Chief Inspector) is a very astute cookie, who knows damn well that they have to make an impact on the school.
>
> (Enfield, Crossfield School)

Mr Carrington also singled out David Walcott as a person who had done a great deal to develop the inspectorate, helping to maintain good relationships with the heads, undertaking full inspections and stimulating fresh thinking. The relationship was not soft or cosy but 'they are fair and they are approachable and you can ask for help and they will give you help'. Based upon past experience and a continuing dialogue, Mrs Church expected 'a good working relationship in the future', one which would cope with the greater emphasis upon monitoring the National Curriculum. Mrs Duke also anticipated continuing good working relations with the inspectorate.

Mr Bishop, at Fourgate School, gave an account of changes over the previous four years in the relationships between schools and inspectors. He suggested that there was less emphasis on direction and more on negotiating a school's participation in, for example, an innovation in approaches to teaching and learning. Only Mr Adlington added some cautionary remarks to his otherwise positive account, detecting an 'edginess' among the inspectors: 'When we have conferences, they always feel that they have got to be coming up with answers to problems, even if they know in their hearts there is not a simple answer'. He attributed this to a concern to assist the teachers, although he was anxious that the edginess might be translated into anxiety in the schools. Edginess among inspectors might not unreasonably also arise, of course, because of uncertainty about the role of the LEA and their place within that.

If officers were also to exhibit edginess, the views from these heads suggest it would not be wholly misplaced. From one of the heads came a comment about the need 'for a lot of pruning to be done', another indicated that 'their role really seems more peripheral than it did' and a third said there was 'some cynicism in schools because the LEA doesn't seem to be getting any smaller'. Set against this was the recognition by a fourth that setting up LMS would have cost a lot and that 'the LEA has had to work a lot harder because they have had their training problems, they have had to transfer a lot of their expertise to schools'. What also emerged, however, were more specific comments about some officers, notably those who, according to several of the heads, had failed to understand the shift in power to the school from the LEA. Some 'have found it very difficult to accept the fact that a lot of power that they once held has gone; and we still get the occasional officer trying to pull rank against the little things they can't do any more'. By comparison there were positive comments about others and, most commonly, the group of officers and less senior staff responsible for implementing LMS.

The shift of responsibilities to the schools brought about by LMS, together with statements from the DES that too many LEAs are retaining too many resources at the centre has created a context where the scale and effectiveness of central resources are likely to be questioned. The statements of these heads suggest a value-for-money attitude to these services. Their comments about the inspectorate showed a good deal of satisfaction with the service, no one suggesting that the funding for inspectors be delegated to schools. By contrast, the dissatisfaction with some of the officers led to comments about the level of resources at the centre and the wish for a more streamlined centre: 'I certainly think there will come pressure sooner or later, sooner from my point of view, pressure on the centre to really become streamlined and really serve the needs of the schools quite specifically and quite directly'; and, from another: 'I think that's where the next big cuts are coming – in office staff'.

Parental Involvement

Awareness among the headteachers of the greater potential significance of parental choice as a result of the 1988 Act is exemplified in the attention being given to marketing. However, when the six heads were asked directly about changes in relationships with parents, there was less evidence of immediate change and rather greater expectation of changes to come.

Mr Enfield's comments illustrate the limited extent of change in direct parental involvement. His remarks on voluntary financial contributions and on religious education showed little obvious change in the parent role. Only on reporting procedure was there notable change and this seemed to arise from the school's own anticipation that recent reforms required the school to review its arrangements:

> it has altered our thoughts on our reporting procedures, certainly,
> and it's tied in very much with the Records of Achievement that we
> have for the youngsters. I don't think there is any other topic that we
> have devoted so much staff INSET and discussion time, as the
> changes we have had over the last two or three years over reporting

to parents. . . . And it is interesting that we have not been satisfied
with any of the results and neither have the parents . . . probably
because we went over the top on pupil assessment; parents want to
know what teachers say, not what their own kids say.

(Enfield, Crossfield School)

At Southbridge, Mrs Duke also referred to reporting as an important area. It
was reasonable that parents receive information on national curriculum assessment but there was some concern that whole-school assessment be given a
context. In any event, schools should ensure that the published data were properly explained and that there was a job to do, 'being prepared to speak up and to
educate and make statements about that'.

At Meadow School, Mrs Church cited greater interest in the school's budget
at the annual meeting, parents beginning to question it much more carefully than
in the past. She also mentioned two formal requests from parents for access to
the schemes of work in all the subjects their children were following. While recognizing that these were only two requests from 1,000 children, she did feel that
there would be a greater demand 'as parents realize their rights under the Act and
under LMS'. This is an area which, among others, is likely to affect the headteacher's role in relation to the school's curriculum. This interrelationship
between curriculum and LMS and the impact of statutory duties with respect to
the National Curriculum was a reason for inviting the heads to comment on the
impact of the National Curriculum on their role.

MANAGING THE NATIONAL CURRICULUM

There were some sharp differences of view about the impact of the National
Curriculum upon their individual roles. At Fourgates, Mr Bishop felt he now had
a greater awareness than in the past of the school's actual transaction of the
curriculum. He now saw himself more as managing the curriculum:

Formerly I did expect departments to perform efficiently and the
alarm bells did not go off unless the results were poor, which is,
perhaps, a retrospective way of planning curriculum. If I had a bad
crop of examination results or a queue of parents coming in to see
about such and such a teacher or subject, then I tended to deal with
things. That's not the way it should have been but there was an
element of that. Now I have to ensure that the parts are put into play
systematically . . .

This process of implementation meant that there was much more information on
schemes of work, more attention to cross-curricular co-ordination than hitherto.

Mr Adlington at High Crest also claimed a greater awareness of the practice
of the curriculum in the school. He was more aware of needs in different subject
departments and with respect to cross-curricular issues. His reflections included
comments on the effectiveness of some of his heads of department:

I have got a much better grasp of what the weaknesses actually are. I
didn't realize how bad they were, until national curriculum planning
forced me, in a way, to send in the cavalry; to do simple things like

manage meetings, co-ordinate, to see that targets were actually
specified and achieved.

(Adlington, High Crest School)

Two deputy headteachers were playing a leading role in supporting two departments in this process of change. Elsewhere, he described the changing role of
some of his senior pastoral staff:

For instance, my head of lower school, who previously had adopted a
purely pastoral focus – and done it very well – has now altered the
job descriptions and focus of her heads of year who, in turn, have
done the same with tutors, so that [they are] working to monitor the
limitations of National Curriculum Key Stage 3 in maths, science and
technology, and English.

(*ibid.*)

At Meadow School and at Southbridge, the heads did not see the National
Curriculum as having had a major impact upon their knowledge of the curriculum,
each indicating that they were fairly well informed about the practice of the
curriculum in their school. None the less, the implementation process had made
them better informed. The information 'didn't come as a real road to Damascus
job when I read it, but it gave me a bit more precise information as a planning
tool' (Mrs Duke). This included, for example, a review of careers education which
raised concern both about the negligible amount of work in National Curriculum
Years 7–9 and about the understanding of the concept of careers education in
some of the work being done. It was also Mrs Duke who remarked that 'the
National Curriculum has frightened me by its subject emphasis and I really see it
[the school's curriculum] as being a collaborative effort of a school'. There had
been a major effort to shape the National Curriculum's proposals to the school's
conception of its own ten teaching areas.

At Meadow, the head claimed the changes were requiring the teaching staff
to clarify:

very precisely what they were teaching. Now, I'm sure they would
seize me by the throat if they heard me say that, but I think there is
some truth in it and, certainly, . . . there would be quite substantial
amounts of work to be done on specifying what pupils should know,
what skills they should develop and so on.

(Church, Meadow School)

At Crossfield, Mr Enfield's account was also of a head who stressed familiar-
ity with the development and the practice of the curriculum, a lengthy account
explaining the review of the curriculum which he had implemented on becoming
head and which made the school well placed to adjust to the requirements of the
National Curriculum. Annual reports from heads of department and annual department discussions with these heads of department, curriculum-mapping exercises,
all combined to provide information on the school's curriculum.

Much less extensive was the account from Mr Carrington at Langford School
who, none the less, made an interesting distinction in the capacity of different
departments to engage in evaluating and recording their implementation of

programmes of study: 'Maths and science find it easier because they are quite used to building blocks, they quite like going from A to B to C to D, but English doesn't: it likes to weave around and go sideways and miss out a thing. They're finding it difficult, therefore, to evaluate and record'. He also noted the virtue of having local management as a tool which allowed him to give additional resources to those departments which were leading the implementation of the National Curriculum, a combination of industrial sponsorship, central funding and the school's budget allowing him to give £41,000 to technology in the current year. It is an example which highlights the positive dimension of the opportunities afforded by local management for the provision and process of the curriculum. What is more important, however, is whether this typifies the overall outcomes of reform for the curriculum opportunities of all children.

CONCLUSION: A NEW ACCOUNTABILITY?

I have argued elsewhere that the 1988 Education Reform Act assumes a greater coherence if we recognize that one of its principal purposes was to challenge the 'producer interest', reducing the influence of professional educators in decisions about education purposes, provision, processes:

> By centralizing control over some aspects of policy, such as for the school curriculum, the reforms attempt to reduce the control of professional educators in this area. By decentralizing control over human and physical resources to governing bodies of schools and colleges the reforms reduce the power of education administrators in local government and require headteachers and principals to work more closely with governors. Moreover, because the particular form of decentralization selected introduces more competition – allowing parents, pupils and students more choice over school places – the power of the client is enhanced in relation to that of the producer.
> (Thomas, 1992, p. 3)

What do these accounts tell us about the immediate impact of these new forms of accountability on secondary schools in England and Wales? Clearly, given the small number of interviews, at best they provide us with some clues, possible intimations of what the future may look like. These intimations do suggest, however, that the greater accountability required through a statutory national curriculum and the accountability-through-competition of LMS is already shaping the response of schools and the work of headteachers.

According to the accounts of the headteachers in these six schools, teachers are being held to account by their headteachers for the ways in which they discharge their curriculum responsibility. Several spoke of more time spent in reviewing departments and schemes of work, 'sending in the cavalry' and, if needed, making three teachers redundant while appointing another to meet the curriculum requirements of the school. In this last school there was an explicit recognition of the 'Us and Them' effect of the need to increase hierarchical control over the teaching staff. What we do not know is whether this relationship will become more typical. It is possible that the need to plan together, as described at Fourgates, may create a stronger sense of community and of collaboration which offsets the increased formal power of the headteacher and of the governing body to which she or he is the leading professional adviser.

Despite the increased statutory powers of the governing body, it is not evident that the governing bodies of these schools are, as yet, providing a major route of external accountability. In these accounts they are, at best, still coming to terms with their new roles and responsibilities. In three schools there are signs of heads taking a positive view of governing bodies actively discharging their duties. In the other three schools there is no coherent account of governors acting as a corporate body influencing the school. We know too little about the capacity of heads to act as gatekeepers regulating the access of governors to real involvement in the government of the school but we might be wise not to underestimate their potential significance in that role.

Heads may also be pivotal in shaping relationships with LEA officers and inspectors. The monitoring role of the inspectorate was recognized in these interviews and, in this respect, they represent a formal process of accountability. More prevalent in the accounts of the LEA, however, was of a new relationship which placed schools, and their needs, at the centre. The local inspectorate were highly valued in this respect but, by comparison, there was more scepticism about the role of some officers and questions about the scale of resources at the centre. Here the focus of accountability changes, much as the authors of the legislation might desire, the heads evaluating the quality of service provided and believing that they should have more opportunity to control resources, selecting those central resources they wish to use. This might be expected as a result of reforms which also introduce accountability-through-competition and the attention given to marketing is evidence of the impact of this form of accountability. Indeed, parents occur in these accounts principally as agents of school choice and it is this issue of competition which leads to questions about the relationship between the schools making up the local system. What views did these headteachers have of relationships between themselves and their schools?

While there was no direct question about these relationships it was raised by several. At High Crest, Mr Adlington was quite dispassionate in his assessment of the consequences for two competing schools of increasing his own school's standard number and wondered whether he might be able to strengthen its enrolment at the expense of others by developing its community role. There was little obvious concern at the prospect of a school closure brought about by the pressures of competition. At Fourgates, Mr Bishop outlined an underlying wariness in relationships: 'They are a pretty gentlemanly and ladylike lot, but I can't help feeling that there is a subterranean desire to sort of carve the breast and eat the largest part of the turkey but nothing is ever said collectively about it', and, after an account of their own work with feeder schools, he went on:

> We don't advertise the school in a vulgar fashion . . . but there are one or two schools that might go a bit over the top. I am aware of one school that has put a thing up in the Library, so I understand (I have not seen it myself), which says that 'such and such' school, a school of excellence . . .

(Bishop, Fourgate School)

194

Whether or not this will contribute to a progressive loosening of links between schools only time will tell but Mr Enfield's comments might reflect a sea change. The mutual support which they had provided through the years of industrial action, the co-operation from TVEI cluster groups, was declining. This could be explained by new appointments, a factor mentioned by Mr Carrington in his reflections on competition:

> Where we're talking about marketing, and I know I see it there in the back of your mind, you're saying: 'Why aren't they co-operating like they did when they were working in TVEI?' Well, the competition wasn't there then . . . it's almost a gentleman's agreement that they don't really cut each other's throats – at the moment; but there's a lot of new heads in there, a lot of new heads . . .
>
> (Carrington, Langford School)

He then went on to speculate about the possible emergence of a hierarchy of schools arising from this competition and an outcome where:

> the bottom rung of that could have a school which makes *The Blackboard Jungle* look like a teddy bears' picnic. And that is the danger, but I am afraid I see no alternative, I see no alternative, if you're put into this competition scene; the only way you're going to reverse this is going back to your catchment areas.
>
> (*ibid.*)

This is a view of the school system which does not take into account the continuing powers of LEAs to use catchment areas as a means of regulating admissions to schools which are oversubscribed (DES, 1988), arrangements which can be used to retain the 'neighbourhood' character of schools. Mr Carrington's concern is that a competitive environment will disadvantage those children attending schools least able to use market freedoms and he doubts whether schools can co-operate and limit the extent of competition. This is possibly the most demanding and difficult part of local management and of the role and responsibilities of headteachers. What are the boundaries of their accountabilities and professional commitments? If they are confined to the children who attend their own school, does this threaten a secondary school system which may work well only for those children attending high-status and high-enrolment schools?

References

DES (1988) *Admission of Pupils to County & Voluntary Schools*. Circular no 11/88.

DES (1990) *Developing School Management. The Way Ahead*. A Report by the School Management Task Force.

Hughes, M. (1973) 'The professional as administrator: The case of the secondary school head' *Educational Administration Bulletin*, **2** (1), 11–23.

Thomas, H. (1992) 'The update to module 2 E333', in *Policy Making and Education Reform*. Milton Keynes: The Open University.

Chapter 12

System Restructuring, School-based Management and the Achievement of Effectiveness in Australian Education

Judith Chapman, Jeffrey Dunstan and Brian Spicer

RESPONSIBILITY FOR AUSTRALIA'S SCHOOLS

In Australia, schooling is compulsory for all young people aged 6 to 15 years. Constitutionally, state and territory Ministers for Education have responsibility for all school education in their respective states and territories. However, the commonwealth plays an important role in considering the broad purposes and structure of schooling, and in promoting national consistency and coherence in the provision of schooling. In co-operation with the states, the commonwealth addresses resource equity and quality issues through its general recurrent, capital and specific purpose programmes. In addition, it has specific responsibilities for migrants and Aboriginal people, the provision of financial assistance to students, and Australia's international relations in education.

There are more than 9,000 schools attended by over 3 million students in Australia. Two basic sectors of schooling operate: a governmental sector with approximately 72 per cent of all students and a non-government sector with about 28 per cent of the students. Within the non-government sector in each state there is usually a Catholic school system, other non-government systems and independent schools.

Constitutionally, the government school system in each state must provide educational opportunity for all children of school age regardless of physical and intellectual ability, social and economic circumstances, cultural background or beliefs. Parents have the right, however, to choose non-government schooling for their child if they wish, and many do so for educational, religious, cultural or other reasons. Parents electing to take up the non-government option are usually called upon to provide financial input to the school of their choice.

RESTRUCTURING OF EDUCATIONAL MANAGEMENT: QUALITY, EQUALITY AND CONTROL

While independent schools in Australia have always had a high degree of auton-omy in terms of their self-governing nature, this has not been the case for government and, to a lesser extent, Catholic schools. While the language of restructuring varies from state to state and system to system, some common threads are evident. In all states, a decentralization of decision-making and devolution of control over resource decisions has been taking place, generally bringing the locus of decision-making either to schools, or as close to schools as possible, and reducing the size of central, or state, bureaucracies.

A wide range of administrative changes have been introduced as part of the decentralization and devolution process. In most states the devolution of control over resources through administrative reforms is seen to support school quality in the following ways:

- supporting local decision-making;
- providing for potential savings and increased investment earnings;
- allowing greater flexibility in funds management;
- allowing increased responsiveness to changing and emerging needs at the school level.

Generally, all states are seeking greater involvement of parents in school decision-making. Communities are being encouraged to become active partners in the management of schools, although the role of existing and proposed school councils/boards varies considerably across the states. Devolution of decision-making involves varying degrees of control for schools themselves over educational and curriculum matters, management of school physical and financial resources, and management of aspects of human resources and work organization.

At the same time, while being able to explore a greater degree of self-management and pursue locally articulated school goals, schools in these systems must also continue to meet community expectations of equity and access, and of the delivery of quality, consistent educational programmes with the accompanying responsibility for students' learning outcomes. Clear state policies and guidelines continue to play a critical role in helping to ensure an effective functional relationship between school self-management, accountability to the local community and accountability to the broader community of the system and state.

A flurry of publications has issued from states, systems and schools during the current period of reform. Many of these are in the form of strategic plans, or even vision statements, for education at a variety of levels from local to state-wide. They provide sets of principles and policy guidelines to support schools, districts, regions and other education units in the formulation of their own development plans, whether they be for a one-, three-, or five-year period. In fact, most systems and schools are choosing to develop both short- and long-term plans, particularly in order to make progress towards long-term goals easier to monitor and measure. School development planning has been taken up in tandem with a more distinctive role for school councils in the government sector, providing impetus to increased community participation in education, and broadening the locus of local accountability for effectiveness of schooling and educational resource management.

Though the language and terminology may vary across states, systems and schools, here too there are common threads. School development plans, school renewal plans, action plans for school improvement are all planning documents developed by schools to help them mesh their particular needs, conditions and intentions with system priorities. They are collaboratively developed to cover a designated period of time, with planning participants including the school executive, teachers, parents, community members and students in a variety of combinations. School development plans generally require the commitment of school principals to greater and lesser degrees, depending on the role of the planning group in terms of governance in that particular school or system. They are founded on school and system goals and aspirations, and bring together the complexities of educational policies, programmes, human, physical and financial resources, as well as strategies for monitoring, evaluating and reporting on progress against the development plan. Most states and systems provide schools with a range of documents and support resources to assist them with the process of formulating their school development plan.

In terms of monitoring, evaluating and reporting, a range of approaches are in use. South Australia and New South Wales, for example, have both adopted the use of programmes of educational review, involving a visiting review panel, to help schools monitor and evaluate their performance. While practices may be less public or formal in some systems, schools are generally required to report on their progress annually, at least to district level.

In the area of human resource management many changes in the way teachers work in the day-to-day operations of schools are taking place in all sectors. Reform and restructure of curriculum lead to new configurations of teachers both within and across faculty areas in secondary schools, and to teaching approaches drawing on different groupings of students and teachers for a variety of reasons in both primary and secondary schools.

Broad changes in curriculum emphasis, especially in the post-compulsory years, have also resulted in changes in teachers' work, through programmes like Joint Secondary Schools TAFE, and increased access to vocational education and training in schools generally. Students now undertake more of their studies off the school site, with training experiences, job placement and the like taking them, and increasingly their teachers, out of the classroom and into new teaching/learning environments.

While these developments are exciting and provide great stimulus to creativity and innovation in teaching/learning, they are also a great challenge to schools organizationally, and at times can test the boundaries of established employment and industrial relations' policies and practices. Programmes like the National Schools Project through the National Project on the Quality of Teaching and Learning have provided a framework where all parties from all sectors can trial new approaches to these issues.

Changes in the human resources management of schools have the potential to rejuvenate the structures and organization through which education is delivered, with consequent educational benefits for students, teachers and the community. There is also the potential for enhancement of teacher professionalism and career structures. In a number of states and systems there is now a degree of local staff selection and wider use of merit selection principles, generally of executive staff or principal, which is undertaken with the involvement of teachers and community members. This also helps give schools a greater sense of self-determination and self-management.

In the area of financial resource management devolution of increased decision-making responsibilities to school level has generally included greatly increased access to and control over funds for operating and related costs. Although many systems have tended to keep responsibility for major capital works and some maintenance at the centre, schools now receive an annual budget, to be managed within agreed accounting and accountability practices, and often supported by a computer-based, system-developed administrative, accounting and management information package. An emerging need for principals has been professional development in the area of financial management, which states' systems and schools have responded to in a number of ways, including training and in-service courses, and in some cases, additional infrastructure such as the appointment of bursars, or similar financial administrators, whose services may be shared across a cluster of schools.

The capacity to make informed judgements about anticipated costs, and identify operational, educational and professional priorities on a school-wide and collaborative basis, not just annually, but with an eye to the three-year or five-year school development plan, allows schools to respond in a far more focused and immediate way to the needs of the school community and within system priorities. Final responsibility for financial management tends to rest with school principals, but school councils or boards are now able to play a significant role in the government sector of many states in resource allocation in schools. Inevitably, the amount of funds that are truly discretionary will tend to fall short of schools' wishes, but to be informed and able to articulate their decisions over the financial aspects of schooling brings the self-managing school closer to reality and supports effectiveness of schooling and resource management.

THE RESEARCH

In this context of system restructuring and increased school-based management, research was undertaken to investigate the impact at the school level of the most recent policies and reforms designed to enhance the effectiveness of schooling, and of the effectiveness of educational resource management.

Five government schools, two Catholic schools and one independent school in the state of Western Australia were subject to intensive study. The selection of schools was undertaken in consultation with employing authorities to provide a breadth of experience across primary, secondary and special schools, urban and rural schools, privileged and disadvantaged schools, and schools with a range of student enrolments. Details of the schools in the study are included in Table 12.1.

Interviews were conducted at school, regional and central levels by an experienced research team, a diversity of personnel being interviewed by one to two members of the research team during the week spent at each school location. In order to understand better the relationship between the school and system state-wide authorities, interviews were also conducted with senior staff from central offices of the Ministry of Education and the Catholic Education Office, and with regional personnel in two regions serving more isolated schools in the state. One hundred and seven interviews were conducted.

Table 12.1 *Details of schools included in the study*

School	Type of school	Enrolment	No. of staff [F/T]	[P/T]
Leichhardt	Government Primary	365	16	2
Hartog	Government Primary	326	14	6
Tasman	Government District High	169	12	2
Eyre	Government Senior High	982	65	8
Gregory	Government Educ. Support Centre	22	4	0
Stirling	Independent School K-12	1013	73	0
Giles	Catholic Primary	514	18	0
Warburton	Catholic Secondary	350	26	0

Data included interviews with school, system and community personnel, analysis of school documents, and observation of meetings, classes, assemblies and other school operations. Interviews were tape-recorded, and supplemented by extensive handwritten notes. Confidentiality of the outcomes was assured. A summary of findings was returned to participant schools and system personnel for verification, comment and response.

An interview schedule was used to focus data collection. The interview schedule allowed the case studies to focus on a range of policies within each functional area (e.g. responsibility at the school level for governance, curriculum, human resources and finance) as well as a consideration of those policies with regard to linkages across functional areas.

THE CONCEPT OF EFFECTIVENESS: THE IMPORTANCE OF GOALS AND PRIORITIES

In the minds of those interviewed in this study, effectiveness of schooling refers in the broadest terms to the major expectations held for a school or school system. It is within these broad perspectives that schools undertake the development of their general aims and objectives and their more specific strategies for implementation. Broad perspectives of effectiveness generally concentrated on student impacts and outcomes, 'the value added notion of schooling'.

A complex interplay of elements was seen as inherent in the development of effectiveness. Many people in this study talked about three, four or five of these elements in relation to their own school at any given time, maintaining that it is not one single factor that leads to effectiveness, but an aggregation of contributing elements, including:

- maximum outcomes for all students;
- the contribution of sport, music and other activities to schools;
- parent and community support for the school;
- transition from year level to year level;
- pastoral care and quality relationships;
- school climate;
- support from the leadership team;
- management policies and practices clearly enunciated so that doubt is removed;

- commitment of staff.

Particular stress was placed on the importance of clearly formulated school goals. All schools associated with this study had determined goals appropriate for their school. They were variously called goals, aims, purposes and objectives, but they always represented a long-term vision of what the school believed it should be seeking to achieve, and were referred to in relation to concepts of the effectiveness of schooling.

An analysis of the data shows a number of goals seen to be of major significance. These appeared to fall into two categories – those associated with student outcomes (Figure 12.1) and those associated with the ways those outcomes might be achieved (Figure 12.2).

SCHOOL-BASED MANAGEMENT AND SCHOOL EFFECTIVENESS

In recent years across Australia, policies have been introduced at the national, state and school levels to enhance the effectiveness of schooling. Our research attempted to identify those which have had the greatest impact on the effectiveness of schooling. We found that these policies can be grouped according to seven discrete categories:

1 School development planning.
2 Management of student behaviour.
3 Partnership in decision-making.
4 Regular review of curriculum provisions.
5 Outcomes-based education.
6 Devolution and local school management.
7 The management of resources.

School Development Planning

School development planning is being undertaken by schools as one means by which the effectiveness of schooling might be enhanced. In both government and non-government schools, school development planning is resulting in:

- clearer enunciation of school goals;
- the identification of specific current priorities;
- the introduction of successful implementation arrangements.

Clarity of school goals Our study found that when the process of establishing goals is part of the process of schooling for all who participate, acceptance of the goals, and a sense of ownership of those goals, is developed. Further, if dissemination of the goals to the school community of staff, parents and students is undertaken effectively, the goals become internalized, enhancing a sense of purpose and unity in the school's operation.

It was clear from our study that goals are more effective when they are owned by the school community, ownership being developed through the processes used

Figure 12.1 *Goals relating to student outcomes*

GOALS RELATING TO STUDENT OUTCOMES

- Maximizing the individual academic, social
and physical growth of students:

*'The school will provide each child with the opportunity to maximize
personal development and achievement in the areas of intellectual,
creative, physical and social endeavour.'*

*'To enable students to develop and achieve their individual
and academic potential and to achieve personal excellence.'*

- The development of self-esteem:

*'To promote students' self-esteem and self-concept within the caring
environment of the school.'*

- Enhancement of a sense of community and of public service:

*'To develop a sense of community both within the school and
beyond, and to provide opportunities for service to others.'*

- Development of knowledge and skills for
higher education or the workforce:

*'To equip students with the knowledge and skills which enable them to take
advantage of opportunities to enter the workforce or further education.'*

- Development of each child's ability to adapt, cope and work with change:

*'To provide for students a general education which aims to develop each student's
ability to adapt to, cope with, and work within our constantly changing world.'*

- Development of skills needed for self-motivation:

*'There is a need for students to learn the skills necessary for self-motivated
and self-directed activity.'*

- Fostering Christian faith and values (within non-government schools):

*'To integrate all areas of learning with knowledge and experience of the
Christian values of Catholicism.'*

*'To foster the Christian faith and values so that individuals may later have
the freedom to choose their own belief system and way of life.'*

Figure 12.2 *Goals which relate to means whereby student outcomes might be achieved*

GOALS RELATED TO MEANS WHEREBY STUDENT OUTCOMES MIGHT BE ACHIEVED

- Valuing the dignity of the individual:

'To provide a caring, responsive and supportive environment in which students develop a positive attitude and response to individual differences, and an appreciation of the worth of diversity amongst their fellow students and other members of the college community.'

- Providing an appropriate curriculum:

'To provide a curriculum where there is coverage of the guidelines set down by state and Catholic Education authorities, and where there is awareness of the realities of today's society and the children's need to adapt to change.'

- Establishing appropriate relationships:

'A warm and caring environment which is conducive to learning, accepts and respects their beliefs, encourages understanding and tolerance of differences.'

- A need to work with the family in goal achievement:

'To work with the family in encouraging the full development of the child.'

- A need for a positive, warm and caring environment:

'To develop a positive school environment that will maximize each student's potential.'

---

to establish and review the goals.

We also found that goals are more effective when they are internalized by the school community, internalization meaning not only a knowledge and understanding of the goals, but an acceptance of their appropriateness for the school and a commitment to assist in their achievement. Internalization is developed through the processes used to disseminate and reinforce the goals. To assist internalization, all schools involved in this study had published their goals in documents that were available to either the staff, students or parents, or to all three groups. Internalization is enhanced also when the goals and expectations are reinforced regularly not only through such publications as handbooks, the school magazine, school newsletters and the school prospectus, but also through school programmes and practices.

All schools translated these goals into more specific short-term objectives, including the establishment of annual priorities for action. No difficulties in iden-tifying, articulating or gaining acceptance of the goals were identified in schools in this study. Moreover, once the process of goal-setting had been undertaken, all schools showed strong commitment to goal achievement.

The identification of priorities In system guidelines issued to government schools, selection of school priorities was made a responsibility of school decision-making groups. Priorities were to be based on an analysis of student outcomes and on other information available about the school's effectiveness. Staff and parents were encouraged to submit potential areas of curriculum development or organi-zational improvement to school decision-making groups for consideration in the development of local priorities. These would supplement the system priorities communicated to each school for consideration on an annual basis through the Ministry's corporate plan. The inclusion of priorities in the school development plan, and the need for schools to monitor and report to District Superintendents on the student outcomes in two priority areas were enshrined for government schools in a Memorandum of Agreement between the Ministry of Education and Teacher Unions.

As an element within school development planning, schools are taking action to determine annual priorities relating to student outcomes or organizational issues. Where this occurs, teachers co-operate across all subject and faculty areas to effect improvement in the chosen priority areas. The range of priorities estab-lished by schools for 1993 is presented in Table 12.2. All but one school identified three priority areas.

Table 12.2 *Priorities established by schools*

School	Priority 1	Priority 2	Priority 3
Giles	First Steps – Reading	Self-esteem	Reporting and assessment
Leichhardt	First Steps – Writing	Self-esteem	Oral language
Hartog	First Steps – Reading	Mathematics	Physical Education
Tasman	Learning to learn	Technology	Oral communication
Eyre	Numeracy	Post-compulsory education	Literacy
Stirling	Curriculum review	Self-esteem	Excellence
Gregory	Individual development	Parent empowerment	Establishing the role of the school in the community
Warburton	Capital development	Mission statement	Curriculum review

Although organizational issues had been suggested as potential priorities in Ministry guidelines, in no instance was such an issue included as a direct result of school decision-making. All selected priority areas related directly to outcomes for students, and were generally associated with curriculum. Two schools focused on development of self-esteem, and one school on assessment and reporting arrangements.

The diversity of priorities selected by schools is a positive indication of the benefit of local decision-making. Externally imposed priorities clearly would not have addressed specific local circumstances. It is interesting to note that the identification and dissemination of system priorities occurred only in December 1992 for school year 1993, and was considered by schools to be too late for consideration in their own priority development. This view is confirmed by the observation that only two schools included one Ministry priority each in their own priority listings.

It is clear that identification and dissemination of system priorities will need to be achieved with significantly longer lead times if schools are to reflect emerging government policies and guidelines for change in their priorities and if the Ministry intends that schools will take such priorities seriously.

Implementation strategies Of course, acceptance of annual school priorities by the principal, the school decision-making group and the staff provides no guarantee of successful outcomes. School development planning also involves a consideration of implementation arrangements to achieve objectives in selected priority areas. Successful introduction of implementation arrangements, we found, depended on decisive leadership, a comprehensive implementation strategy, opportunities for professional development and a strong commitment by the school community.

For example, implementing their 'First Steps' priorities in writing, spelling and oral language, Leichhardt Primary School, Hartog Primary School and Giles Catholic Primary School emphasized a clear vision of directions which had been introduced through access to an external consultant from the Ministry of Education and through their own principal and leadership team. They identified comprehensive strategies which included objectives, time-lines, resource implications, data collection arrangements, teaching and learning strategies, in-service education activities, and evaluation techniques. They also appreciated professional development activities which included a ten-day external programme supplemented by programmes on school development days. A strong commitment was evident through acceptance by teachers of positions as project leaders, volunteer membership of project committees, attendance at staff meetings in their own time and regular informal sharing of progress.

Concluding comment In responding to policies designed to introduce school development planning, our data revealed that schools in this study more clearly enunciated their school goals, used a range of approaches to identify current specific priorities and introduced successful implementation arrangements. In doing so, schools exercised greater self-determination and accepted increased responsibility, the rationale for the introduction of school development planning provided by the Ministry of Education.

School-based Management of Student Behaviour

Our study also revealed that the effectiveness of schooling is enhanced if schools are able to achieve their goal of affirming the dignity of the individual student. This goal is generally related to 'managing student behaviour', a phrase commonly used in schools to embrace the issue of student discipline and more broadly encompassing all approaches to student attitudes and relationships within the school. Policies and practices in this area of schooling are developed and implemented to:

- minimize disruptive behaviour that would otherwise limit the learning programme for students;
- assist the development of positive attitudes in students;
- identify specific student problems requiring special attention;
- recognize special effort.

The allocation of significant resources of time, money and personnel to each of these elements of student development reveal the key importance attached to them by schools, an importance reinforced by the inclusion of at least one element as a current or very recent priority by a majority of schools in school development planning.

Minimizing disruptive behaviour   Schools involved in this study had developed student behaviour policies, usually on theoretical bases developed by Glasser. The aim of such policies is two-fold: to have students understand the consequences of their behaviour, and to allow uninterrupted student-teacher interaction in the teaching-learning situation by ensuring that the students' right to learn and the teachers' right to teach are protected. Policies provide for clear sets of rules to be followed, with clear consequences for students who fail to adhere to the rules. The consistency which results is of great benefit in resolving disciplinary problems.

Our data reveals that the basis of effective student behaviour policies lies in negotiation between staff and students concerning what is acceptable and what is not acceptable behaviour, and the sanctions which should apply. In addition, close liaison with parents is maintained through regular reports which record both positive and negative student behaviour.

In our case study schools, student behaviour policies made teachers more secure in their relationships with students. In a recent staff bulletin at Eyre Senior High School, teachers were reminded of the importance of managing student behaviour (MSB) policies:

> 'No MSB, No peace;
> Know MSB, Know peace.'

Minimizing disruptive behaviour that would otherwise limit the learning programme for students is thus addressed primarily through the development of student behaviour policies which principals and staffs believe are instrumental in enhancing the effectiveness of schooling.

Developing positive attitudes   Schools realize the significance of identifying specific strategies for the building of self-esteem and self-confidence in their students. Many schools have established self-esteem as a current priority and have developed interesting strategies to achieve their objectives. For example, a deliberate priority was introduced at Stirling College to overcome some negativism which had been identified. A teacher comments:

> One innovation to receive widespread acclaim has been the determination to eliminate 'put-downs', the use of sarcasm, the downgrading of a student by students or staff, aggressive bumping, any expression of superiority over a person, either verbally or physically. Suggested by the School Counsellor, the policy has been widely implemented within the school community, being the subject of remarks by the Headmaster at the opening assembly of the year, by the use of signs around the college, and even now by parents. The goal is the building up of the self-esteem of students, and the elimination of destructive actions in relationships. The Headmaster claimed that the success of the 'no put-downs' policy was in part in its timing. The need for action to overcome an emerging aggression among students was identifed by the outgoing Year 12 students. The suggestion by the School Counsellor matched the need at precisely the right time.

But it is clear that initiative needs to be taken through a range of school practices to reinforce the self-esteem focus. In this regard the lead given by the Principal was recognized by teachers at Giles Catholic Primary School, who asserted that: 'Self-esteem is a big consideration at this school. The Principal gave us a talk, urging that whatever we take on must enhance the self-esteem of the pupils. It was a powerful staff meeting, and a powerful message. Because he reinforces it all the time, we act on it.'

The focus on pastoral care and student self-esteem at a staff residential in-service conference at the same school reinforced the theme as the 'giftedness of self'. The Principal noted the lines from *Shirley Valentine* as reflecting the school's target for each child: 'I've come to like meself [*sic*], really ... I think I'm all right'.

The determination in a school to ensure that each child develops a sense of self-worth must, however, be backed up by decisive action. 'You must plan activities that bring your school together', was the advice of the Principal at Warburton Catholic Secondary College.

Identifying special student problems   In association with the concern to improve student behaviour, arrangements established in schools to assist students with specific problems included an emphasis upon pastoral care, individual worth, student welfare and maintenance of a caring environment with quality relationships.

The house system, supported by the roles of the Chaplain and the School Counsellor, is a major influence at Stirling College. It enables the school to be 'really focused in pastoral care'. Major changes to the house system have been introduced by the Headmaster in recent years, primarily to improve student welfare and to ensure a caring environment.

The formalized structures for caring for students, however, need co-ordinated consideration, as there is a strong belief that:

> Kids do not accept authority any more. You must earn respect now. It's not given because you're a teacher. Kids come to school more argumentative and with a whole range of social problems not noticed before: single parent families; unfed; late to class, as Mum and Dad are not at home when they leave for school; not well-dressed; and with limited parental support. A teacher is far more a counsellor now.

Formalized structures which need to be co-ordinated include a form teacher system; a year-level co-ordinator system; an attendance checking system; a discipline system to manage student behaviour; merit awards in all subjects; special education provisions for handicapped, underachieving, low-achieving and academically able students; and the services of a school psychologist, youth education officer, school nurse and social worker. All of these structures were in place at Eyre Senior High School.

Some staff within secondary schools particularly need to be specifically identified with the pastoral care role. Year level co-ordinators at Eyre Senior High School have accepted that role, with responsibility shifting from their former discipline role to one of student support. At Stirling College the role is accepted by housemasters.

The acceptance by schools of both a pastoral care role and the establishment of caring environments is doing a great deal towards achieving the goal of enhancing the dignity of the individual in the school setting and beyond.

Recognizing student effort Our study showed that the provision of regular opportunities to show appreciation for student progress or a significant student contribution to the school is a major factor in developing student dignity.

A system of student awards operates within many of the schools under investigation. Merit certificates are presented to students 'deemed worthy by class teachers' at Leichhardt, Eyre and Giles schools, with an understanding that during each year it should be possible to have some achievement noted for each child. 'A proper use of these certificates and other devices will encourage students to do the "good things"'.

For similar reasons teachers were 'encouraged to send students to, or invite to classes, the Principal, Deputy Principal or Head of Department so that they can acknowledge the student's work, efforts or achievements'. Assemblies also provided excellent opportunities specifically to recognize student performance.

This range of school initiatives reinforces the importance attached by schools to recognition of special student effort. The initiatives in each instance are products of local school action rather than the meeting of system requirements or policies.

Concluding comment From the data collected in the course of this study, we conclude that systems need be in place in schools and school systems to recognize the achievements of students. It must not be left to chance or whim. Deliberate endeavours should be made in regular ways, through planned channels, and within clearly determined policies, for special student effort to be recognized. It should be added, however, that achievement in all its forms should be acknowledged – in the aesthetic, the physical, the social as well as the academic. Further-more, it is clear that achievement must be conceived of in terms of personal capacities and not by an absolute standard against which only the privileged few can excel.

School communities clearly believe that effectiveness of schooling is enhanced through careful attention to student behaviour management. Despite the uniform emphasis currently being given in each school to these policies, however, some questions remain unanswered:

- whether the emphasis on self-esteem has improved learning outcomes of students;
- whether the focus on self-esteem and self-confidence has an effect on the development of thoughtfulness in relation to other individuals and groups;
- whether an emphasis on reward, recognition and appreciation develop feelings of inadequacy in those recognized less frequently;
- how an appropriate balance can be achieved between pastoral care and a caring environment on the one hand and self-reliance of the individual on the other hand.

Partnership in Decision-making

Our study clearly revealed that effectiveness of schooling is enhanced when a part-nership is developed between parents, principal, staff and students in a school community. Decision-making practices which variously draw on this partnership to establish the membership of decision-making groups, and which apply the bene-fits of that decision-making partnership across all functional areas of the school's operation, lead to a strong sense of mutual support, a strengthening of purpose, a commitment to decisions made, and an empowerment of participants. We found that partnerships have a particular impact upon:

- school culture and ethos;
- parent-school relationships.

Influence of partnerships on school culture and ethos Action by principals to involve staff, students and parents in opportunities for decision-making on important issues within the school was found to meet with positive appreciative responses in all the case study schools.

The development of a charter of rights made a great impact on the school culture and ethos at Hartog Primary School, both in the method of its develop-ment, and in its availability to the school community as a model of rights and responsibilities. The Principal asserted that it is seen as:

> the centrepiece of the school. It grew out of a desire to get people to
> work well together. It is a one-page accountability document, not a
> checklist. It is our school vision. We work co-operatively here, so we
> built it up together. We asked, 'What do you think the school should
> be? How should we behave to achieve it? A small subcommittee of

staff initiated the work, followed by full staff input, involvement of
non-teaching staff, then a survey of parents, and it came back
through the school decision-making group and the Parents and
Citizens' Association. A working party finally brought it all together.
We try to talk it up all the time.'

Participation is further encouraged by a spreading of the management base
to involve more people; a management base of 16 heads of department and eight
housemasters is a more effective involvement of personnel within Stirling College
than the former arrangement of only four heads of department and four housemasters.

An increase in staff and parent participation in decision-making and the
hastening of a culture of partnership has developed in government schools
through the impetus given by the 'Better Schools' programme. One teacher at
Hartog Primary School expressed a widely held view that: 'You need a staff who
want to work towards something, owned by them, participatively. Things should
be decided in a group situation, with good leadership, not necessarily the
Principal's'.

Influence of partnership on parent-school relationships The establishment of school decision-making groups in government schools, the changing
role of parents and citizens' associations in some schools, the appointment of a
specific home liaison officer through the Priority School programme in one school,
and the principals' emphasis on parent involvement are all indications of a drive
to further develop the effectiveness of schools through enhancing the parent-
school relationship.

A key question, however, concerns the degree to which parents on the school
decision-making group are able to represent the parent community of the school,
and whether this represents partnership with parents. To what extent are they
powerful representatives, and viewed as such by other parents?

Strong praise for the operation of the school decision-making group was
reflected by one parent representative at Hartog who asserted that it was: 'the
basic backbone of the education within the school – a great communicating system
for staff and parents to work with. Education for parents is involved, broadening
it out so that parents can contribute and make the school most effective for their
students'.

However, not all comment was as positive. In some schools criticisms reveal
a need to address an expansion of decision-making powers, of methods of reporting to constituencies and of membership arrangements. School decision-making
groups in these settings tended not to be making decisions. There was not a
constituency to which members could report. There was a very small percentage
interested, and there are more at parents and citizens' meetings where the role is
less significant. Little value was seen in information-sharing with such a small
group. The concerns of two parents express a widespread unease. One saw the
school decision-making group as:

a toothless tiger. Parents were demanding a say in how schools were
run, like at a private school, after all they were paying for it. All we

do is meet and be informed. We don't have a say. My opinion is that we should have a say in how the money is spent. People in the community can be a big help to a principal who has no financial training. There is no real involvement in the running of the school . . . a real frustration.

At a second school, a teacher member of the school decision-making group called the group:

a sham. It pretends it has participative decision-making, but it doesn't. You nod your head, you sign a paper and you go back to teaching. It's a rubber stamp, for example, on budget issues. There is no participative decision-making, no discussion why each point was so, just presented. If you do contribute, it ends up to your detriment . . . so you do your job and don't put your foot outside the circle.

The operation of school decision-making groups in non-government schools has a longer history. The role of the school council is to appoint the Principal, to manage the business affairs of the college, including the management and administration of the college's real and personal property, and to carry on the business operations necessary to provide the education set out in the constitution's aims. The Headmaster at Stirling College has undertaken a comprehensive analysis of his council's role, finding that of 142 council decisions during one year, 85 decisions were of a housekeeeping nature, and only five could be classified as policy decisions. The Principal wrote that:

The College Council makes most of its decisions in connection with the financial, property and personnel areas of their responsibilities, and makes very few decisions regarding academic programs and student affairs. It is the principal who is charged under the constitution with the full direction and organization of the College. Governing bodies are not equipped by knowledge, experience or socialisation to govern the academic enterprise.

The last sentence of the Principal's comment was strongly supported by other principals in both government and Catholic schools, who guarded jealously their right to manage the educational side of the school's operation. It was supported also by teachers who, as previously noted: 'are still finding it hard in some cases to come to grips with parents being involved in decision-making'.

Yet at Hartog Primary School the fullest involvement of parents, even in educational debate and discussion, had not been daunting to principal or staff, but had been welcomed as contributing to the school's effectiveness. At Gregory Education Support Centre, where parent involvement centred on helping the students, there was no professional antagonism or 'rubber stamping of decisions', but a clear sense of common purpose.

Concluding comment Shared decision-making involving staff, parents and students is gathering momentum in schools. Even small shifts from the experience of far more autocratic school management are seen as dramatic change. Even where the principal is still the decision-maker in relation to the operation of school decision-making groups, many people would say they appreciated the opportunity for participation.

Certainly, effectiveness of schooling is enhanced when a partnership is developed between parents, principal, staff and students in a school community. Decision-making practices which variously draw on this partnership to establish the membership of decision-making groups, and which apply the benefits of that decision-making partnership across all functional areas of the school's operation, lead to a strong sense of mutual support, a strengthening of purpose, a commitment to decisions made and an empowerment of participants.

Action which has been taken to support partnership arrangements includes an encouragement of participation opportunities; new approaches to parent-school relationships; the opening of curriculum provisions to parent involvement; new models of education resource management; and changing patterns of general school decision-making.

Regular Review of Curriculum Provisions

Schools striving to develop effectiveness of schooling regularly review their curriculum provisions to ensure that:

- current research and development findings are implemented;
- emerging changes in patterns of school enrolment are addressed;
- changing student needs and community expectations are fully addressed.

Implementing current research and development findings Our study revealed that no school has the time or resources to undertake expensive and extensive curriculum revision for itself. Such revision is dependent upon expert external advice. The outcomes of curriculum research and development undertaken by the State Ministry of Education are therefore widely imemented. Teachers in government schools, and to a great extent those in non-government schools, look to the Ministry for curriculum leadership through provision of course guidelines and supporting materials, and through related in-service and professional development activities. The quality of that leadership is often widely applauded and respected by teachers, as in the case of the 'First Steps' developments in the primary school curriculum in Western Australia, leading to the acceptance of the programme also in Catholic and independent schools.

An outcome of curriculum development at system level, 'First Steps' builds on the long-held view that teachers must cater for individual differences among students in their classrooms and provide for development learning. By taking this theoretical base into account in planning course structures, materials and developmental stages in writing, reading, oral language and mathematics, the Ministry has produced materials which provide a strong incentive for schools to review their current provisions.

The introduction of Unit Curriculum into Years 8, 9 and 10 in secondary schools in Western Australia in recent years is a further example. Based on extensive research and development within the Ministry of Education, Unit Curriculum emerged as the recommended means whereby schools could introduce more relevance and greater breadth into the lower secondary years. Its acceptance also by many Catholic schools reinforces the value of research and development activities in stimulating curriculum review.

It is noteworthy that Stirling College asserted its independence on this particular issue deciding, after a review, not to proceed with Unit Curriculum. Warburton Catholic Secondary College introduced Unit Curriculum into its programme, but later rejected it as a result of a staff decision. A remote school in northern Western Australia introduced Unit Curriculum for two streams of students, but maintained traditional subject orientation for a third stream. Of significance, however, is the fact that both of these schools made their decision not to proceed only after reviews of their curriculum provision. Other schools proceeded with implementation, although serious concerns were expressed about a number of factors: the lack of additional resources for other than the pilot schools; the limitation on class size through the Conditions of Work Agreement which coincided with the introduction of Unit Curriculum; the simultaneous elimination of subject superintendents resulting in additional responsibilities for principals and heads of departments; the introduction of the 'Better Schools' programme; and budget cuts. That schools were prepared to review their curriculum provisions when faced with a coincidence of so many other adverse factors highlights both the importance they attach to state-wide research and development for curriculum review, and the unreasonable expectations of the Ministry of Education in simultaneously imposing on schools such an array of change issues. It is clear that the Ministry of Education has a responsibility to provide up-to-date curriculum advice based on research and development of the highest quality if schools are to regularly review their curriculum provisions and enhance the effectiveness of schooling.

Addressing emerging changes in patterns of student enrolment

When student enrolment patterns are changing in a school, a review of curriculum provisions is necessary to ensure continuing effectiveness. Increasing numbers of students are staying on to Years 10, 11 and 12 in government, Catholic and independent schools. At Eyre Senior High school, for example, 97 per cent of students are now staying on to Years 10 and 11 although, as one teacher pointed out, '20–30 per cent would leave tomorrow if they could get a job'. It was a surprise to discover that 15–20 per cent of students in Years 11 and 12 do not come to school every day, with Monday and Friday being particularly notable for absenteeism. Five years ago that cohort of students, was not in schools; now that they are in schools there is a critical need to review curriculum provisions to ensure increasing relevance and interest. The needs of many of these students are different from the needs of the smaller numbers who stayed on to Years 11 and 12 in the past primarily as a pathway to higher education. So breadth and depth of subject offerings and a variety of pathways to diverse career and higher education destinations each dictate a need for curriculum review.

An increase in overseas fee-paying students, particularly from Asia, is another current change being experienced in the pattern of school enrolments. This is adding a new dimension to the existing need, through migration policies, for schools to consider curriculum provision and student needs within a multicultural context. At Stirling College, 50 additional overseas students have been enrolled, of whom 31 are boarders, creating new demands because of the need for English language training and for different emphases in pastoral care. The introduction of Indonesian into the curriculum as a 'Language other than English' is also a direct outcome of the changing nature of the student population.

Meeting changing student needs It is also clear that the needs of students a decade ago are not the same needs as those of today and that this has implications for curriculum review. Technology advances have accelerated, leading to keyboard skills becoming one of the basic skills. Students are less likely to gain employment on leaving school than they were just a few years ago, so that expectations about their own career future, the economy and the shape of the world of work are all in process of change. The need to provide an education to equip young people for change, for adaptation and for development of a range of interests and skills has become paramount, including provision for development of leisure and recreational interests to cater for the expectation that further reductions in hours of work will accompany technological developments.

At Stirling College, one major evidence of change has been the Lower School curriculum, introduced to expand learning options in Years 8, 9 and 10 as a result of higher retention rates throughout the school. A realistic alternative programme is now offered to those students not seeking to move on to higher education, programmes being tailored to match the interests and abilities of students.

The decision to implement the International Baccalaureate is another evidence of regular curriculum review at Stirling College. This will be introduced as an alternative tertiary preparation programme for students in Year 11, making the last two years of secondary schooling, according to the Headmaster, 'far more academically rigorous and challenging than it is for particularly capable students'.

Addressing changing community expectations Schools should, as community organizations, deliver effectively the outcomes a community expects. These expectations, however, undergo change over time, and are moulded and fashioned in varying ways through the media, through emerging consciousness of need, through pressure groups and through social, industrial, commercial or political developments. A community awareness of declining physical fitness thus led to the establishment of a daily fitness programme in a number of schools following a review of their curriculum provisions. Publicity about the extent of child abuse led to the establishment of preventative education programmes in the curriculum. The increasing awareness of the world as the 'global village' and the growing appreciation of Australia's role in Asia led to the expectation that community languages will be offered in schools.

Only as schools undertake regular reviews of their curriculum provisions on the basis of the above expectations will their effectiveness be maintained and extended.

Concluding comment Curriculum is at the very heart of schooling. What a school teaches through its formal and informal programmes determines its effectiveness. Data from this study show that to remain effective schools must consistently review their curriculum provisions to ensure implementation of current research and development findings to ensure that emerging changes in patterns of student enrolment are addressed, changing student needs are met and that community expectations are achieved.

Outcomes-based Education

In considering effectiveness of schooling, school communities are beginning to focus their attention not on the process of what is being done, but on what is being achieved by the individual student. The focus has for so long been on courses and methodology, not on outcomes. The evaluation of results which emerges through the school development planning process is providing a new means of determining teaching effectiveness. It is a new emphasis and expectation in considerations of the effectiveness of schooling.

The successive stages of goal-setting, planning, determination of strategies for implementation, resource allocation and provision of evaluation arrangements are each being addressed specifically and thoughtfully by schools, often based on the 'Better Schools' model. Increasingly, however, the end point of that process is being seen as the progress made by the individual student, the value added to the student's development during a particular period of schooling. Schooling is becoming increasingly 'outcomes-based'.

Despite the attention currently being given to outcomes, the issue is clouded in secondary schools because future directions are unclear for many students. Over the past five years students have experienced new pressures. Changes in higher education arrangements have led to uncertainties about subject choice as well as certainty about the need for the highest possible tertiary entrance score; unemployment factors have created lower expectations of employment; problems with the next generation taking over a family business or farm have increased; and the benefit of a full secondary education appears to have been devalued in the eyes of students because it no longer acts as a guarantee of entry into tertiary education or the workforce. There has simultaneously been a sharper emphasis on the development of appropriate competencies.

The issue is clouded also in special schools for students with disabilities, where students do not reach the first level of outcomes on state-wide continua. Special schools are comfortable with outcome statements only where they are developed specifically for students with disabilities, are behaviourally based and reflect realistic goals.

It is clear from our study that the attention to outcomes has led to:

- emergence of student outcomes as a whole-school responsibility;
- encouragement of individualized learning arrangements;
- stimulation of individualized assessment strategies such as student profiles;
- emergence of new approaches to aggregating student outcomes as a means of evaluating goal achievement;
- reconsideration of arrangements for reporting to parents.

Outcomes as a whole-school responsibility The focus on student outcomes in priority areas has been reinforced by the nationwide emphasis on achievement of competencies. Student outcomes are presented as a responsibility of all staff: oral language is not the exclusive responsibility of the English staff; mathematics is seen to permeate all subject areas; and self-esteem must be reinforced by whole-school approaches and attitudes.

Standardization of certain aspects of mathematics that come into all areas of the curriculum was introduced at Eyre Senior High School. An examination was undertaken by the School Development Committee where student learning could be reinforced and improved by standard approaches being used by all teachers. This led to advice to all teachers concerning, for example, standard approaches to graphing definitions and characteristics of bar graphs, column graphs and pie graphs to ensure consistency, and in nomenclature of mathematical forms and symbols such as in measurement. At other schools, similar school-wide approaches to the achievement of goals in priority areas were pursued: the 'put-down' policy at Stirling College, the oral language emphases at Tasman District High School and the home liaison programme at Leichardt Primary School are some examples. All had clear outcomes identified as a focus of attention and action for all staff.

Encouraging individual learning The introduction of 'First Steps', the new curriculum initiative developed by the Ministry of Education in reading, writing, oral language and mathematics for primary schools provides an example of the current encouragement of individualized learning. Teachers regularly claimed that 'First Steps' was better tuned to students' needs and that it enhanced individual development because of its presentation of a continuum of outcomes. The child's mastery of successive stages in the continuum is evidence of positive outcomes, and provides the basis for the next learning stage. Emphasis is on developmental learning as students are placed on the continuum in each specific learning area. For teachers this has increased their awareness of the whole developmental process and reinforced the psychology of individual differences and individualized learning. When individualized learning approaches are adopted, the focus on outcomes becomes child-specific, providing both a clear view of current achievement and a sharp prediction about the next stage of growth. This emphasis was particularly appropriate at Gregory Education Support Centre, where the progress of students with learning disabilities depended heavily on individualized learning programmes.

Stimulating individualized assessment strategies Both national and state authorities are concentrating attention on student outcomes in their preparation of student profiles in each subject field, arguing that being explicit about outcomes is critical to improvement. An accountability document issued by the state authority notes that essential aspects of curriculum will be contained in student outcome statements provided through the national profiles, and schools and teachers will be accountable on the basis of these. The profiles will provide a basis for student assessment and reporting and will provide a focus on outcomes rather than processes.

The work on the 'First Steps' curriculum initiative done at state level predated the work on profiles at national level, but the same force is driving both trends: the developmental view of learning and the importance of student outcomes. The continua in 'First Steps' are seen to be consistent with the national profiles because outcome statements build in a macro-level of outcome: 18-month intervals are staged, and become developmental markers, of great value not only in gauging student progress, but for school development planning and the establishment of priorities.

Student outcome statements are viewed by state authorities as particularly important in the face of devolution of responsibility to schools. Methodology, resources and content are recognized as being a school responsibility, but senior state administrators believe that accountability to parents and students should be based on student outcomes established by the Ministry to ensure state-wide consistency and standards.

It is asserted that at this stage, however, some of the indicators are vague and there is no shared understanding of their meaning, but refinement is occurring, and in-service education activities are providing opportunties for staff to clarify perceptions. Criticism was levelled that insufficient consultation by the system authorities has occurred in the development of profiles, and that their introduction was far too hurried. One teacher at Eyre Senior High School 'didn't know how you could own something if it has only had lip-service paid to consultation'. Nevertheless, 'there is no doubt in people's minds that outcomes for students are a top priority in this school'. Development of profiles for students with disabilities presents specific problems, but underlines the importance of individualized assessment.

At a number of schools in this study, concern was expressed that the arrangement of continua within levels on student outcome statements frequently meant that a student stayed at a particular level for an extended period of time, even up to two or three years. This made principals and teachers wary of reporting to parents in terms of the student outcome statements, as 'there is not seen to be much growth between level two and level three over a two- or three-year period because of the limitations of the descriptors'.

Aggregating student outcomes Schools are developing technologically based management information systems to assist in evaluating goal achievement. These approaches to aggregating student achievement data are providing objective information on which school development planning can proceed, and from which goal achievement can be assessed.

At Leichhardt Primary School 'collated results are indicating patterns of strength and weakness in the school and assisting the staff and parents to determine school priorities'. The management information system for the school development plan features an analysis in March and September of the children's progress along the writing development continuum using key indicators, an evaluation of the self-esteem of the students and a collated report on the results of the teachers' assessments against the school's ten performance indicators. Not only does the analysis highlight gaps between achievement and potential at whole-class and whole-school level, but opportunity is provided also for identification of similar gaps where they exist for individual students.

Schools are beginning to take seriously the evaluation of progress towards established performance indicators within their set priorities. At Tasman District High School, at the outset of work on their oral language priority, a survey was undertaken of student responses to the greeting by staff, 'Good morning (Jane)'. A baseline of reactions by students was aggregated, incorporating for example, no response, a grunt, 'Morning', or 'Good morning Mr Smith'. Formative data is being assembled during the semester, and a summative assessment is planned to evaluate improvement over the year. In other priority areas, progress towards achievement of performance indicators is similarly being monitored through data analysis, although as the principal stated: 'We can't demonstrate yet that our data is valid "as in research valid", but it is helping us to determine our directions'.

Reporting to parents It has been the experience of schools in this study that changes in the format of reports to parents on student progress are necessary to meet increasing parent expectations. As broad an array of data as possible should be included on the premise that the more information provided to parents, the greater their awareness of their child's progress and thus a greater awareness of effectiveness. Schools are welcoming increased parent interest and pressure, believing that it forces the school to become more effective in terms of both academic and personal development. A significant accountability issue at Stirling College was the awareness of a parental attitude that said: 'I want results. If not all As, then at least there should be significant comment on attitudes development. Parents are coming to see that.' 'When I first came,' the Headmaster reported: 'the focus was on the percentage result in examinations! Now we are writing fuller, franker, more detailed comments'.

At Giles, the Principal established a staff committee, and regularly consulted with parents to develop a new system for reporting student progress, based not on numerical results but on appropriate wording to highlight recent individual progress. No marks, no grades were included, but advice about each child's development stages in different subjects. This had the additional benefit of educating parents.

Teachers are still using traditional reporting methods at Hartog Primary School, but student outcomes based on national profiles in each subject area are now being considered.

Concluding comment Outcomes-based education is one response to the challenge to show that resources allocated to education are achieving objectives set for them. Data from this study confirm that student outcomes are increasingly being seen as a whole-school responsibility; that individualized learning arrangements are encouraged; that individualized assessment strategies such as student profiles are being stimulated; that new approaches to aggregating student outcomes are emerging as a means of evaluating goal achievement; that cost-effectiveness of allocated resources is being challenged; and that arrangements for reporting to parents are being reconsidered. At the same time, a need for caution is expressed. Schools are concerned that the emphasis on outcomes may not only restrict their freedom and creativity, but provide a public measurement of a school's performance which does not take into account the differing characteristics of student populations, intake variables and progression over time.

Devolution and Local School Management

Effectiveness of schooling is encouraged when responsibilities previously maintained by systems at central level are devolved to schools themselves. A powerful momentum for increased effectiveness is a school's recognition that it can undertake new responsibilities. As a senior system administrator stressed: 'You (i.e. school personnel) are responsible for how good your school is. The responsibility for school improvement must reside in the school.' The benefit of independence in allowing a school to pursue its aims without bureaucratic constraint was asserted by the Headmaster of Stirling College, an independent school throughout its history. The college appreciates its freedom to respond to the needs of students as it deems appropriate. The strong feeling was expressed that the college enjoys a freedom not available to systemic schools, and so is able to develop its own character, make its own decisions in relation to staffing, financing, facilities and curriculum, as well as introduce a wide range of co-curricular activities, thus expanding the opportunity for success for students. Nevertheless, there are some clear constraints on the college's independence. The curriculum for Years 8 through 10 is constrained by the requirements of the Secondary Education Authority for Years 11 and 12. Some concern was expressed that the Public Schools Association timetable for sport was very heavy indeed, constraining the college in determining its own sports agenda. Financial constraints brought on by the recession were also quoted as being a current constraint on actions the college might otherwise want to take.

So too with government schools, devolution and local school management do not imply full independence for schools. They remain in a system where equity, access and a community expectation of some consistency are crucial. The process of devolution has been the process of enabling as many decisions as possible to be transferred to the school level, while insisting that schools still operate within clear state policies and guidelines.

The changes resulting from devolution and local school management are influencing the effectiveness of schooling through a school's:

- ability to use available resources more flexibly;
- capacity to develop its own management arrangements;
- opportunity to involve a wide range of personnel as it undertakes the new responsibilities.

Flexibility in resource usage Whereas formerly the Ministry of Education met all school accounts for gas, electricity, water, postage and telephone, they are now negotiating with Leichhardt Primary School, and many other schools, so that these payments will be devolved to school level. The agreed present level of annual costs will be provided as a grant to the school, which will then be in a position to manage locally those resources. Experience has shown that local management of energy consumption increases responsibility and reduces costs, thus introducing a degree of flexibility for schools in utilizing money saved. The Registrar at Leichhardt believed that 'if the school has to look after the money it will provide better stewardship. The Ministry is being very fair with baselines'.

This policy is consistent with action already taken to devolve financial arrangements to schools. Schools are receiving grants for teaching aids, equipment, subject requirements and consumables, minor building works, office requisites, for gardening and cleaning stock, and for library expenditure where formerly many of these items were distributed from a central store. Grants are provided direct to schools as a block grant, with schools being free to budget and buy within the total grant according to their needs, with no strings attached. By this arrangement, system authorities argue that a school has resource flexibility, though school administrators claim the degree of discretion is limited after mandatory expenditures have been met.

Development of management arrangements System officials believe that while the policies and guidelines for devolution through the 'Better Schools' programme have been well planned, their implementation, particularly in secondary schools, has not been widely successful. This is despite the fact that first, schools are receiving direct grants through which they are able to support their school development planning; and secondly, policies and guidelines have been provided for school decision-making groups to involve local parents and communities in school planning. Senior system administrators are concerned that devolution processes seem to have stalled, and a review is currently being undertaken to consider further staged development. In particular, attention is being directed to the introduction of one-line budgeting including the cost of school staffing, increased flexibility for the mix of teaching staff, and for changes to the process of staffing schools.

There is, none the less, a degree of frustration that devolution has not yet extended significantly into the administration of non-teaching personnel or facilities areas. It is clear, as indicated by the Principal at Hartog Primary School, that schools would appreciate more flexibility about the kinds of staff available to them: 'We may not need a gardener full-time, as appointed by the Ministry, but would prefer a teacher aide. We should be able to make that decision.'

However, there is considerable nervousness about the devolution of teaching staff administration to schools, many believing that for equity reasons the appointment of teaching staff to schools is best left as a centralized function. Concern is expressed also that under devolved arrangements, the transfer of teachers from difficult locations to more comfortable ones would be constrained.

The Principal at Tasman District High School expressed the concern of small communities:

> There are many less desirable areas that would find it difficult to
> attract teachers, and once there they would never get out. If you get
> a bad teacher now, you can blame the Ministry. What if you hire them
> yourself? And a school council would perpetuate parochialism and
> conservatism. If this community were selecting staff they would
> select teachers with strong religious views, and would allow them to
> permeate all the teaching. There is need for a breadth of perspective
> in all areas. I'm happy to let the Ministry do it.

Already elements of personnel administration have been devolved, however, with decisions about promotion positions within schools now being made at the school level, with appraisal of beginning teachers being undertaken by principals, and with discipline and dismissal procedures initially being handled at school level.

Devolution meant the abolition of the Curriculum Branch and the position of subject superintendents at central level. Teachers, with hindsight, speak warmly of the role subject superintendents undertook, referring to co-ordination of schools, knowledge of staff members in their subject faculty, assistance in appointment of staff and the supervision of large groups of teachers involved in writing and assembling curriculum materials for the benefit of subject teachers in schools who had neither the time, opportunity or experience to do it themselves. With the passing of the superintendents, the responsibility for management of curriculum issues has passed to heads of departments in schools, and to the development of networks between schools.

Involvement in resource management The principal and the school bursar have traditionally been the school's educational resource managers. Many teachers and parents are now becoming involved in school decision-making and management. This involvement is arising through membership of a school's representative finance committee, through opportunities for preparation of submissions by teachers and heads of departments, through appointment as a cost centre co-ordinator in a school, or through membership of the school decision-making group or the parents and citizens' association. Each of these groups or individuals is increasingly being involved in decisions about the use of resources available to the school, a significant trend as the percentage of the cost of running a school which is provided through the school grant continues to rise.

Because of the representation involved, awareness and understanding of resource management within schools is extending. This is reflected well in the processes used at Giles Catholic Primary School where the Principal, realizing the resource implications involved in introducing 'First Steps', made the following arrangements:

1 To approach the parents and friends' association for a commitment to initial funding and longer-term annual funding of $6,000–8,000 to meet the costs of an external presenter and manuals required to implement the programme, as well as additional books and resources for teachers.

2 To gain the support and approval of the school board for in-service education funding for the programme.

3 To encourage the support teacher's approach to the co-ordinator of the 'First Steps' programme at the Ministry of Education to seek approval for the introduction of the programme to Giles.

4 To approve the support teacher being utilized full-time in implementation, thus allocating the salary of one teacher towards the programme. The Principal believed that unless a teacher was available to monitor implementation, the momentum would die.

Her time was used in classrooms advising and supporting teachers, and in small group work.

In order to facilitate the programme teachers contributed great amounts of time for teacher development after hours, as it was inappropriate to use instruction time for the purpose.

Concluding comment The changes resulting from devolution and local school management are influencing the effectiveness of schooling through a school's ability to use available resources more flexibly; a school's capacity to develop its own management arrangements; and a school's opportunity to involve a wide range of personnel as it undertakes new responsibilities.

The Management of Educational Resources

Educational resource management in schools is undergoing major change in the current context. Not only is there increasing partnership in decisions about resource allocation, but also increasing attention is being given by principals, staffs and parents to the processes used in the allocation of resources. These processes have significant implications for schools as understanding of resource management extends from principals and bursars to teachers and parents as a part of whole-school planning. Data reveal four related findings:

1 Processes are being established to ensure that decision-making concerning resource allocations becomes part of school development planning.

2 Budget planning should reflect the most appropriate utilization of all the resources known and expected to be available to the school.

3 From the aggregate of educational resources available to a school to manage, a very limited percentage is discretionary. Schools would like this percentage to be raised.

4 The discretionary resources should be targeted primarily to priority areas in a given year.

Resource allocations and school development planning Processes are being established by schools to ensure that decision-making concerning resource allocations becomes part of school development planning. The stimulus for this development in government schools has been the publication of the booklet *School Financial Planning and Management* by the Ministry of Education (1991b) as part of its 'Better Schools' programme.

The processes for resource allocation being developed by schools are increasingly participative, thorough and open. Submissions developed by teachers and heads of departments are generally considered by the bursar, the principal, a representative finance committee and the school decision-making committee before a decision is finalized. A strong claim was made at some schools that no one person has any more weight than anyone else and that at each stage of the process there is a genuine opportunity for amendment. The previous year's budget is frequently used as a starting point for discussion, and proposals for change emerge based on new priority areas. Often the final proposals are submitted to the parents and friends' association with a recommendation for support, and a request that they fund particular components for the year as their contribution to resources.

Aggregation of resources Because of the advent of forward planning and the allocation of resources based on priorities, the resources available to a school should be known wherever possible at the time of budget planning. For both government and non-government schools the achievement of this goal is being enhanced through refinements to the administration of government grants, including a movement to one-line school grants for government schools by which schools are given increasing flexibility and control over recurrent budgets.

System officials confirm that schools' recurrent costs, now met from system budgets, will progressively be incorporated into one-line school grants to assist and encourage local school decision-making. The basic premise is that: 'Schools themselves should decide their priorities for cleaners, mathematics teachers and computers, for example, and have the one-line budgets and flexibility to do different things.'

A differential funding and resourcing model is currently being considered, including flexibility with staffing provisions. It is claimed that the present grant arrangements are of limited sensitivity to differences between schools, based as they are on numbers of teachers and students, numbers of new graduates and distance from the capital city. The objective is a global budget with differential resourcing based on differential needs for greater equity, shifting a little from over-resourced to underresourced schools.

Local funds raised by parents and friends' associations to support their schools are not always identifiable at the time of budget planning. However, the priority process is beginning to involve the work of these associations. At Hartog Primary School, the school decision-making group: 'discussed the budget in the light of the school priorities for next year. The recommendation is to be made to the parents and friends' association that $7,000 be raised in 1993 to fund the priority areas of mathematics, reading, physical education/health and K-2 programmes'.

At some schools there is still a tendency for parents and friends' associations to determine for themselves how their funds should be deployed in the school. This led in one school to some tension as to whether funds should be expended on air conditioning (the desire of the parents and friends' association) or on reading materials (the desire of the principal and staff). The development of clear and open communication between principals and parents and friends' associations led to discussion about school priorities and the part which parents could best play in support for those priorities.

Where resources to be available to a school for the following year can be identified at the time of budget planning, more logical and considered decisions can be made about priority expenditure. It is recognized that this is not always practicable. In Catholic and independent schools, where government grants are based on student enrolment, difficulties arise. At Warburton Catholic Secondary College, for example:

we lost something like 19 students from one class between the start of the year and the finish of the year. If you start the year with 90 and finish it with 70 and your recurrent grants from the state and the commonwealth are averaged over 12 months, then those 20 students can translate into $65,000. It plays havoc with your budget.

Limited discretion available to schools From the aggregate of educational resources available to a school to manage, a very limited percentage is discretionary. Schools would like this percentage to be raised.

Despite the view of system officials that 'schools have the resources to back up their school development plan, through a school grant with no strings attached', and despite an appreciation by principals that devolution is giving more financial responsibility to schools, new ideas often cannot be resourced because unallocated funding is too small. A current system review of devolution is addressing this concern as attention is directed to a range of further financial delegations to schools, including relief teacher payments and finance for works and services.

There is a strongly held view that 'if the school has to look after the money, there will be better stewardship'.

Targeting of priority areas The establishment of current priorities by schools is providing a basis on which resource allocation decisions can be made. At Hartog Primary School the resources policy was unequivocal: 'Human, physical and financial resources will be budgeted and deployed to reflect the agreed priorities of mathematics, reading, physical education/health and the K-2 programme'.

Since the appointment of a mathematics co-ordinator and the identification of mathematics as a priority at one school: 'there are 20 times as many resources for teachers and students in the classrooms'. Reference books, up-to-date information and in-service education opportunities are now available also:

> The co-ordinator has impact, she is efficient, caring, has a mathematics brain, sees mathematics as a priority and is prepared to give it time. She comes to classrooms in allocated time to bring in equipment and share information, gives ISE information, organizes specific time to be allocated at staff meetings, organizes the maths resource room, and mathematics outcomes have improved as a result.

This action highlights the benefit of allocating personnel, finance and facilities resources to a priority area in support of the school development plan.

But the trend to base resource allocations on priorities needs to be monitored carefully. Data show that staff responsible for priority areas can often get what they need without question, because it is a priority. The need for justification prior to purchase, and for ongoing evaluation after purchase requires emphasis. Processes must also be introduced to ensure that priority areas are not supported to the exclusion of areas currently held on maintenance funding.

Concluding comment The management of educational resources is undergoing major changes at school level. New structures are being established, including cost centre co-ordinators and finance committees, thus expanding the knowledge about available resources and extending the influence of school personnel on decision-making about resource allocation. The placement of resource management into the context of school development planning introduces a rational framework for effective utilization of resources, including the targeting of priorities, provided that the resources available to the school are known sufficiently in advance, and allow enough discretion in spending to justify the time and energy required. The effectiveness of resource management is enhanced when the wide range of personnel involved are accorded appropriate training.

DISCUSSION

Implications of Increased Decentralization School-based Management for School Effectiveness

Whether there is a causal link between increased school-based management and school effectiveness is difficult to determine, as the level of management information and outcomes data on which to base such judgements is low. Nevertheless, even though such 'hard' data is unavailable, anecdotal evidence in this study strongly supported the link between the exercise of greater management responsibility at the school level and the increase in effectiveness of schooling. Anecdotal evidence showed the link to be forged by a number of factors:

1 *The benefit of choice being made on the basis of local knowledge.* It is asserted that effectiveness of schooling is enhanced because better choices are made, choices that are appropriate for the setting, and made by people fully familiar with all factors impinging on the decision. The expenditure of funds available to a school provides one example of devolved decision-making which can enhance school effectiveness. Providing resources in a one-line budget gives to schools a substantial increase in flexibility to make better choices between competing priorities.

2 *The development of 'ownership' through the exercise of greater responsibility at the local level.* Greater management responsibility at the school level brings with it an increasing sense of responsibility at that level for educational decision-making. It is asserted that the effectiveness of schooling is enhanced because value is placed on people's contributions. They are empowered through the exercise of greater responsibility and by 'owning' their decisions. They learn to recognize that effectiveness of schooling is dependent on their own decisions and actions, not on external influence and imposition.

3 *The development of increased accountability at local level.* The increased accountability of school decision-making groups and of principals at the local level has accompanied increased devolution of management responsibility to the school site. It is asserted that effectiveness of schooling is enhanced because such accountability

is immediate, identifiable, and based on a full understanding of circumstances. Furthermore, immediate follow-up action, including assistance and support, is both possible and likely, thereby further adding to the potential for greater effectiveness.

4 *Greater control over the work environment leads to greater satisfaction and better performance.* Senior administrators in employing authorities report that they have been influenced in their thinking by findings of studies in the behavioural sciences which affirm the value of giving to workers greater control over their own work arrangements, with resultant increases in effectiveness.

Of course, enabling things to happen does not ensure that they will happen. Devolution of management responsibility to the school level provides an opportunity for improving the effectiveness of schooling, but it should be noted that it does not necessarily lead to such improvement, unless a whole host of factors are in operation at both school and system level.

The Positive and Negative Impacts on Effectiveness of Devolving More Management Decisions to the School

A range of positive and negative impacts on effectiveness of devolving more management decisions to schools is identifiable from the data collected as part of this study. Whether the impact of a devolved management responsibility is viewed at school level as positive or negative depends to a great extent upon the readiness of school personnel to accommodate the new responsibility.

Positive impacts Positive impacts include the following:

1 Schools have been able to target local needs more effectively as a larger proportion of funds have been provided to schools 'with no strings attached'. There is a strong feeling that this flexibility in resource utilization has led to greater effectiveness through better use of resources.

2 The specific needs of principals and teachers are being met through professional development activities selected and funded at the school level. Rather than participating in system-imposed programmes, schools are themselves determining areas of involvement where the greatest benefit can accrue to staff, and therefore to students, thus enhancing effectiveness.

3 The knowledge base of teachers is increasing, leading to better decisions being made in relation to finance and curriculum issues at school level. Involvement of teachers is now encouraged in areas of school decision-making previously guarded as the province only of the principal or the system. The wider knowledge base is encouraging fuller debate, development of a greater range of options for action, and more-informed decision-making.

4 The knowledge base of parents is also increasing as their involvement in decision-making issues increases at school level. Their involvement is also encouraged in areas of school decision-making previously guarded as the province only of the professional educator.

5 Schools have begun to develop whole-school approaches to planning and implementation where priorities are set on the basis of data about student needs, development and performance and general concerns for social and economic factors. Teachers are convinced that targeting needs which have been specifically and participatively identified at the level of the individual school is having significant positive impact. Whole-school approaches are also seen as reducing some of the rigidities in the organization and structure of schools and of teaching and learning.

6 Successful student and school outcomes have become more widely known and recognized as a new culture of involvement has been generated by devolution of more management decisions to school level.

7 Effectiveness is enhanced where there is unity of purpose and endeavour. The acceptance of greater responsibility at the school level has created the potential for greater effectiveness, both through the principal's leadership in the establishment of goals and objectives, and through the development of team spirit within the school whereby commitment to achievement of outcomes is supported.

Negative impacts Negative impacts include the following:

1 The devolution of more management decisions to schools has been based on an expectation that all schools would be ready to accept these additional responsibilities and would welcome them. Schools have different characteristics: their readiness to accept more management decisions and their ability to cope with them vary, and account needs to be taken of this variability as systems move towards a more devolved approach to educational decision-making.

2 Principals and teachers have been placed under considerable pressure because of the time which is needed to undertake additional management responsibilities. The time needed for consultation on decision-making issues is loading many teachers very heavily, and is causing a distraction from their primary function of teaching and student learning.

3 Low morale among school staff has emerged when devolution of management decisions has been recognized as devolution of clerical administration, of 'administrivia', with little change in responsibility or real decision-making at the school level. This attitude has been reinforced when additional duties have not been

matched by additional human resources, or when financial grants have not been indexed to allow required payments to keep up with inflation.

4 Because of their history in a centralized system, schools have not been attuned to doing things independently. Regrettably, as systems have moved towards changed arrangements in management and decision-making, little attention has been paid to changing the culture and climate in schools. While school attitudes maintain the culture that 'The centre tells you what to do', devolution of responsibilities tends to be responded to with suspicion and some cynicism.

CONCLUSION

In recent years government schools in Australia have been given a great deal of the responsibility formerly held at central level. Devolution has tended to be gradual and limited, but generally well absorbed by schools as they have accepted accountability for more money in school grants, and been given more freedom to budget and buy according to their own needs. There are expectations at both school and system levels of increased devolution of responsibilities to school level to further develop school self-management.

Acceptance of devolution on the part of some schools has been unequivocal: 'Give us the money and we will get on with it'. In these schools, school personnel have been positive in accommodating the extra workload, spending the extra time needed and learning new skills on the basis that they could then show initiative in meeting local needs more appropriately. Other schools have been prepared to undertake the new responsibilities through goodwill, doing so however with neither excitement nor opposition.

Account needs to be taken, however, of a third group of schools which have not been willing recipients of greater management responsibility. They are a group who maintain that the changes are politically and economically motivated, imposed by system authorities to reduce pressure on the central office. They argue that:

- inadequate provision has been made for the additional workload created by the changes;
- there is no educational rationale related to teaching and learning to support devolution;
- it is making principals into managers instead of educational leaders.

This group is suspicious of any proposals for change which do not clearly lead to benefits in classroom relationships and processes. Their perception is that parents now see teachers working harder at management tasks than on educational tasks, with enormous amounts of time devoted to such matters as selection of teachers for responsibility positions in the school and to budget decisions. In order to achieve the benefits of local decision-making, great demands on time and energy have resulted, creating a degree of disenchantment in school communities.

Unwillingness to accept greater management responsibilities also relates to a widespread suspicion that funds provided at the time of devolution of specific responsibilities will not keep pace with inflation. Although grants are acknowledged to be generous at their instigation, there is a general belief that indexation to inflation tends to be short-lived.

No matter to which category a school belongs, both system and school personnel agree that the devolution process has been 'hard going every step of the way'. Yet goodwill and co-operation have minimized potential disruption.

System officials recommend that future action in devolving responsibilities to schools should be on the basis of consultation, not by administrative fiat. Within the Western Australian system, flexibility of decision-making, a continuum of devolution and an evolutionary approach is suggested so that additional responsibilities could be accepted according to the specific interests and capacities of each school.

No matter what the commitment to devolution, there is widespread agreement that in conjunction with ongoing decentralization and devolution, equity, accountability and cost-effectiveness across systems must be preserved.

ACKNOWLEDGEMENTS

This chapter is derived from a study funded by the Australian Commonwealth Government, Projects of National Significance Fund, undertaken as part of Australia's involvement in Stage Two of the OECD Activity on The Effectiveness of Schooling and of Educational Resource Management.

Lines from *Shirley Valentine*, by W. Rushton and published by Reed Books, reproduced with kind permission.

References

Australian Education Council (1992) *National Report on Schooling in Australia, 1991*. Carlton: Curriculum Corporation.

Ministry of Education, Western Australia (1987) *Better Schools in Western Australia: A Programme for Improvement*. Perth: Western Australian Government Publishers.

Ministry of Education, Western Australia (1989) *School Development Plans: Policy and Guidelines*. Perth: Western Australian Government Publishers.

Ministry of Education, Western Australia (1990) *School Decision Making: Policy and Guidelines*. Perth: Western Australian Government Publishers.

Ministry of Education: Western Australia (1991a) *School Accountability: Policy and Guidelines*. Perth: Western Australian Government Publishers.

Ministry of Education, Western Australia (1991b) *School Financial Planning and Management: Policy and Guidelines*. Perth: Western Australian Government Publishers.

Name Index

Subject Index